BEHAVIORAL GUIDE TO
PERSONALITY DISORDERS (DSM-5)

SETON HALL UNIVERSITY
UNIVERSITY LIBRARIES
SOUTH ORANGE, NJ 07079

ABOUT THE AUTHOR

Dr. Douglas Ruben is a forensic and licensed psychologist, and national consultant in Applied Behavior Analysis, Personality Disorders, Addictions, and Parenting. His seminars on parent empowerment, personality disorders, schools, and adult children of alcoholics appeared nationwide through Cross Country University. He literally has given over 3000 workshops across the United States from Portland, Maine to Portland, Oregon. Dr. Ruben is author and coauthor of over 70 scholarly and self-help books and over 100 professional articles. Among his recent behavioral practitioner books include *Tantrum Survival Kit: The Definitive Guide to Tantrum Management; Effects of Bad Parenting and What to do About It; Treating Adult Children of Alcoholics: A Behavioral Approach; Assessing and Treating Addictive Disorders; Handbook of Childhood Impulse Disorders and ADHD; New Ideas in Therapy, Current Advances in Psychiatric Care; Transitions: Handbook of Managed Care; Family Addiction;* and *Aging and Drug Abuse.* His self-help books recently included: *Parent Guide to Children of Alcoholics (COAs); 25-Secrets to Emotional Self-Healing; Forever Sober; No More Guilt: 10 Steps to A Shame-Free Life; Bratbusters: Say Goodbye to Tantrums and Disobedience; Avoidance Syndrome: Doing Things Out of Fear;* and *Family Recovery Companion.* He is on the editorial board of *The Forensic Examiner* and runs a private practice (over 30 years) in Okemos, Michigan.

BEHAVIORAL GUIDE TO PERSONALITY DISORDERS (DSM-5)

By

DOUGLAS H. RUBEN, Ph.D.

CHARLES C THOMAS • PUBLISHER, LTD.
Springfield • Illinois • U.S.A.

RC
554
·R83
2015

Published and Distributed Throughout the World by

CHARLES C THOMAS • PUBLISHER, LTD.
2600 South First Street
Springfield, Illinois 62704

This book is protected by copyright. No part of
it may be reproduced in any manner without written
permission from the publisher. All rights reserved

© 2015 by CHARLES C THOMAS • PUBLISHER, LTD.

ISBN 978-0-398-09087-6 (paper)
ISBN 978-0-398-09088-3 (ebook)

Library of Congress Catalog Card Number: 2015024644

With THOMAS BOOKS *careful attention is given to all details of manufacturing
and design. It is the Publisher's desire to present books that are satisfactory as to their
physical qualities and artistic possibilities and appropriate for their particular use.*
THOMAS BOOKS *will be true to those laws of quality that assure a good name
and good will.*

Printed in the United States of America
SM-R-3

Library of Congress Cataloging-in-Publication Data

Ruben, Douglas H.
  Behavioral guide to personality disorders (DSM-5) / by Douglas H. Ruben,
Ph.D.
      pages cm
  Includes bibliographical references and index.
  ISBN 978-0-398-09087-6 (pbk.) -- ISBN 978-0-398-09088-3 (ebook)
  1. Personality disorders. 2. Behavioral modification. I. Title.
  RC554.R83 2015
  616.85'81--dc23
                                                                    2015024644

In Warmest Memory of
Charles Ruben

PREFACE

We live in turbulent times. Over the last five years, the influx of mental health problems from a jobless economy, returning war veterans, and deluge of refugees resulted in staggering numbers of psychiatric outpatient and hospital admissions. These unprecedented mental health needs compel a more thorough and scientific understanding of clinical psychopathology. The *Behavioral Guide to Personality Disorders* offers one solution to this exigency.

Behavioral Guide to Personality Disorders is the first behaviorally-based reference guide on Personality Disorders and their applicability in vocational, therapeutic, and other rehabilitation service agencies. Chapters cover (a) each personality disorder from a learning theory perspective; (b) the *Dos and Don'ts* on how to manage personality types in service delivery systems (called "personality management"); and (c) predictors of each personality disorder for vocational, therapeutic, and rehabilitation outcomes. The objective of the book is simple. It provides practical and ready-to-use clinical information for practitioners and advanced students facing the high demand for triage and treatment decisions. It helps the paraprofessional and professional measurably identify individual behavior problems in clients and consumers, and predict their trajectory of outcome success or failure under certain circumstances or when provided a litany of rehabilitation services.

Behavioral Guide also culls from evidence-based research and application to ensure the viability and acceptability of the analysis. For simplicity of reading and rapid reading comprehension, the design of this book is called a *power-point book*. It allows for self-paced learning with power-point (graphic-visual) reminders embedded in the text with study questions listed afterwards.

As for social validity, this book is the product of over 3000 workshops given statewide and nationally by the author on either (a) Personality Disorders or (b) Parenting-Family Guidance over the last 15 years. Workshops were tailored for a highly diverse pool of professionals in interdisciplinary mental health fields. Questions asked by the workshop attendees reflected the current zeitgeist for concrete, tangible, measurable, observable, and more functional explanations of behavior. These explanations were consistent with conceptualizations seen in applied behavior analysis, experimental analysis of behavior, cognitive behavior therapy, and the integrated field analysis of behavior, or interbehaviorism. As attendees observed, most books on Personality Disorders found in the scholarly and practitioner marketplace recycled existing models of psychopathology. The classic textbooks explained the etiology, course, and intradynamics of the disorder relative to cultural and community models. Models explored were generally eclectic, heavily covering perspectives that were psychoanalytic, neo-psychoanalytic, lifespan, trait, and humanistic; less emphasis was upon cognitive, behavioral, and social-learning perspectives.

This was not always the case. About 40 to 50 years ago, behaviorally-based books on personality were prolific. In 1961, Lundin's book *Personality: An Experimental Approach* rattled the field with its tenacious departure from the traditions of psychoanalytic theories. Lundin revived this momentum in 1969, with *Personality: A Behavioral Analysis.* In 1975, Ullman and Krasner pioneered a behavioral approach extended to all of types of psychopathology in their highly acclaimed and seminal text, *A Psychological Approach to Abnormal Behavior.* From 1972 to 1984, revisions kept alive another spectacular behavioral treatise of abnormal behavior and personality disorders, that of Bootzin and Acocella's *Abnormal Psychology: Current Perspectives.*

Like its predecessors, *Behavioral Guide to Personality Disorders* offers a return to the behavioral framework to understand the intricacies of psychopathology. It explains the behavioral underpinnings of each personality disorder, both to debunk the mythical reasons or *reifications* distorting the etiologies, and to advance a more respectful scientific outlook on personality disorders. Within a scientific framework, professionals in the allied health fields can more confidently predict the outcome success or failure of individuals with personality disorders, who receive mental health treatment, vocational rehabilitation, or other allied health services.

CONTENTS

Preface vii

Chapter

1. CURRENT CLASSIFICATIONS OF PERSONALITY
   DISORDERS. 3
   Background and Learning Theory. 3
   Classification of Personality Disorders 5
   Clusters of Personality Disorders. 7
   Paranoid Personality Disorder 11
   Schizoid Personality Disorder. 13
   Schizotypal Personality Disorder 15
   Antisocial Personality Disorder 18
   Borderline Personality Disorder. 20
   Histrionic Personality Disorder 23
   Narcissistic Personality Disorder 25
   Avoidant Personality Disorder. 30
   Dependent Personality Disorder 40
   Obsessive-Compulsive Personality Disorder 42
   Contingent and Noncontingent Effects of Punishment 43
   Functional Outcomes of Punishment 49
   Avoidance and Escape Patterns. 52
   Superstitious Behaviors. 52
   Rule-Governed Behaviors 54
   Other Personality Disorders. 60

2. DSM-5 CHANGES IN OTHER DISORDERS
   COMORBID WITH PERSONALITY DISORDERS 65
   Neurodevelopmental Disorders. 66
   Autism Spectrum Disorders. 66
   Schizophrenia Spectrum and Other Psychoses. 67

Depressive Disorders 68
  Disruptive Mood Dysregulation Disorder 69
  Persistent Depressive Disorder (Dysthymia)................. 69
  Premenstrual Dysphoric Disorder 70
Bipolar and Related Disorders................................. 71
Obsessive-Compulsive and Related Disorders 72
Sleep-Wake Disorders.. 74
  Circadian Rhythm Disorder................................. 75
  Rapid Eye Movement (REM) Sleep Behavior Disorder 75
Disruptive and Impulsive Control Disorders 77
Substance-Related and Addictive Disorders 78
  Abuse-Dependence Continuum................................ 78
  Stimulant-Depressant Effects 84
  Cluster A Personality Disorders........................... 84
  Cluster B Personality Disorders........................... 85
  Cluster C Personality Disorders 86
  Gambling Disorder... 88
Neurocognitive Disorders...................................... 89
  Delirium 90
  Traumatic Brain Injury (TBI).............................. 91

3. DECISION TREE FOR PERSONALITY
   MANAGEMENT...................................... 97

4. DOS AND DON'TS OF PERSONALITY DISORDERS:
   APPLYING PERSONALITY MANAGEMENT............. 105
Cluster A Personality Disorders............................... 106
  Dos with Cluster A Personality Disorders.................. 106
  Don'ts with Cluster A Personality Disorders............... 110
Cluster B Personality Disorders 115
  Dos with Cluster B Personality Disorders.................. 116
  Don'ts with Cluster B Personality Disorders............... 123
Cluster C Personality Disorders 131
  Dos with Cluster C Personality Disorders.................. 132
  Don'ts with Cluster C Personality Disorders 142

5. PREDICTORS OF PERSONALITY FOR SPECIFIC
   VOCATIONAL, THERAPY, AND REHABILITATION
   OUTCOMES 151
Program Attrition 152
Absenteeism 152

Motivation 153
History of Transient Jobs 153
Coworker Relations 154
Supervisor Relations 155
Substance Abuse 155
Violence 156
Office Crime 157
Program Compliance 158
Cluster A Personality Disorders (Paranoid, Schizoid,
    Schizotypal) 158
    Program Attrition 158
    Absenteeism 160
    Motivation 161
    History of Transient Jobs 162
    Coworker Relations 164
    Supervisor Relations 165
    Substance Abuse 166
    Violence 167
    Office Crime 169
    Program Compliance 170
Cluster B Personality Disorders (Antisocial, Borderline,
    Histrionic, Narcissistic) 172
    Program Attrition 172
    Absenteeism 174
    Motivation 176
    History of Transient Jobs 178
    Coworker Relations 187
    Supervisor Relations 188
    Substance Abuse 194
    Violence 196
    Office Crime 199
    Program Compliance 201
Cluster C Personality Disorders (Avoidant, Dependent,
    Obsessive-Compulsive) 205
    Program Attrition 205
    Absenteeism 207
    Motivation 209
    History of Transient Jobs 211
    Coworker Relations 214

Supervisor Relations 218
Substance Abuse 221
Violence 224
Office Crime 226
Program Compliance 228

References 233
Name Index 247
Subject Index 249

BEHAVIORAL GUIDE TO PERSONALITY DISORDERS (DSM-5)

Chapter 1

CURRENT CLASSIFICATIONS OF
PERSONALITY DISORDERS

Background and Learning Theory

The progressive evolution of the *Diagnostic Statistical Manual of Mental Disorders (DSM)* has paralleled a rapidly diversified society. From its origins in the 1890s under the eras of Mesmer and Breuner, and through a vast metamorphosis over 100 years, the DSM underwent five revisions to reflect the cultural changes and medical sciences of civilized man. Terminology changed, classification labels softened, or were replaced with less offensive language. Trends noticeably shifted from labeling the *person with a disease* to labeling *the behavior of a person.* This transformation of language pivoted from *problematic person to problematic behavior.* This was most visible in the subsection of the DSM concerned with *Personality Disorders.*

The *Personality Disorders* consist of 10 typologies assembled to show pervasive patterns in a human organism, from late adolescence or early adulthood through to late adulthood. Pervasive patterns mean an (a) enduring pattern of inner experience, that (b) deviates markedly from the expectations of the individual's culture, (c) is stable over time, and (d) leads to distress or impairment. They are qualitatively distinct syndromes consisting of similar or some overlapping symptoms visible in the individual's everyday experiences. Symptoms directly affect cognitive, emotional, physical, and behavioral modalities, the totality of which impedes an individual's interpersonal functioning, impulse control, decision making, medical health, and career, educational, and other vocational longevity.

From a behavioral perspective, Lundin (1961), an early behavioral systems theorist, explained personality as the unique behavior equipment which one has acquired through a history of learning. Such a view of personality considers it to be a part of the general field of learning, dealing in particular with those learning processes which are involved in man's adjustment to his environment. Here, Lundin focused on an individual's *interaction with the environment,* a theme echoed by Kantor in his preface in a book on clinical psychology (Ruben & Delprato, 1987). Kantor claimed individuals are converted from ordinary hominoids to personalities. They behave and *interbehave* (*intermingle*) with the earth, climate, atmosphere, and with things and events in numerous situations of a social, economic, moral, scientific, and aesthetic nature. In this way, as individuals reciprocate with the world around them, their personalities evolve. Some evolve predictably or causally, other individuals evolve randomly or so-called improperly, deviating from the community norms. Kantor believed no two people were exactly alike, exposed to a multiplicity of unique individual experiences.

The fundamentals of Kantor's concept of Personality are visible in many contemporary behavioral analyses of personality (e.g., Morris & Midgley, 1990; Nelson-Gray & Farmer, 1999; Ruben, 1983, 2001; Sato, 2001). The one commonality especially enduring is that pathology in personality remains a function of the culture. Just as the traditions and rituals of a society in one part of the world does not fit in another part of the world, so the perspective of personality abnormality may vary by the cultural matrix. In the definitions presented herein of the 10 personality typologies classified in the DSM, emphasis is on the operational aspects of the personality relative to an individual's environment. How adaptive or maladaptive the individual is, in other words, entirely depends on the individual's prior history with, discernment of, and integration of the contingencies governing the individuals' lives. Such contingencies describe the functional relationship or "if-then" causal connection mediating between the organism and its surrounds.

Operational or *functional definitions* of personality types comport with the DSM-5's new focus on the *cultural syndrome of personality,* which is shaped by the endemic cultural traits, values, orientation, practices, rituals, and norms of the community. The specific components of the cultural syndrome are known as "markers." These markers are predictors of personality progression and consist of (a) genetic markers, (b) biomarkers, (c) family traits, (d) neuro-markers, (e) family predictors, and

(f) clinical predictors. Together, these markers help distinguish the contingencies underlying not only personality types, but also the reasons why personality types exacerbate or diminish over time.

Classification of Personality Disorders

Let's begin by looking at how the classification of personality disorders changed from DSM-4-TR, the last revision of DSM, to DSM 5. There are three ostensible changes made. First, the 10 personality disorders in DSM-4-TR remained exactly the same despite a storm of controversy surrounding proposals to reduce the 10 personalities to six personalities and reformulate the system to assess personality disorder (Frances & Widiger, 2012). The DSM-5 Task Force reconciled this dispute by laying out their theoretical proposal for the reformulated model of personality in Section III of the DSM-5, entitled, *Emerging Measures and Models.*

Second, the multiaxial system used to organize diagnoses into five levels was eliminated. This meant, instead of listing Personality Disorders on Axis II, psychological reports or other documents would list a Personality Disorder alongside other prominent disorders, including medical problems. This changed the layout from sequential rows designated by Roman numerals, to a non-numerical sequence as appears below.

Multiaxial system of stating diagnoses before DSM-5:

Axis I: 309.13 Cyclothymic Disorder
Axis II: 301.40 Obsessive-Compulsive Personality Disorder;
301.82 Avoidant Personality Disorder
Axis III: none known
Axis IV: (social functioning): stable housing, on probation
Axis V (GAF):   50

Recommended new system of stating diagnoses with DSM-5:

Diagnosis: (309.13) Cyclothymic Disorder, with anxious dis-
                  tress; (301.40) Obsessive-Compulsive Personality
                  Disorder; (301.82) Avoidant Personality Disorder.
Medical: none known
Psychosocial/Contextual Factors: stable housing, unem-
                  ployed, support system.
**Disabilities (WHODAS): 50 (general disability score, 40 =
                  average)**

Notice, as well, in the DSM-5, the Global Assessment of Functioning Scale was eliminated. It was replaced by the World Health Organization Disabilities Assessment Schedule (WHODAS).

Third, in DSM-5, wording in the description of Personality Disorders was more clearly conceptual and related to empirically based models. Emphasis increased on correlating experimental and applied research with the diagnosis, prevalence development and course (prognosis), culture-related issues, gender-related issues, and criteria to differentiate one personality disorder from another personality disorder.

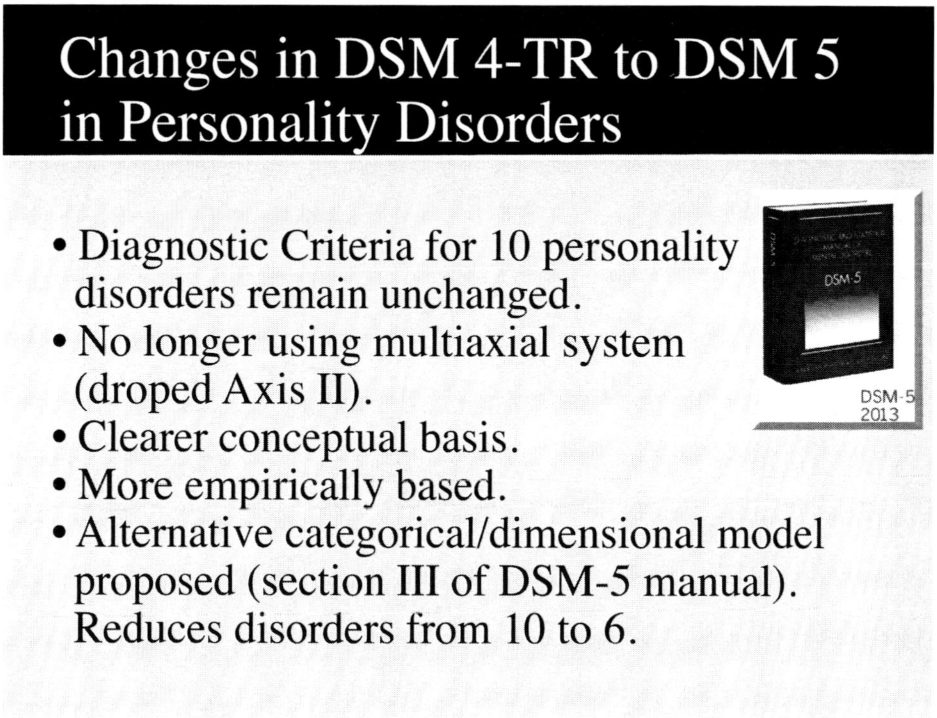

Changes in DSM 4-TR to DSM 5 in Personality Disorders

- Diagnostic Criteria for 10 personality disorders remain unchanged.
- No longer using multiaxial system (droped Axis II).
- Clearer conceptual basis.
- More empirically based.
- Alternative categorical/dimensional model proposed (section III of DSM-5 manual). Reduces disorders from 10 to 6.

DSM-5
2013

Figure 1.1.

C'mon, remind me:
1. The diagnostic criteria for Personality Disorders remained

   _____.
2. Personality Disorders had a clearer _____ basis.
3. In DSM-5, the multi-_____ system was eliminated.
   Answers:

Clusters of Personality Disorders

Personality disorders conveniently divide into three *clusters,* or groupings. Each grouping or cluster has similar features. Cluster A consists of the Personality Disorders of (1) Paranoid Personality, (2) Schizoid Personality, and (3) Schizotypal Personality. Since these disorders all share behavior parameters that are socially "odd," "eccentric," or poorly developed, we conveniently use the first letter "A" to remember the word *Awkward.*

Cluster A = Awkward

Cluster B consists of Personality Disorders of (4) Antisocial Personality, (5) Borderline Personality, (6) Histrionic Personality, and (7) Narcissistic Personality. Common denominators among these disorders are "drama," "intense," and excessive or "ballistic." A convenient semantic cue for this cluster is to use the first letter B for the word *Ballistic.*

Cluster B = Ballistic

Cluster C consists of Personality Disorders of (8) Avoidant Personality, (9) Dependent, and (10) Obsessive-Compulsive. Recurrent behavior patterns among these disorders include anxiety and interpersonal deficits, or cowardice. Consequently, a very easy way to remember Cluster "C" is the mnemonic *Cowardice.*

Cluster C = Cowardice

Again, a fast learning tool to recall the three clusters of Personality Disorder based on their categorical similarities is the ABC, which stands for:

Awkward
Ballistic
Cowardice

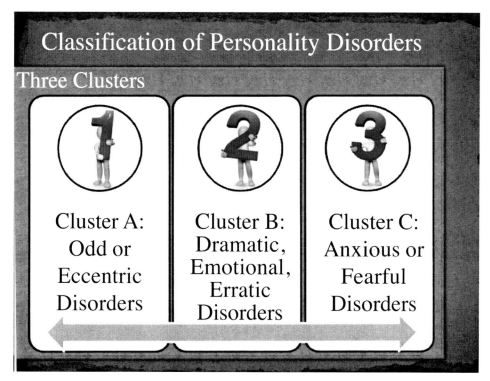

Figure 1.2.

C'mon, remind me:
4. Cluster A of odd, eccentric disorders can be remembered by the word _____.
5. Cluster B of dramatic, emotional disorders is remembered by the word _____.
6. Cluster C of anxious or fearful disorders can be recalled by the word _____.

On a closer look, let us consider the three Personality Disorders under Cluster A, or *Awkward*. These cover Paranoid Disorder, Schizoid Disorder, and Schizotypal Disorder. The reason these disorders are clustered together is because there is a (a) distortion of thoughts, (b) incongruence of behavior with social norms, and (c) persistent detachment from realistic contingencies. Most importantly, Cluster A personality types exemplify individuals who engage in unreliable, unpredictable, but repetitive patterns that amplify problems, create difficulties, or distract from rather than assists in finding solutions to problems. Excesses or "behavior extremes" include inflated and disorganized statements, and strange or bizarre speech or gestural behaviors. Deficits, or underdeveloped skills include poor social skills, apathy or depression, and avoidance.

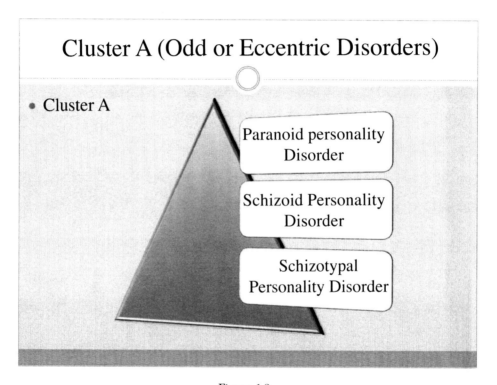

Figure 1.3.

C'mon, remind me:
7. Cluster A, for Awkward, consists of Para-_____ Personality Disorder.
8. A second Cluster A Personality Disorder is _____.
9. A third Cluster A Personality Disorder is _____-typal Disorder.

Paranoid Personality Disorder

Let's examine the first Cluster A Personality Disorder, the Paranoid Personality Disorder. The hallmark of paranoia is a pervasive distrust and suspiciousness of others. The individual interprets other people's motives as malevolent, a pattern evolving from childhood. Etiologically, paranoia emerges from childhood exposure to arbitrary and capricious (non-contingent) punishment. The random or unpredictable surprise of punishers aroused anticipation, or *anticipatory anxiety*. Anxiety increased super-alertness to the child's and later adult's environment, to the point where the individual *always expected something bad or felt foreboding*. Another way of saying "foreboding" is distrust or suspiciousness.

A second feature of paranoia are inferences generalized about people or situations all pointing to distrust. These inferences make up "rules" or *rule-governed behaviors* (Hayes, 1987) descriptive of the past or present punishment contingencies. The individual forms beliefs from the anxiety, not only that *something bad might happen* but that there are evil people out there who conspire to make bad things happen. They overanalyze, obsess over minor details, and come to unfounded conclusions. Once the individual reaches these conclusions – feels mistrustful – little can change the individual's mind. Acts of distrust are unforgivable and unforgettable. Outwardly the individual is not aggressive. He or she is cynical, sarcastic, and passively attacks the reputation of another person, say, through Facebook or blogs, or some other anonymous source. Most importantly, mistrust is a normal feeling for this individual.

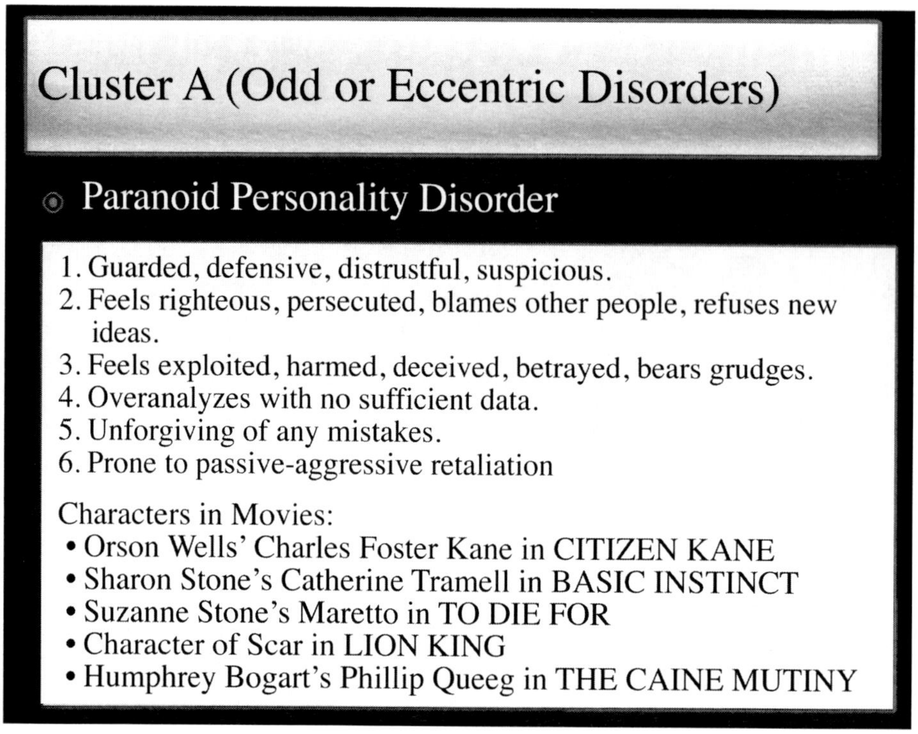

Cluster A (Odd or Eccentric Disorders)

⊚ Paranoid Personality Disorder

1. Guarded, defensive, distrustful, suspicious.
2. Feels righteous, persecuted, blames other people, refuses new ideas.
3. Feels exploited, harmed, deceived, betrayed, bears grudges.
4. Overanalyzes with no sufficient data.
5. Unforgiving of any mistakes.
6. Prone to passive-aggressive retaliation

Characters in Movies:
- Orson Wells' Charles Foster Kane in CITIZEN KANE
- Sharon Stone's Catherine Tramell in BASIC INSTINCT
- Suzanne Stone's Maretto in TO DIE FOR
- Character of Scar in LION KING
- Humphrey Bogart's Phillip Queeg in THE CAINE MUTINY

Figure 1.4.

C'mon, remind me:
10. Features of Paranoid Personality included guarded, _____, distrustful, suspicious.
11. Individuals with Paranoid Personality are _____ of any mistakes.
12. Individuals with Paranoid Personality are prone to _____ _____ retaliation.

Examples of Paranoid Personality appear in famous people such as former FBI Director J. Edgar Hoover or President Richard Nixon. In Hollywood movies, character roles depicting Paranoid Personality abound. Some notables include Charles Foster Kane in *Citizen Kane*, Catherine Tramell in *Basic Instinct*, Maretto in *To Die For*, Scar in *The Lion King*, and Phillip Queeg in *The Caine Mutiny*.

Schizoid Personality Disorder

Schizoid Personality Disorder is uncommon in the general population, affecting 1 percent of clients seen. It is a pervasive pattern of (a) detachment from social relationships, (b) a restricted range of expression of emotions with others, and (c) general indifference. Defining criteria most specifically include (1) neither desires nor enjoyment from close (intimate or other) relationships, including being part of a family; (2) choice of solitary activities; (3) little interest in sexuality; (4) little pleasure in any activities; (5) lacks close friend or confidants; (6) appears uncaring of praise or criticism; and (7) shows emotional coldness or flattened affect. Early signs of schizoid personality may surface in childhood or adolescence but be confused with Autism Spectrum Disorder (ASD). In ASD, however, unlike with Schizoid Personality, prominent patterns include ritualism, stereotypy behaviors, or fixation on objects of events.

Origins of Schizoid Personality may be traced to sensory, emotionally, or interpersonally deprived youngsters raised either in parent-hostile or parent-absent environments. From parent-hostile environments, for example, around excessive punishment, children habituated or grew numb to the torrent of verbal or physical adversity to the point of dissociating from it. If from parent-absent environment, child *never learned* developmentally appropriate skills and adapted to needs through crude, primitive, or solitary reliance. In other words, conditioned reinforcers were few or nonexistent for the youngster who failed to create generalized or more extensive reinforcers in his or her life.

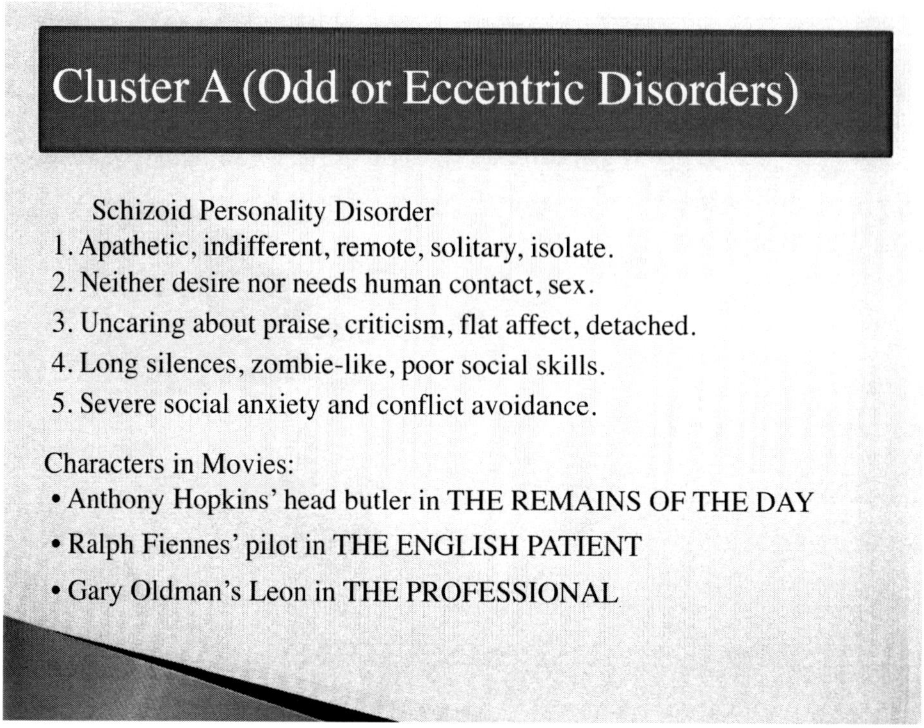

Cluster A (Odd or Eccentric Disorders)

Schizoid Personality Disorder
1. Apathetic, indifferent, remote, solitary, isolate.
2. Neither desire nor needs human contact, sex.
3. Uncaring about praise, criticism, flat affect, detached.
4. Long silences, zombie-like, poor social skills.
5. Severe social anxiety and conflict avoidance.

Characters in Movies:
• Anthony Hopkins' head butler in THE REMAINS OF THE DAY
• Ralph Fiennes' pilot in THE ENGLISH PATIENT
• Gary Oldman's Leon in THE PROFESSIONAL

Figure 1.5.

C'mon, remind me:
13. Individuals with Schizoid Personality show no _____.
14. They seem _____ about praise, criticism, flat affect, detached.
15. They suffer severe social _____ and conflict _____.

Examples of Schizoid Personality depicted in characters in Hollywood movies might include Anthony Hopkins' portrayal of the head butler in *The Remains of the Day*, actor Ralph Fiennes' pilot in *The English Patient*, and Gary Oldman's role of Leon in *The Professional*.

Exclusions of Schizoid Personality are important to note. Symptoms *do not occur* (a) during a schizophrenic episode, (b) during a mood disorder, (c) along with a pervasive developmental disorder, (d) during a psychotic episode, and (e) due to direct physiological effects of a medical condition.

Schizotypal Personality Disorder

Schizotypal Personality Disorder is also uncommon in the general population, affecting less than 3 percent of clinical clientele. Like Schizoid Personality, it involves a pervasive pattern of social and interpersonal deficits and extreme social anxiety. Unlike Schizoid Personality, patterns include (a) eccentricities of behavior, (b) acute discomfort with close relationships, (c) little capacity (poor skills for) close relationships, and (d) cognitive or perceptual distortions including belief in magical powers or talents. More concretely, individuals exhibit (1) ideas of reference (not delusions) or beliefs, (2) odd thinking and speech, (3) suspiciousness or paranoia, and (4) appearance is odd or facial-hand, body movements are odd, peculiar.

A learning theory etiology of Schizotypal Personality resembles the history of physical, sensory, or emotional deprivation seen above in Schizoid Personality. Here, however, underdevelopment of socially appropriate behaviors were replaced by maladaptive speech or body mannerisms, and superstitious thinking. The superstitious or reified thinking resulted from incorrectly associating or correlating events together that seemingly predicted bad outcomes. Rule-governed behaviors emerging from these repeated and invalid associations convinced the individual he or she possessed special powers, gifts, talents, or can exert mind or energy control over people. Psychics, for example, claiming extrasensory (paranormal) abilities, frequently connect arbitrary or idiosyncratic nuances of the environment with people's behaviors, concluding that one causes the other.

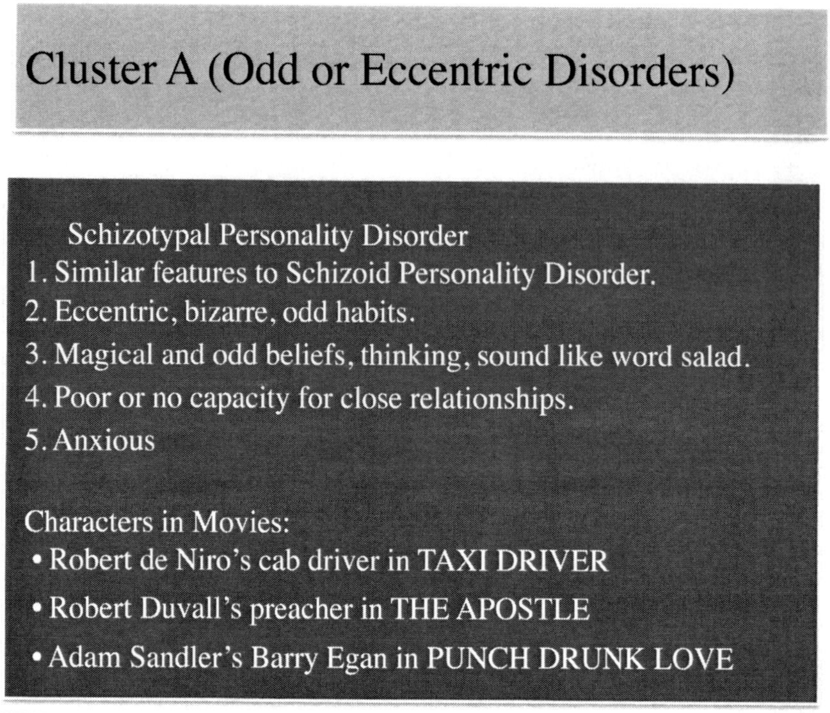

Cluster A (Odd or Eccentric Disorders)

Schizotypal Personality Disorder
1. Similar features to Schizoid Personality Disorder.
2. Eccentric, bizarre, odd habits.
3. Magical and odd beliefs, thinking, sound like word salad.
4. Poor or no capacity for close relationships.
5. Anxious

Characters in Movies:
• Robert de Niro's cab driver in TAXI DRIVER

• Robert Duvall's preacher in THE APOSTLE

• Adam Sandler's Barry Egan in PUNCH DRUNK LOVE

Figure 1.6.

C'mon, remind me:
16. Schizotypal Personality Disorder has patterns similar to _____ Disorder.
17. Individuals claim _____ and odd beliefs.
18. They show poor or no capacity for _____ relationships.

Examples of Schizotypal Personality depicted in characters in Hollywood movies might include actor Robert de Niro's cab driver in *Taxi Driver*, Robert Duvall's role of the preacher in *The Apostle*, and Adam Sadler's portrayal of Barry Egan in *Punch Drunk Love*.

Exclusions of Schizotypal Personality are identical to that of Schizoid Personality Disorder. Symptoms *do not occur* (a) during a schizophrenic episode, (b) during a mood disorder, (c) along with a pervasive developmental disorder, (d) during a psychotic episode, and (e) due to direct physiological effects of a medical condition.

Let's consider Cluster B. Cluster B stands for *Ballistic.* The term "ballistic" aptly describes the impulsive, explosive, reckless, and irrational behaviors produced by four Personality Disorders. These four personality typologies include Antisocial Disorder, Borderline Disorder, Histrionic Disorder, and Narcissistic Disorder. The common thread shared among Cluster B personality disorders is the immaturity of emotions and behaviors exhibited. Behaviors typical of childhood or early adolescence involving rebelliousness, selfishness, codependence, and over-reactivity persist into adulthood, with escalating intensity over minor disappointments. Cluster B personality types exemplify individuals who engage in unreliable, unpredictable, and random patterns that directly incur problems, create difficulties, or distract from rather than assist in finding solutions to problems. Excesses in behavior may deflect people away from helping the individual. This deflection often arouses anxiety in the individual who feels alienated or abandoned from any supporters.

Cluster B (Dramatic, Emotional, or Erratic Disorders)

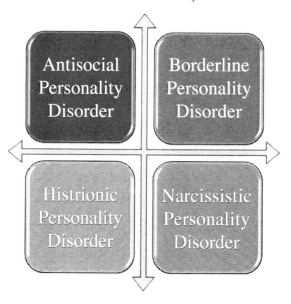

Figure 1.7.

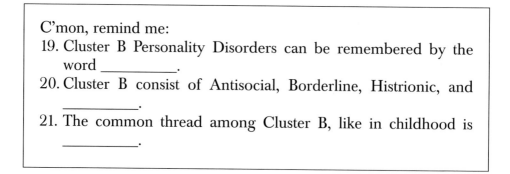

C'mon, remind me:

19. Cluster B Personality Disorders can be remembered by the word _____.

20. Cluster B consist of Antisocial, Borderline, Histrionic, and _____.

21. The common thread among Cluster B, like in childhood is _____.

Antisocial Personality Disorder

Antisocial Personality Disorder affects 3 percent of the general population, and up to 30 percent of clinical populations. It is a pervasive pattern of disregard for and violation of the rights of other people, often emerging in childhood or early adolescence. When repeated disregard for rules, polices, and promulgated norms occurs in youth, often resulting in police convictions, the diagnosis given is *conduct disorder*. The progressive course from Conduct Disorder to Antisocial Personality Disorder, after 18 years of age, depends on the following criteria being met: (a) failure to conform to social norms, (b) deceitfulness, (c) impulsivity, (d) irritability and aggressiveness, (e) reckless disregard for authority, (f) reckless disregard for safety, (g) consistent irresponsibility, and (h) lack of remorse. Observers may characterize the Anti-Social Personality type as (1) untrustworthy, (2) immature, (3) self-centered, (4) charming or smooth talker, (5) a liar, and (6) manipulative.

Note that a common error in semantics is between *antisocial* and *asocial*. In the modern self-help literature, people who are not social or introverts frequently get mislabeled as *antisocial*. Antisocial, we saw above, means, a dereliction of social responsibility and violation of social rules. The proper term describing a nonsocial, introversive, or solitary person is *asocial*. The "a" in *asocial* means "without social."

In learning theory, etiologies for the Anti-Social Personality are manifold (Connor, 2002; Nelson-Gray, Lootens, Mitchell, Robertson, Hundt, & Kimbrel, 2012). The basic tenant holds that children exposed to inconsistent reinforcement and punishment contingencies, often reacted in excessive ways (e.g., tantrums, noncompliance) to generate *any contingency*. Since reinforcers were inaccessible unless prompted excessively, that meant children engaged in high rates of behavior (ratio schedules) for extensive periods of time (interval schedules) to generate parental reactions. Higher rates of behavior meant higher frequency or aggressive behaviors. Extensive periods meant longer durations or unabated persistence of (unwanted) behaviors. When the contingency involved random delivery of punishers, children learned to be pre-emptive, or to respond in advance of anger to avert or avoid the punishment. Such pre-emptive responses appeared as *anticipatory aggression*. Anticipatory aggression was misinterpreted as the child "was always angry." Anticipatory aggression also resulted in numbness or habituation to the punishment contingencies, to a point where the aggressor became indifferent or showed no reaction to the contingencies (i.e., was unemotional, unremorseful).

Cluster B (Dramatic, Emotional, or Erratic Disorders)-Antisocial Personality Disorder

1. Impulsive, deviant, unruly, adventure-seeking.
2. Deceitful, manipulative, liar, charmer.
3. Intimidator, instigator, aggressor, stalker, predator.
4. Conduct disorder in childhood.
5. Mistreats partners-infidelity, domestic violence
6. High risk of juvenile, adult crimes

Characters in Movies:
- Anthony Hopkin's Hannibal Lechter in SILENCE OF THE LAMBS
- Angelina Jolie's Lisa Rowe in GIRL INTERRUPTED
- Malcolm McDowell's Alex in A CLOCKWORK ORANGE

Figure 1.8.

C'mon, remind me:

22. Antisocial Personality means no _____, guilt, empathy and blames others.
23. Individuals with this personality disorder are _____, deviant, unruly.
24. Individuals with Antisocial Personality may _____ partners.

Examples of Antisocial Personality depicted in characters in Hollywood movies might include actor Anthony Hopkins' Hannibal Lechter in *Silence of the Lambs*, Angelina Jolie's Lisa Rowe in *Girl Interrupted*, or the movie classic *A Clockwork Orange*, featuring Malcolm McDowell's role of sociopathic Alex.

Exclusions of Antisocial Personality are when symptoms occur (a) during a schizophrenic episode, (b) during a manic (hypomanic) episode, or (c) due to direct physiological effects of a medical condition.

Borderline Personality Disorder

Borderline Personality Disorder represents only 2 percent of the general population, affecting about 10 percent of outpatient clinical populations. It involves a pervasive pattern of instability in mood and self-image emanating from early adulthood. Specifically observed are (1) frantic efforts to avoid real or imagined *abandonment*; (2) rapid vacillation between overidealization (glorifying) and devaluation (demonizing), also known as *splitting*; (3) negative self-image or feelings of imposterism; (4) impulsiveness (e.g., addictions, adrenaline-rush); (5) recurrent suicidal threats; (6) cyclicity of moods (resembling Bipolar I Disorder); (7) chronic feelings of emptiness; (8) inappropriate or intense anger including displays of erratic temper; and (9) transient, stress-related paranoid thoughts. Hallmark characteristics seen by most outsiders are that individuals with Borderline Personality are (a) demanding; (b) hostile, while also codependent; (c) vaguely threatening; (d) dramatic; (e) manipulative; (f) rageful; (g) rigid; (h) never apologetic; (i) migratory with jobs, friendships, and intimate partner relationships; (j) intolerant of both separation and intimacy; and (k) recurrently depressed or agitated (i.e., never happy).

A learning theory model of Borderline Personality (i.e., Linehan, 1993) hypothesizes four factors causally responsible for symptom development. First, children lost or were separated from parents (guardians), resembling the etiology of Reactive Attachment Disorder (or Disinhibited Social Engagement Disorder). Here, the essential feature was absent or grossly underdeveloped attachment between the child and putative caregiving adults. Second, children exposed to random (arbitrary and capricious) punishment developed inappropriate ways to respond both to the anticipation and actual arrival of the punishment. Efforts to prevent punishment were futile; in other words, efforts were unavoidable and inescapable arousing helplessness (i.e., conditioned suppression, Seligman & Campbell, 1965; Seligman & Johnston, 1973).

Third, children exposed to alcoholic, drug abusive, or dysfunctional parents (mood cycles, severe anger) survived by adapting or navigating around the maze and deluge of a chaotic life. Fourth, children exposed to domineering or overprotective parents and denied or greatly limited in autonomy (e.g., floundering, making personal mistakes) grew clingingly dependent on adult parents for emotional decisions. As adults, overattachment onto other adults (e.g., friends, partners, authorities) provided similar comfort in knowing a secured "caretaker" will render the hard decisions. Abandonment by the caretaker aroused a frenzy of anxiety in the Borderline individual and scornful resentment toward the caretaker. Abandonment also aroused a distorted sense of "emptiness," "loss," "futility," and sadness in the Borderline individual, evolving into depression. This acuity of depression often accompanies presuicidal, parasuicidal, or actual suicidal patterns.

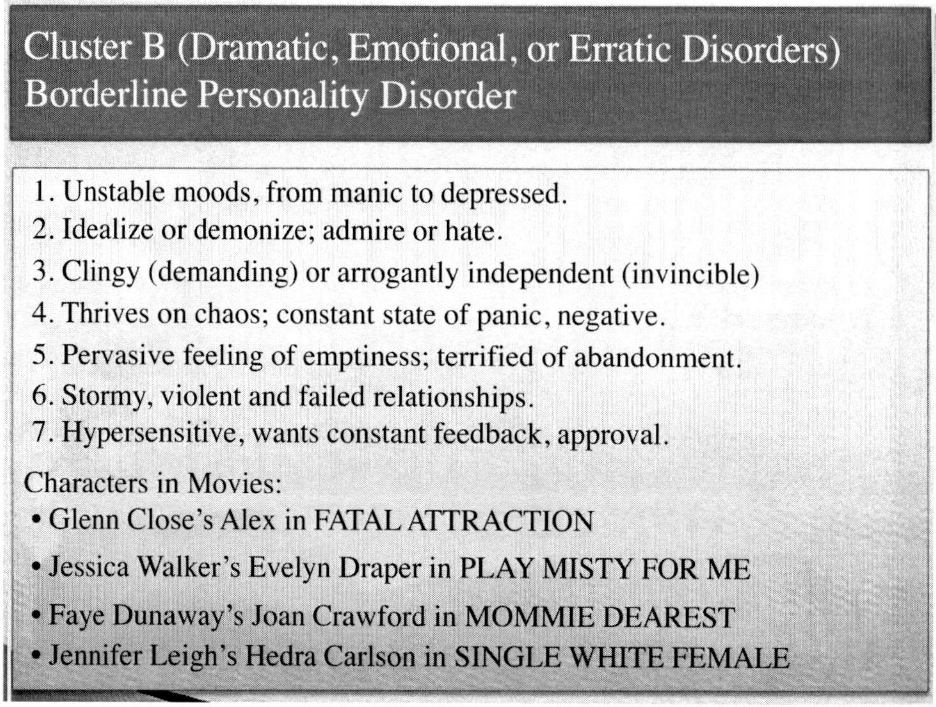

> ## Cluster B (Dramatic, Emotional, or Erratic Disorders)
> ## Borderline Personality Disorder
>
> 1. Unstable moods, from manic to depressed.
> 2. Idealize or demonize; admire or hate.
> 3. Clingy (demanding) or arrogantly independent (invincible)
> 4. Thrives on chaos; constant state of panic, negative.
> 5. Pervasive feeling of emptiness; terrified of abandonment.
> 6. Stormy, violent and failed relationships.
> 7. Hypersensitive, wants constant feedback, approval.
>
> Characters in Movies:
> • Glenn Close's Alex in FATAL ATTRACTION
> • Jessica Walker's Evelyn Draper in PLAY MISTY FOR ME
> • Faye Dunaway's Joan Crawford in MOMMIE DEAREST
> • Jennifer Leigh's Hedra Carlson in SINGLE WHITE FEMALE

Figure 1.9.

C'mon, remind me:
25. Borderline Personality means no _____ moods, from manic to depression.
26. Borderlines may idealize you in one moment and _____ you in another.
27. Borderline individuals typically have stormy, _____, and failed relationships.

Examples of Borderline depicted in characters in Hollywood movies might include actor Glenn Close's portrayal of Alex in *Fatal Attraction,* Jessica Walker's classic role of Evelyn Draper in *Play Misty for Me,* Faye Dunaway's historic portrait of Joan Crawford in *Mommie Dearest,* and Jennifer Leigh's Hedra Carlson in *Single White Female.*

Histrionic Personality

Histrionic Personality affects 10-15 percent of the clinical population. It only appears in an estimated 2-3 percent of the general population. It involves a pervasive pattern of excessive emotionality and attention-seeking behaviors, traceable to early childhood. Common patterns include: (a) need for the "spotlight" or center of attention; (b) seductiveness or provocativeness; (c) rapidly shifting moods and shallow expression of emotions; (d) use of physical appearance to draw attention to self; (e) speech is impressionistic and lacking in detail; (f) acts are dramatic, theatrical, and exaggerated; (g) individual is highly gullible or influenced by other people or circumstances; and (h) perceives relationships as promising more intimacy or attachment than really exists. For example, histrionic individuals are prone to erotomania, or the misperception of another as amorously attractive to the Histrionic person, without any evidence or proof that this attraction is true.

A behavioral explanation of Histrionic Personality concerns three factors. First, children exposed to inconsistent reinforcement (contingencies) exerted much effort (e.g., high ratio strains) to generate either the promise of or actual delivery of the reinforcers. Early demonstrations of tantrums and attention-seeking behaviors formed the pattern of *persistent, sequential, durable,* and *excessive behaviors linked together to generate favorable outcomes.*

During the tantrum sequence, when a child observes attention withheld for his or her antics, the child may oversolicit attention by apologizing or physically clinging on to the parent in between episodes of the robust temper. This interlude between tantrum bursts is called a *tag, since it is tagged onto the cyclical response sequence of the tantrum* (Ruben, 2014). Specifically, tags consist of panic-like, desperate, and exaggerated pleas for forgiveness (i.e., attention), often produced with visceral intensity (e.g., crying) and elaboration of promises ("I will be good, you'll see"). The topographical and functional characteristics of the tag (i.e., syncronicity, duration, sequentiality, content, intensity, frequency, magnitude, etc.) *all strongly resemble and predict histrionic-like behaviors in adults.*

Second, histrionics embody impulsiveness. Children exhibiting attention-seeking behaviors were impatient, spontaneous, demanding, and impulsive. That is, parents overresponded quickly to the attention-seeking child rather than delaying a response to the child. Consequent-ly, early childhood diagnoses comorbidly included Oppo-sitional Defiance Disorder (ODD) or Attention Deficit Hyperactivity Disorder (ADHD) (see Ruben, 1993). Even in adulthood, histrionics show osten-sible tendencies for "childlike" reactions that are superficial, dramatic, showy, needy, and often entail sidetracking onto other topics (i.e., dis-tractibility).

Third, attraction to self or "seductiveness," including using physical appearance to draw attention, is an artifact of conditioned impulsive-ness. One way a preteen or adolescent discovers rapid attention from adults (or peers) is when flaunting his or her body. Ostentatious dis-plays of physical attention may range from dying the hair a strangely bright color, wearing odd combinations of clothing, to wearing mini-mal clothing to expose the individual's natural body shape, contours, or features. The level of deviation in clothing or physical seductiveness all depends on the individual's *reactional biography*, or history of condi-tioning of knowing *how far to risk exhibitionistic behaviors without teetering on social condemnation or police arrest.*

Cluster B (Dramatic, Emotional, or Erratic Disorders)-Histrionic Personality Disorder

1. Dramatic, catastrophic-thinking, thrives on chaos.
2. Seductive, overbearing, demanding, attention-seeking.
3. Shallow, worries about irrelevant features sidetracks.
4. Clingy, needy, immaturely childlike.
5. Perceives self as victim.

Characters in Movies:
• Vivien Leigh's Scarlett O'Hara in GONE WITH THE WIND
• Mike Myers as Austin Powers in series
• Kathleen Turner's voice for Jessica Rabbit in WHO FRAMED ROGER RABBIT

Figure 1.10.

C'mon, remind me:
28. Histrionic Personality means dramatic, _____, or thrives on chaos.
29. Such individuals are seductive, overbearing, _____, attention-seeking.
30. The Histrionic individual perceives self as a _____.

Examples of Histrionic Personality depicted in characters in Hollywood movies might include actress Vivien Leigh's seminal role as Scarlett O'Hara in *Gone with the Wind,* Kathleen Turner's voice-role for Jessica Rabbit in *Who Framed Roger Rabbit,* and comedic actor Nathan Lane in his madcap role as Albert in *The Bird Cage.*

Narcissistic Personality Disorder

Narcissistic Personality Disorder occurs in less than 1 percent of the general population. Ironically, that percentage spikes among clinical populations (16 to 30%). It involves a pervasive pattern of grandiosity driven by a need for self-admiration. Patterns include (a) exaggeration of self-importance; (b) preoccupation with fantasies of unlimited success, power, brilliance, or ideal (self) love; (c) belief of oneself as special, only understood by some; (d) requires excessive admiration from followers; (e) sense of entitlement; (f) interpersonally exploitive; (g) lacks empathy – unwilling to recognize or identify feelings in other people; (h) envious of other people; and (i) righteous and arrogant. Other collateral features frequently observed include (j) mood fluctuations mirroring self-esteem, (k) goal-setting based on gaining approval or falsely high standards, and (l) relationships (friends, intimacy) are largely superficial and exist to serve self-esteem (personal vanity).

A learning model of Narcissistic Personality addresses two major etiologies. The first is an operational chronology by which a self-gratifying child receives continuous reinforcement through childhood and adulthood (e.g., Ruben, 1987). From inner proprioceptive kinesthesia (sensations) that are "inside the skin," to ostensible self-stimulatory behaviors appearing "outside the skin," a progression occurs of self-pleasure through different levels (i.e., hierarchies) of unconditioned reinforcement. Once self-gratification is visible or "outside the skin," observable to parents or the public, censorship (negative social feed-back) rapidly controls most of the flagrantly inappropriate behaviors. For example, a child publicly masturbating would be rebuked by teachers or friends, or in severe cases, by youth probation officers after the child's arrest for indecent exposure.

However, self-gratifying (unconditioned reinforcing) behaviors that go uncensored, and even receive positive support or social reinforcement, may accelerate through adolescence and early adulthood. This is when unconditioned reinforcers, such as masturbating, pair with neutral situations (people watching a person masturbate), and create social or conditioned reinforcers (spectators admiring his or her masturbation). For the behaver, two results occur. First, the behavior "feel good" naturally (unconditioned or *primary* reinforcer). Second, now other people respond favorably to the behaver for engaging in self-gratification (conditioned or *secondary* reinforcer). For example, publicly masturbating adolescents may produce self-pornography uploaded on YouTube, or through payable live streaming. They build up a fan-base of paying customers enabling or reinforcing their continued pornography. As they enter adulthood, pay-for-view pornography abounds. The frequency of their promiscuity may earn higher payoffs by prostituting, or by becoming an escort or gigolo. As social reinforcers increase in many forms (i.e., *generalized reinforcers*), the self-gratifying individual finds multiple ways to generate and maintain self-centered attention.

A second learning model etiology of narcissism can be found in overprotective or excessively "pampering" parents. Children raised with unlimited and noncontingent privileges learn to expect rewards purely by entitlement (Ruben, 2013). The overgiving of love and resources to children by parents does not inspire adventurousness, motivation, individualism, and self-discipline. Just the opposite occurs; the oversaturated child becomes a predator of continuous reinforcement. Abundantly loved and showered generously with accolades, children exert minimal effort for their accolades, growly quickly dependent on the accolades, and consequently demanding the reinforcer-givers (parents) to unselfishly continue the deluge of accolades. Consequently, there are four major side-effects of overflexible parents who overre-ward their children:

1. *Children are immune to rewarding and punitive consequences.* Children praised for everything they do and are rarely or never punished for misbehavior act with great persistence. They may continue a

good behavior excessively or engage in inappropriate behaviors excessively without boundaries. They lack boundaries since they are unaffected by rewards and punishers used to discourage their behaviors.

2. *Children act impulsively, selfishly, angrily, and insensitive to limitations.* Children accustomed to getting their way are resistant to people who say they cannot get their way. They act spontaneously, self-centeredly, and without concern for rules governing their behaviors. Resistance may turn to mild or aggressive anger, whereby the stubborn child adamantly defies authorities by overstepping a rule or finding alternative and deceptive ways to satisfy their wants without the adult knowing about it.

3. *Children resent their parents and other authorities when forced to comply.* Free spirited children oppose pressures of conformity and may challenge the adult forcing them into unwanted action. Opposition is either by arguing, debating, and threatening retaliation. If forced to surrender, they may calculate manipulation by appearing congenial outwardly and planning defiance later. Such passive-aggressive adolescents pass into adulthood and show this pattern in jobs. They struggle with working for employers who tell them what to do against their better judgment. They view obedience as robbing them of individuality and brainwashing.

4. *Children refuse to take responsibility for their mistakes and expect exoneration for wrongful acts against society.* The biggest consequence of overflexible rearing is children who do not feel accountable for their actions. They grow up without household chores, completing tasks, or following through with promises. Mistakes they make, from breaking objects to lateness, all are excused as "normal stages of growth" and absorbed by the overpampering parent so the child will not feel guilty. Without learning "shame" for simple infractions, the vindicated child goes through life never assuming culpability for his or her mistakes and blaming everybody else for the his or her misfortunes.

Cluster B (Dramatic, Emotional, or Erratic Disorders) Narcissistic Personality Disorder

1. Selfish, self-absorbed, arrogant, sees self as superior.
2. Need for admiration, competitive, sees people as envious of him.
3. Angry, explosive, irritable, defensive.
4. Dominates and exploits partners; unfaithful, promiscuous.
5. Lack of empathy, demeaning, self-righteous, lacks remorse.
6. High risk of adult crimes and polysubstance abuse
7. Impulsive, adrenaline-junkie

Characters in Movies:
• Michael Douglas' Gordon Grecko in WALL STREET
• Jesse Eisenberg's Mark Zuckerberg in THE SOCIAL NETWORK
• Barbara Hershey's mother in THE BLACK SWAN
• Ralph Fiennes' Amon Goth in SCHINDLER'S LIST

Figure 1.11.

C'mon, remind me:
31. Narcissistic Personality means self-absorbed, arrogant, sees self as _____.
32. Such individuals get angry, explosive, irritable, and _____.
33. Narcissistic individuals tend to be impulsive and _____-junkies.

Examples of Narcissistic Personality depicted in characters in Hollywood movies might include actor Alan Alda's character in the movie *Crimes and Misdemeanors*, Michael Douglas' portrayal of Gordon Gekko in *Wall Street*, Jesse Eisenberg's Oscar-nominated role of Facebook pioneer Mark Zuckerberg in *The Social Network*, and Ralph Fiennes' role as Nazi commandant Amon Göth in *Schindler's List*.

The last cluster of personalities is Cluster C, for *Cowardice*. This cluster covers three personality disorders: Avoidant, Dependent, and Obsessive-Compulsive. The common threads stringing these personalities together include (a) anxiety (fears); (b) interpersonal deficits; (c) conflict-avoidance; (d) inhibitions; and (e) hypersensitivity to criticism, disapproval, or rejection. Typologies describe generally shy, docile, passive, submissive, and socially underdeveloped individuals who are people-pleasers. Personal histories are replete with (a) childhood or adult trauma; (b) physical, verbal, emotional, or sexual abuse; (c) parental mistreatment or exposure to substance abusive or randomly punitive parents; and (d) overdependence on people, situations, or invented rituals.

Cluster C (Anxious or Fearful Disorders)

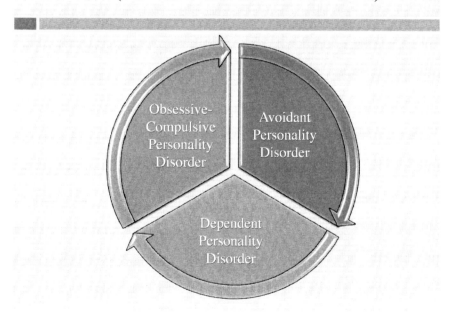

Figure 1.12.

C'mon, remind me:
34. Cluster C stands for _____ or anxious or fearful disorders.
35. Cluster C includes Avoidant, _____, and Obsessive-Compulsive.
36. Cluster C includes _____ disorders.

Avoidant Personality Disorder

Avoidant Personality Disorder occurs in about 10 percent of a clinical population. In the general population, nearly 3.8 million people (1.8%) meet criteria for Avoidant Personality. Symptoms reflect a pervasive pattern of social inhibition. The main diagnostic standards include: (a) feelings of inadequacy; (b) poor interpersonal skills; (c) hypersensitivity to criticism, conflict, rejection, or abandonment; (d) unwillingness to get involved unless certain to be liked (approved); (e) self-suppressed or inhibited in friendships and intimate relationships; (f) preoccupied with being judged negatively; (g) self-perception of inferiority; and (h) reluctant to take risks for fear of embarrassment.

A behavior analysis of Avoidant Personality Disorder and the complex constellation of behaviors accompanying it appear extensively in the evidence-based research (e.g., Dymond & Roche, 2009; Garber & Seligman, 1980; Harper, Iwata, & Camp, 2013; Ruben, 1993b). Reasons expound upon four variables responsible for the genesis of avoidant tendencies. These include: (1) avoidance and escape; (2) hyperalertness or "hypervigilance" to subtle, superficial, or reified properties of the environment; (3) anticipatory avoidance and anticipatory aggression; and (4) interpersonal deficits (introversion). Briefly:

Avoidance and escape. Avoidance and escape revolve around the fear of punishment. Punishment is aversive. It can take many forms from parental and spousal rebukes, to peer and supervisor confrontations. Avoidance describes an integrated sequence of responses sequentially engineered to avert, prevent, or delay contact with the punishment. Escape implies contact already occurs, and now the goal changes. The goal is to disrupt or eliminate the punishment. Increases in avoidance or escape behavior all depend on the success or failure of the action attempted. When avoidance and escape fail repeatedly, exposure to punishment arouses anxiety at first and then, as the individual habituates to the punishment, anxiety titrates to nonresponsiveness or *tolerance*.

Hyperalertness or hypervigilance. Hyperalertness (hypervigilance) is a heightened awareness of environmental cues that signal the impending arrival of punishment. Cues vary in context and content, ranging from conspicuous to inconspicuous, and from real to fake. Spouses married to domestically violent partners may pair or associate the violence (aggression) with the aggressor and with many real or imagined properties of the aggression. Pairings occur shortly before, during, and after the aggression. A conspicuous cue may be the garage door opening as the aggressive partner returns home. Inconspicuous cues are noises that sound similar to but not exactly like the garage door that opens when the partner returns home (i.e., metaphorical extension, see Skinner, 1957). Real cues are measurable, tangible, and observable ones. Fake or imagined cues are cues that lack any defining features of the fearful cue and are concocted or perceived as valid as the fearful cues (e.g., metonymical cues, Skinner, 1957). The spouse "thought he or she heard the garage door" and did not know what was heard, but reacted as if the partner returned home.

Anticipatory anxiety and aggression. Anticipatory anxiety and aggression are both pre-emptive actions. When punishment seems inevitable, two common coping strategies are either to avoid and escape it, or confront it head on. Avoidance and escape requires an individual to be hyperalert or use "mental" radar to scan for signs of oncoming punishment. Overattention arouses a visceral or anxious state as the person is "waiting" for the punishment. This is called *anticipatory anxiety.* On the obverse, directly confronting the punishment entails an overreaction. An individual may get angry, defensive, or fiercely aggressive to change the inevitable course of the punishment. *Anticipatory aggression* attempts to intimidate or stop the angry person or situations promising aggression. For example, an employee who anticipates being reprimanded by the supervisor for incorrectly assembling parts, may burst out in an explosive rage. This outburst is to delay, interrupt, or prevent the supervisor from issuing the verbal or written reprimand. At the moment the supervisor delays the reprimand or forgives the employee and does not issue the reprimand, the adult employee ceases the aggression and restores normal work behavior.

Interpersonal deficits (introversion). A common denominator among individuals with Avoidant Personality is underdevelopment of interpersonal social skills. Social skill deficits vary from unassertiveness, inhibitions, lack of conflict-coping skills, and self-suppression, to poorly interpreting interpersonal cues during social exchanges (i.e., speech pragmatics). In severe cases, deficits in speech pragmatics may be found along the spectrum of Autism Disorder; in milder cases, misinterpretation of cues may relate to differences in cultural and familial norms and values, uncorrected during normal interactions. For example, a Honduras refugee who only speaks Spanish and now lives with his cousins in Miami, Florida, may poorly decipher the visual cues or subtle intraverbals used by English speakers. Certain colloquialisms, idiomatic expressions, or facial reactions accompanying phrases may be absent in the refugee's indigent language.

Then, too, children raised in isolation from their peer mainstream during preteens and adolescent years, in homeschooling or in Amish families, may develop some but not all of the age-normative social skills to function comfortably in the macrocosm. A third example includes children repeatedly rejected from their social peer groups in school or in community functions, and who spend enormous time playing massively multiplayer online role-playing games (MMORPGs). Intragame communication may foster some interpersonal communication skills and build tenacity in reaching out to international game-players. However, the esoteric language used in game-playing exchanges does not generalize well into the complex world of nongame peer interactions.

Examples of Avoidant Personality depicted in characters in Hollywood movies might include Woody Allan's role as Zelig in *Zelig*, actor Donald Sutherland's portrayal of Calvin Jarrett in *Ordinary People*, and Leonardo di Caprio's brilliant biographical presentation of Howard Hughes in *The Aviator*.

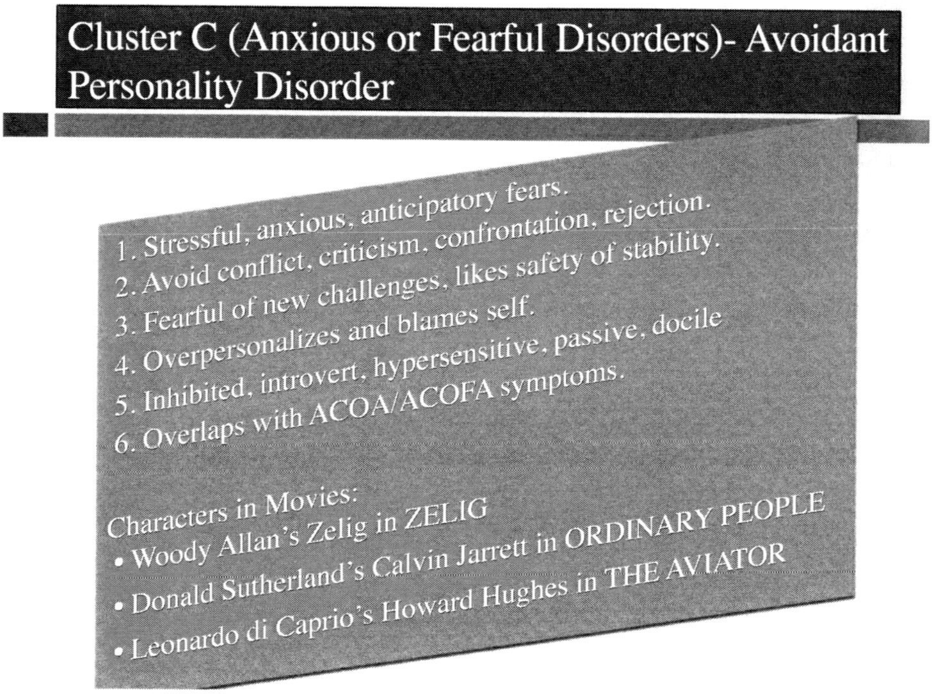

Cluster C (Anxious or Fearful Disorders)- Avoidant Personality Disorder

1. Stressful, anxious, anticipatory fears.
2. Avoid conflict, criticism, confrontation, rejection.
3. Fearful of new challenges, likes safety of stability.
4. Overpersonalizes and blames self.
5. Inhibited, introvert, hypersensitive, passive, docile
6. Overlaps with ACOA/ACOFA symptoms.

Characters in Movies:
• Woody Allan's Zelig in ZELIG
• Donald Sutherland's Calvin Jarrett in ORDINARY PEOPLE
• Leonardo di Caprio's Howard Hughes in THE AVIATOR

Figure 1.13.

C'mon, remind me:
37. Avoidant Personality means fearful of new challenges, likes _____ of stability.
38. Avoidant individuals overpersonalize and blame _____.
39. Avoidant Personality overlaps with _____ and _____ symptoms.

Avoidant Personality overlaps with a subgroup of clinical symptoms originating in childhood and causing severe psychopathology in adulthood. Symptoms emerge from children exposed to alcoholic (or drug abusive) parents or parents with chronic emotional or behavioral disturbance. Such children, when they grow up, are called *Adult Children of Alcoholics* (ACOAs) and *Adult Children of Family Abuse* (ACOFA). Although these subclassifications of troublesome behaviors have received much attention in the social science literature (Ackerman, 1983;

Black, 1982; Brown, 1988), only in the last decade has there been a behavioral analysis to operationally explain the developmental phenomena underlying these clinical syndromes (Ruben, 1992, 2001).

Analysis of the continuous developmental process of children raised in alcoholic or nonalcoholic households reflects three potential contingencies between parent and child. First, children may be exposed to one drinking or drug abusing adult and one nonsubstance-abusing adult. Second, children may be exposed to two diametrically different parent personalities. One parent may be loud, aggressive, dogmatic, and critical, whereas the second parent may be docile, passive, submissive, and placating. Third, children may be exposed to one or two parents (or guardians) who are quiet, timid, introversive, and conflict-avoidant. In the first case, of substance-abusing parents, children navigate around random and distrustful contingencies; they never can predict the timing or severity of punishment, which fosters anxiety. In the second case, the aggressively loud or violent parent is more predictable, which fosters habituation or desensitization (tolerance) to the anger. Tolerance rapidly evolves into helplessness, a prodromal step to depression. In the third case, silent households never teach healthy conflict interchange. Into adulthood, conflict-deprived (adult) children grow anxious around peer groups who are assertive, more blunt, and confrontational.

Ten behaviors compromise a pattern of ACOA or ACOFA symptoms resulting from these three contingencies. This constellation of behaviors include: (1) passivity or aggressiveness, (2) trouble expressing feelings, (3) cannot seem to relax, (4) are loyal (codependent) beyond reason, (5) are overly responsible, (6) fear of losing control, (7) difficulty with relationships (friendships, intimacies), (8) fear of conflict, (9) overly self-critical, and (10) becoming addictive to excitement.

1.   *Personality is one of two major types: Passive or Aggressive.* Dichotomy of behavior is predictable. ACOAs or ACOFAs raised under a random, untrusting, and frequently punitive environment adapt by responding in one of two major ways. First, rebellion toward that environment appears in the form of challenging the abusing adults. Expressed anger is outwardly aggressive, violent, or oppositional in terms of severe tantrums, noncompliance, running away, lying, stealing, and hyperactivity. In adolescence, when verbal skills are complex, refusals and defiance intensify as the child completely distrusts his parents and assumes total control over personal goals and gratification. Into adult-

hood, this controlling behavior appears manipulating, domineering, and attractive to inept or deficient partners desperate for caretaking partners. Aggression subsides a bit but the person maintains low tolerance to frustration and is easily upset by disruptions in rigidly-planned schedules or decisions. Hostility shown over disruptions, however, *is not to evoke conflict.* Conflict remains avoided at all costs.

The other extreme is more gentle, docile, passively withdrawn from social decisions, confrontations, and ambitions. In childhood this person withdrew from familial antagonism or turned into a mediator, trying to arbitrate peace among hostile parties. Placating aggressive urges of adult parents denied the child his own personal pleasures, opportunities for peer growth, and instilled fear over being autonomous outside the household. Kept within family boundaries, the frightened child developed hypersensitivity to receiving parental approval through personal sacrifice. Approval becomes identified as the only source of love, affirmation, and proof of the child's worthiness. Seeking approval by pleasing, caretaking, or assuming unwanted responsibility further averted conflict.

The irony in both personality patterns is that conflict is absolutely anathema. Conflict threatens the fragile balance of confidence and self-hatred that already is shaken by frequent doubts and distrust among adults. Feared most from adults is criticism for any reason. Aggressively controlling ACOAs anticipate or dismantle conflict by exhibiting aggression pre-emptively against their alleged predators. Rude remarks, hostile provocations, using predators as brunt of jokes, and even "egging on" the predator until he or she explodes, all function to delay or prevent confrontation. Passively controlling ACOAs seek the same goal exactly and thus their behaviors operationally are identical: To defuse rising hostility. However, efforts at defusal are the opposite. Efforts involve satisfying the legitimate or illegitimate needs of predators in anticipation of conflict. They may surrender unwillingly to peculiar wants and needs imposed upon them by predators, hoping the outcome will instantly restore peace. How long this peace lasts is irrelevant.

2. *Trouble expressing feelings.* ACOAS and ACOFAS stuff their feelings internally and refuse sharing anything personally vulnerable. Expression would risk exposure of faults, of looking incompetent, of being disapproved or causing anger in others. Consequently speech is very selective, labored, edited, and words expressed are replayed in

thought over and over to test whether they upset the listener.

3.   *Cannot seem to relax.* ACOAS and ACOFAs appear highly active, constantly busy, and unable to slow down their pace for fear of feeling unproductive, wasteful, and lazy. Even sitting is accompanied by fidgeting, working on projects, and thoughts are racing. Slow, calming, or vegetative actions evoke sudden panic and shame. Panic is from the expectation of punishment coming from an authority or significant other (boyfriend, girlfriend, spouse), even if the person lives alone. Feelings of impending criticism overwhelm the person and mobilizes him or her into immediate action to relieve the anxiety. Reactions of guilt or shame arise from *wanting to just relax but believing it is awful and immoral.* Anticipatory fears evolved from never having opportunities to relax or play by oneself, if compelled to be responsible for other siblings or constantly helping other people.

4.   *Are loyal (codependent) beyond reason.* ACOAS and ACOFAS become dependent personalities who are terrified of abandonment and would do anything to hold onto a relationship not to re-experience the painful separation felt from living with people who never were emotionally there for them. Loyalty also means self-appointed commitment to any cause, group, or friendships no matter how problematic or dysfunctional the situation becomes. The adult must stay aboard that *Titanic* even if everyone else abandons ship. This martyrdom affirms beliefs that the adult is incomparably superior in loyalty and well deserves the praise and approval of her recipients.

5.   *Are overly responsible.* A corollary to *loyal beyond reason* is taking on far more than the adult can chew. Adults have an overdeveloped sense of responsibility focusing entirely on the welfare of another person rather than on themselves. Shifts from selfishness prevent drawing too much attention to their faults (or assets) and disapproval for being conceited. Helping others, also called *caretaking* or *enabling,* involves total consumption with organizing, solving, or directing lives of other people to guarantee their unconditional approval and ongoing friendship. Forfeiture of personal needs varies from small sacrifices to complete self-neglect, frequently disintegrating down to living or dying depending on whether it pleases another person. Targets for enablers are generally weak people suffering some emotional or physical disability, or underdeveloped socially. It becomes a natural challenge for enablers to commit to the rehabilitation of that person, not for the victory, but for assurance of their approval.

6. *Fear of losing control.* Loss of control translates to panic over look-ing vulnerable. *Vulnerability* poses serious threats to inadequacies kept private and below the surface. Lack of leadership, or denied opportu-nities to direct, coordinate, or organize people or things instills a fear of abandonment. That other people do not need this adult or regard his services as unimportant thereby implies the person is incapable, incom-petent, and has shortcomings. Inferring this rejection, adults believe they failed certain expectations and may immediately rebound with double the amount of energy and commitment aspiring to please the person at all costs.

7. *Difficulty with relationships.* There are two types of relationship failures. First is with social interactions. Second involves the wrong choice of interpersonal and intimate partners. Building social peer groups is difficult because the composition of people must be passive, weak, or amenable to the adult's peculiar idiosyncracies. For ACOAs and ACOFAS who are shy, overprecautious, and passive, groups must already identify an assertive leader who commands authority and com-pliance from members. For ACOAs who are aggressive, perfectionis-tic, and workaholics, groups must be passively receptive to the rigid guidance and offer a surplus of laudable remarks. In intimacy, forming a cohesive relationship again requires attraction to either extreme in a single person. The *failure* exists from discovering that opposite attrac-tions turn sour very quickly or after a series of conflicts.

8. *Fear of conflict.* Aggressive or passive ACOAS and ACOFAS are equally afraid of conflict. Conflict refers to any disagreement, criticism, or opinion lodged against the adult for inappropriate behavior. Conflict resembles childhood situations of inescapable and unavoidable parental punishment causing shame, self-criticism, and desperate need for approval. Hatred of conflict becomes so fierce that adults literally say or do anything to avert confrontation, even if escaping it will ulti-mately pay the price of another, ensuing confrontation.

9. *Are overly self-critical.* Self-deprecation develops from replaying what ACOAS and ACOFAS therapists call "mental tapes." Tapes are essentially obsessive thoughts in the form of religious, moral, or pow-erfully persuasive beliefs on how behavior *should be, ought to be, and must be.* These are rule-governed behaviors discussed earlier or colloquially referred to as *musterbations.* Such "musterbations" (cf., Ellis, 1962) take two forms. One form is constant negative assaults on imperfections or mistakes believed to be preventable or controllable, using the same

words, phrases, or intonations recalled from the adult's parents when they were verbally assaultive years ago. Replays of parental verbal abuse shift from the object-mistake in question to generalized attacks regarding the adult's integrity ("you're so stupid") or unrealistic perception of life ("who do you think you are anyway, you won't amount to anything").

10. *Become addicted to excitement, alcoholics, abusers, or compulsive people.* ACOAS and ACOFAS either become alcoholic, marry an alcoholic (or drug abuser), or both, or find another compulsive personality such as a workaholic or overeater to fulfill their own compulsive needs. Why is this? Attraction to excitement largely occurs when the passive adults are dissatisfied with the monotony of boring daily routines. They are desperate for escapism and lack the skills to achieve this objective without coercion from or caretaking for an energetic person. By contrast, more aggressive ACOAS and ACOFAS at first resist excitable, impulsive people; they seek just the opposite disposition. They gravitate toward reserved, docile, or emotionally disabled persons, who suppress their abuses until the relationship (in friendship or intimacy) develops fully. Whether the ACOAs or ACOFAs are extroverts or introverts, they do share a reason for addiction to excitement. Excitement or any hedonistic-like fun eluded them in childhood; they never had ample opportunities to experience it. They were raised to be overresponsible to compensate for their profoundly impulsive (nonresponsible) parent-adults.

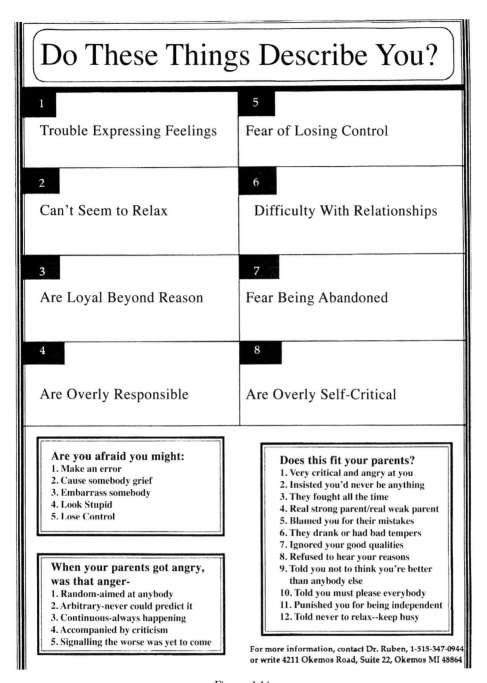

Do These Things Describe You?

1 Trouble Expressing Feelings

5 Fear of Losing Control

2 Can't Seem to Relax

6 Difficulty With Relationships

3 Are Loyal Beyond Reason

7 Fear Being Abandoned

4 Are Overly Responsible

8 Are Overly Self-Critical

Are you afraid you might:
1. Make an error
2. Cause somebody grief
3. Embarrass somebody
4. Look Stupid
5. Lose Control

Does this fit your parents?
1. Very critical and angry at you
2. Insisted you'd never be anything
3. They fought all the time
4. Real strong parent/real weak parent
5. Blamed you for their mistakes
6. They drank or had bad tempers
7. Ignored your good qualities
8. Refused to hear your reasons
9. Told you not to think you're better than anybody else
10. Told you must please everybody
11. Punished you for being independent
12. Told never to relax--keep busy

When your parents got angry, was that anger-
1. Random-aimed at anybody
2. Arbitrary-never could predict it
3. Continuous-always happening
4. Accompanied by criticism
5. Signalling the worse was yet to come

For more information, contact Dr. Ruben, 1-515-347-0944 or write 4211 Okemos Road, Suite 22, Okemos MI 48864

Figure 1.14.

C'mon, remind me:
40. ACOAs and ACOFAs are overly self-_____.
41. Such individuals have trouble expressing _____.
42. They have difficulties with _____.

Dependent Personality Disorder

Dependent Personality Disorder affects about 2.5 percent of the general population. A rare incident rate at best, many of its pervasive features overlap with *avoidant personality.* Dominant patterns include *a need to be taken care of.* Dependent personality types cling desperately or codependently onto receptive hosts, whom they see as confident saviors. They fear criticism, conflict, rejection, and live entirely through the dominant person's judgments or perceptions of life. They morbidly fear *separation and abandonment.* For this reason, dependent personality types often gravitate repeatedly to destructive or violent partner relationships with unawareness and later a generous dose of forgiveness. This repetition of partner attraction is called *Serial Partner Attraction Syndrome (SPAS).*

Learning theory etiologies borrow from the existing literature on Reaction Attachment Disorder (RAD) (e.g., Hall & Geher, 2003). RAD presumes a disturbance formed in the early relationship between child and parent (guardian) in establishing hypersensitivity to physical locality (proximity), and emotional accessibility (i.e., protection). In the absence of parent close-by or providing clear delivery of reinforcers or punishers, a child becomes *anxious, fearful, and dreads separation (abandonment) from the parent.* Poorly adaptive children may attach onto peers or other peers' parents, or other authorities (teachers, police officers, etc.) from whom they can reproduce the same contingencies expected (and denied) from their parents. When substitute or surrogate parents for attachment are not found, the attachment failure arouses constant doubts that *any attachment is possible, with anybody.* Dependent adults thus lack confidence, motivation, ambition, or any semblance of hope unless connected vicariously into another person. The dependent adult lacks an identity per se, and instead absorbs the identity of the host onto whom they are parasites.

Cluster C (Anxious or Fearful Disorders)- Dependent Personality Disorder

1. Helpless, submissive, needy, clingy.
2. Indecisive, solicits opinions from everyone, fear of mistakes.
3. Morbidly fearful of separation, abandonment.
4. Avoids conflict, passive, docile, chameleon-effect
5. Severely caretaking, vicarious, empathic, codependent.
6. People-pleasers.
7. Prone to Serial Partner Attraction Syndrom (SPAS)

Characters in Movies:
  • Isabella Rossellini's Dorothy Vallens in BLUE VELVET
  • Charlotte Rampling's Lucia Atherton in THE NIGHT PORTER
  • Bill Murray's Bobby Wiley in WHAT ABOUT BOB?
  • Jessica Chastain's Celia Foote in THE HELP

Figure 1.15.

C'mon, remind me:
43. Dependent personality types are helpless, submissive, needy, and _____.
44. They avoid _____, and have a chameleon effect.
45. They are prone to Serial _____ _____.

Examples of Dependent Personality depicted in characters in Hollywood movies might include actress Isabella Rossellini's Dorothy Vallens in *Blue Velvet,* Jessica Chastain's dizzy character of Celia Foote in *The Help,* and Bill Murray's comedic house-visitor Bobby Wiley in *What About Bob?*

Obsessive-Compulsive Personality Disorders

Obsessive-compulsive personality affects only 3–10 percent of the clinical population despite its social popularity. It describes a pervasive preoccupation with orderliness, control, and perfectionism. Focus is on details, rules, lists, organizations, schedules, and standards of expected action. Such individuals are overconscientious, scrupulous and rigid about their morals, religious beliefs, cultural values, or system by which they govern their lives. Often their high level of orderliness interferes with normal functional routines of daily life. For example, parents who toilet-train their children may expect soil-free-diapers after two days of training. They impatiently scold their child for *failing to listen, learn, and reach the goals.* Partners in marriage expecting a Disney-fantasy or Utopic relationship may condemn the marriage to foreclosure when every day is not perfect. *Order and rightfulness* are the underlying precepts dictating what is and is not right.

With personality disorders, the theme is always a pervasive pattern, not a specific behavior that is clinically pathological. It is more of a "mind-set" or perception of how *things should be,* which may or may not directly influence specific behaviors. For Obsessive-Compulsive Personality Disorder, the theme or "mind-set" of perfectionism permeates the entire constellation or behaviors. This is very different from the clinical disorder called *Obsessive-Compulsive Disorder.* Here, patterns of behavior uniquely blend together as concurrent or sequential responses that make up a chain (Delprato, 1986; Delprato & McGlynn, 1988; Ruben, 1990). This chain of response occurs in the same way, each time, like a ritual or superstition to prevent loss of control (anxiety). The person who does this chain of responses, however, may not be a perfectionist. They obsess over the responses, and then act on the obsession *compulsively.* For example, excessive hand-washing that occurs 50 times per day may entail a chain or sequential order of exact responses in completing the washing. First, one goes into the bathroom. Then, one lathers both hands with soap, each about 20 seconds. Then, one rinses off the soap between fingers. Then, one dries the hands with a towel. The entire sequence may need to occur twice or three times before the person leaves the bathroom.

This obsessive-compulsive ritual is exhausting and disrupts a normal day. The obsessive-compulsive hand-washer, however, may not believe in orders, rules, or feel his or her life must be perfect. *The behavior is obsessive-compulsive, but the behavior is specific, not general to the entire personality.* In clinical practice as well as in the general public, confusion frequently occurs between Obsessive-Compulsive Disorder and Obsessive-Compulsive Personality Disorder. They are distinct, and one disorder may not overlap with the other disorder. However, like any clinical syndrome, there are many cases where there is a clear overlap.

A behavioral analysis of Obsessive-Compulsive Personality Disorder and treatment for it partly derives from the wealth of literature on behavioral etiology and intervention for obsessive-compulsive disorder (e.g., Foa, Yadin & Lichner, 2012). Four parts comprise the analysis. First, children react to contingent and noncontingent delivery of punishment. Second, postpunishment reactions in children through early adulthood develop avoidance and escape patterns. Third, use of avoidance and escape patterns evolve into development of superstitious behaviors. Fourth, rules develop about avoidance and escape, superstitious behaviors, and ways to avert the punishment; referred to earlier as *rule-governed behaviors.* Let us briefly consider each part.

Contingent and Noncontingent Effects of Punishment

CONTINGENT EFFECTS. *Contingent effects of punishment* are essentially any aversive stimuli (electric, noxious, social) which supports responses that eliminate or reduce such stimulation. That is, there is a clear "link" between stimuli (or setting events) and behavior. A contingent relationship between aversive setting events and responses further denote the presence of *discriminative* and *consequential* cues. These two cues function in different ways, but may or may not occur together. Discriminative cues ("antecedents") forewarn of ensuing stimulation, whereas consequential cues ("consequences") produce an increase or decrease in responding. Discriminative cues may signal onset of aversive stimulation in the form of *time* (when it will occur), *intensity* (how bad it will be), *duration* (how long it will last), *frequency* (how many times it will occur), or *latency* (how much time will elapse before the next onset). Time in between termination of one aversive stimulus and onset of another aversive stimulus is called *Inter-trial-interval (ITI).*

Conditioning of *discriminative* cues can be operant, respondent, or both. If the discriminative cue is operant, it signals ("evokes") an oncoming consequence for some behavior. If it is respondent, it triggers ("elicits") a reflex-like or reactive behavior regardless of the outcome.

In most cases, *both operant and respondent operations occur in what is called intermingling effects.*

In the respondent paradigm, conditioning is usually primary (uncon-ditioned) or secondary (conditioned). Primary aversive stimuli (cues) cause naturalistic, biological, or unlearned reactions, such as electric shock eliciting pain or a loud noise eliciting a startled reflex. When a primary aversive stimulus pairs several times with neutral or benign events, the latter events acquire elicitive properties similar to the pri-mary aversive stimulus. Such stimuli are called *secondary* or *conditioned aversive stimuli.* These secondary or conditioned stimuli now can pro-duce exactly the same behavior as the primary stimulus does. The behavior produced by the secondary (conditioned) stimuli are called *conditioned emotional responses.* For example, a child gets upset (visceral arousal) when his parent yells at him. He hears the yelling (uncondi-tioned stimulus) while also hearing the garage door open up (neutral stimulus). Soon, the child feels upset (conditioned emotional response) just from hearing the garage door open up (conditioned stimulus).

An interesting variation is *how these two stimuli are paired and what may happen as a result.* In other words, does it matter if the garage door opens first, before the parent yells? What happens if the pairing is the other way around? The parent yells followed by the sound of the garage door. *Such qualities describe the temporal parameters of conditioning.* There are four types of temporal pairings. One way is called *delayed condition-ing.* This is where the unconditioned stimulus follows the conditioned stimulus after some delay of time (seconds). It is the *most powerful and durable effect of aversive conditioning.* That is, the electric garage door opens and 30 seconds later mom yells at her child. Consequently, the child will feel fear more quickly, intensely, and longer-lasting when hearing only the garage door open up. The child may also scurry to clean his room more voraciously to mitigate or relieve that fear.

A second way is *trace conditioning.* Here, the unconditioned stimulus follows the conditioned stimulus, *after it pairs simultaneously with condi-tioned stimulus* for a brief second or two. The noise of the garage door opening coincides briefly with mom yelling. The interval of time in between the conditioned stimulus and unconditioned stimulus is called the *trace interval.* If this interval is short, for example, mom yells just as the garage door opens, fear arousal is fast and intense. If mom yells after several minutes, and just about when the noise of the garage door disappears, impact is weaker on the child and his fear is transient. That is, he can recover faster from his fear. For example, hearing the garage may at first arouse fear, and prompt room-cleaning. If he hears mom yelling immediately, it may determine, in the future, how fast and furious he cleans his room; if there is a delay of hearing mom's yelling, he might pause before cleaning his room *or do more cleaning, in the same sequence. He may anticipate that his longer-sequence of cleaning somehow averts or delays mom's yelling.*

A third way is simultaneous conditioning. Here, the unconditioned and conditioned stimuli occur simultaneously. The garage door goes up just as the mom screams at her son. Despite what seems the ideal temporal contiguity for aversive learning, the truth is that just the opposite occurs. The impact effect is very weak. In fact, if the conditioned stimulus already paired several times with the unconditioned stimulus and now it occurs simultaneous with it, the elicitive effects are blocked or impaired (Kamin, 1969). The garage door *loses its fear-inducing properties,* but this phenomenon occurs only briefly. Ironically, the boy may attribute the sudden loss of fear to other factors, such as that he races to clean his room in a certain sequence, or *ritual.* He believes his ritual of cleaning is (magically) responsible for not feeling afraid when the garage door noise starts.

Two interesting variations on trace and simultaneous conditioning can confuse the boy more. After so many pairings between the unconditioned stimulus and conditioned stimulus, either in successive order or simultaneously, the conditioned stimulus is *no longer new or a surprise. It loses its associative strength or fear-inducing properties.* This is based on the Rescorla and Wagner model of classical conditioning (Rescorla & Wagner, 1972). Van Hamme and Wasserman (1994) expanded on the Rescorla and Wagner model by showing that repeated pairings between two conditioned stimuli can also reduce the *associative value* of one or both of the paired conditioned stimuli. Meaning, the boy will become *less* fearful over time when the garage door opens and is paired with his mother yelling or is also paired with noises of the mother throwing objects (e.g., her purse) on the table (i.e., a second conditioned stimulus). However, according to the boy, who is unaware of this conditioning process, he still believes that his diminished fear is due to rapid and meticulous cleaning done in some exact sequence or ritual.

A fourth way is called *backward conditioning.* Pairings occur with the unconditioned stimulus first, followed by the conditioned stimulus. This operation produces an unexpected result over a short period of time. The onset of the conditioned stimulus actually reduces or *inhibits* the conditioned emotional reaction elicited by unconditioned stimulus. Suppose, for example, the boy heard his mother scream at him *first, and then heard the garage door close.* At first he felt anxious, or felt *anticipatory of something bad* (also called "foreboding"). After multiple pairings of his mother's yelling and the garage door, *in that order,* hearing the garage door shut might *calm him or reduce his fear.* As far as the boy knows, he still believes his reduced anxiety owes to fast and clever cleaning rituals as soon as his mother yells at him.

Contingent punishment also involves instrumental (operant) conditioning, or the role of *consequences.* Consequences follow two types. One type is when the aversive event is presented to some response. For example, when the boy hears the garage door go down, and asks "Are you home, mom?," his mother belts out a loud profanity and gets angry at the boy. Delivery of her anger is presented or occurs immediately after her son asks the question. Traditionally, this process is called *positive punishment.* A second type of operant punishment is when an expected aversive outcome is reduced or removed. In our example, the boy does not ask a question when he hears the garage door go down. Instead, upon hearing the garage door, he abruptly yells to his mother, "Mom, I want you to know I started cleaning my room and it's almost done." He made a *mand,* or statement enjoining or persuading the listener (his mother) to withhold, reduce, or eliminate the punishment, in this case his mother's yelling. Historically, the boy found if he told her *what ritual of cleaning he was engaged in, she would not yell at him.* This second type of operant punishment is called *negative punishment.* In theory, effects of punishment – positive or negative – should decelerate behavior. The boy should be doing something less often.

The trouble with definitions of negative and positive punishment in predicting punishment is that they are not mutually exclusive. Positive and negative punishment are not always clear and do not always produce deceleration effects. Consider our young boy who got yelled at when he asked, "Are you home, mom?" While it is true, he probably will not ask that question again ("Are you home, mom?"), he *will spontaneously generate or increase other behaviors.* The boy does not ask the question when he hears the garage go down; instead he flies into an adrenaline rage of cleaning his room as fast as he can. That intensity and magnitude of response effort (cleaning the room) is entirely proportional to his estimation of how long he can delay his mother's yelling. When he works rapidly and methodically to clean his room, both at high rates, he produces multiple effects in himself and on his world. First, physiologically, he increases constriction of his muscles causing (proprioceptive) sensations. Such sensations pair with "working hard to get the job done." He also increases verbal behavior that accompanies his physiological arousal, whether it is flattering ("I am so productive under pressure") or self-deprecatory ("I am so stupid for waiting this long to clean my room"). He also increases a ritualistic sequence of cleaning behavior that runs the entire chain or pattern before he finishes.

Therefore, *punishment can increase as well as decrease behavior.* When it increases behavior, such as avoidance and escape behaviors, the correct terminology to describe this process is *positive reinforcement.* However, the term "positive reinforcement" is commercially very misleading, conjures up different connotations, and will seem counterintuitive to mental health specialists with a paucity of classes or background in behavioral psychology. For this reason, we will stick to the terms *positive and negative punishment.*

TIME SCHEDULES OF PUNISHMENT CONTINGENCIES. Positive and negative punishment only scratch the surface of this contingency matrix. The main problem for this young child who is developing a compulsive habit is whether negative and punishment (contingencies) are on a time schedule. Schedules are either *response-contingent* or *time-contingent.* Response-contingent punishment is when aversive stimulation follows an exact (fixed-ratio) or average (variable ratio) number of responses without delay. Time-contingent punishment is when aversive stimulation follows an exact (fixed-interval) or average amount of time (variable-interval) depending on whether at least one response appeared before the time interval ends. In other words, will his mom yell at him for how much or how little he cleans his room? Or, regardless of quantity (how much he cleans), does mom explode unpredictably after one minute, ten minutes, or hours after he cleaned his room? That is, in the second case, does it even matter at all that he followed a cleaning ritual or did no cleaning, since mom is bound to yell at him, on average, every 45 minutes for *something he did wrong.*

Schedules of punishment share a second feature, as well. They rarely occur in isolation. They are bundled together in an integrated field and often indiscernible to the individual affected by the schedules. Most punishment contingencies occur one after the other, or simultaneously.

Multiple schedules make it more difficult to ferret out or predict punishment and are the reason for complex obsessions and fears slowly developing. Where prediction is possible, it is by naming the four basic types of multiple schedules. These include *multiple, mixed, chain,* and *tandem. Multiple schedules* are generically two or more contingencies having their own ("discriminative") cues and consequences. *Mixed schedules* are two or more contingencies having one cue and two consequences. *Chain schedules* are two or more contingencies having two or more cues but only one consequence. And *tandem schedules* are two or more contingencies having one cue and one consequence. Table 1.1 better schematizes the relationships of these contingencies and its effects of compulsive behaviors.

Table 1.1
Multiple Punishment Schedules for a Boy and his Mother
about a Messy Room (in terms of two contingencies)

Type of Schedule	*# of Cues/Consequences*	*Example*
Multiple	Two cues, two consequences	Told to clean his room, then spanked for failing to do it right. Told how to do it, then overdid the ritual and nobody yelled.
Mixed	One cue, two consequences	Told to clean his room, yelled at when incomplete, and praised when he overdid the ritual.
Chain	Two cues, one consequence	Told to clean his room, told how to do it, and he overcleans it in a ritual. Praised for cleaning his room or no yelling.
Tandem	One cue, one consequence	Told to clean his room, he overcleans it with a ritual, no yelling, some praise.

NONCONTINGENT EFFECTS. Punishment also can occur when it is least or not expected. The occurrence of aversive stimuli that inconsistently follows some behavior is called *noncontingent.* Noncontingent effects are twofold. First, they are arbitrary. Second, they are capricious. Both are examples of random schedules of punishment. Arbitrary means there is no temporal or other environmental marker signaling the impending arrival of the punisher. Capricious means the individual cannot identify any particular personal behavior done to deserve the punisher. When arbitrary and capricious delivery of punishers impact a person's world, no matter the age of the individual recipient, there are several functional outcomes that can be predicted in the recipient. These effects make it very easy to see how obsessions and compulsions develop.

Functional Outcomes of Punishment

Functional patterns start in childhood and evolve unchanged to adulthood as long as that child remains exposed to same or similar circumstances. In childhood, side effects of punishment include the following predictable patterns:

1. *Child learns to react to punishment for attention.* Attention-seeking responses are instantly fueled by negative or aggressive parental discipline. Child learns yelling, anger, interrupting, and tantrums, or noncompliance as his only response to obtain gratification regardless if the consequences are aversive.

2. *Child learns to pair or "associate" the properties of punishment with the person administering the punishment.* Repeated anger, aggression or negativity by parents turns the parent himself into an aversive event. Properties defining the parent such as tone of voice, physical stature, odor, and facial features acquire threatening messages avoided by the child.

3. *Child learns to stay away from (avoid) anticipated or actual punishment.* Repeated exposure to aversive situations sensitizes a child to obvious and subtle cues surrounding the parent or punishing situation. Hearing a drunken parent complain about a messy bedroom might trigger a child to clean a room to perfection, or overcorrect the cleaning. However, due to conditioning discussed earlier, hearing that parent return home at any time, drunken or not, may cue the same cleaning responses.

4. *Child inhibits appropriate behaviors in anticipation of punishment.* Anticipation to aversive situations interrupts appropriate and inappropriate behaviors. Not only does the frightened child quickly clean his room and overdo the cleaning when yelled at, he also avoids (a) saying goodnight to his parents, (b) spending any time with his parents, and (c) wanting anybody in his room. That is, appropriate behaviors that never were punished directly, but were grouped with punished behaviors, now undergo inhibition.

5. *Child learns inappropriate behavior in anticipation of punishment.* Suppression of some inappropriate behavior from punishment does

not prevent the spontaneous learning of other, more inappropriate behaviors. Inappropriate behaviors "spontaneously" arise for two reasons. First is to replace necessary appropriate behaviors that are inhibited. Second is to replace inappropriate behaviors receiving punishment. For example, a child eating food who is punished for eating too fast may stop eating fast. But she also increases other unwanted food-related behaviors such as (a) cuts up food into tiny morsels before eating, (b) avoid meals altogether, (c) sneaks food into her bedroom and leaves it under her bed or in secret places, or (d) eat wrong or inedible substances (pica) out of biological necessity, or (e) talks about food as bad and thinks they are bad for eating food. All of these symptoms prelude anorexic-like compulsions.

6. *Child never learns behaviors appropriate for peer group.* Social or interpersonal behaviors suppressed at home prevent learning basic peer skills. Children punished for speaking or freely playing never learn to (a) express feelings, (b) share objects, (c) trust people, (d) make mistakes, (e) ask questions, (f) explore their curiosity and imagination, and (g) dismiss criticism. Instead, they may spend excessive time alone on computer games, refuse participation in mainstream peer activities, and withhold their opinions or emotions. Self-immersion in their private or solitary world not just alienates them from people, but also eliminates people from seeing inappropriate behaviors the child does. For example, a child hoarder compulsively keeps unneeded papers or items stacked in his room to a point of inhabitability. He never has a friend over to comment on or judge his chaotic debris.

7. *Child becomes sensitive and generalizes avoidance and escape in punishment situations.* Avoidance and escape responses learned at home instantly transfer to other situations where there is no need for avoidance and escape. Punished children refrain from talking, risking changes, and playing with friends at school. The child acts afraid in the classroom, at recess, on field trips, or around teachers or other adults unrelated to his parents. When asked questions, he appears chronically shy, distracted, and may walk or run away to escape the barrage of adults.

WHY GENERALIZATION OCCURS. Although the adults at school or in the community do not look like or act like the adult punishers at home, generalization occurs when either *relevant or irrelevant* properties of the adults at school match the relevant or irrelevant properties of the adult punisher. Skinner's analysis of verbal behavior (1957) and many disciples of his research (e.g., Sundberg, Ray, Braam, Stafford, Reuber, & Braam, 1979) better explained this odd response transferability as due to *generic, metaphorical, and metonymical extensions.* Generic extension is when all of the obvious relevant properties make one cue identical to another cue. For example, a child who compulsively overtalks in front of his punishing father repeats the same behavior in front of his uncle, a monozygotic twin of his brother, who wears the same clothing.

Metaphorical extension is when some of the relevant properties exist in similar but not identical circumstances. Here, the punished child overtalks in front of different-looking male adults who wear sweaters similar to his father, or who even part their hair like the father, but have a different hair coloring. Metonymical extension occurs when there are *no relevant properties present in the new cues.* Here, a punished child over-talks around people showing *irrelevant cues* or cues unrelated entirely to the punishing parent. The properties the child responds to are real or exist, and these cues grouped together in some temporal or other prox-imity with the relevant (aversive) cues. The child overtalks to a female adult, not even a male adult, who looks nothing like or does not even behave like the child's punishing father. But the common denominator here, as odd as it may seem, is that this female adult accidentally brushed up against the left shoulder of the boy, the same shoulder his father brushes up against before the father yells at the boy.

8. *Child learns inappropriate reactions that interfere with not only normal behaviors but also the "opportunities" for normal learning.* Punished children suffer two repercussions from constant suppression. One is develop-ment of spontaneous inappropriate behaviors. A second repercussion is when inappropriate behaviors delay, interrupt, or entirely prevent access to learning opportunities for socially appropriate behaviors. The most significant inappropriate reaction is pre-emptive aggressive behavior referred to as *anticipatory aggression.* Here, the child compul-sively overreacts pre-emptively before the punishment. Anticipatory behavior is a functional avoidance behavior, the purpose of which is to forestall or eliminate the parent from yelling. The downside is that compulsive (pre-emptive) yelling also falsely creates the impression of the child having mood swings, or showing diagnostic signs of Oppositional Defiant Disorder. Aggression, albeit for avoidance pur-poses, also interferes with teachers and parents wanting to show nurtu-rance and guidance to the child.

Avoidance and Escape Patterns

Thusfar the words "avoidance" and "escape" keep recurring. Traditional learning theorists (e.g., Dollard & Miller, 1950; Mowrer, 1950; Solomon & Wynne, 1954), as well as their applied counterparts (e.g., Eysenck, 1979; Stampfl, 1987; Stampfl & Levis, 1967; Wolpe, 1958) have proposed that psychological symptoms can be conceptualized as avoidance behaviors designed to escape from aversive conditioned stimuli. Human laboratory experiments attesting to this phenomenon (Banks, 1965; Dannecker & George, 2009; Malloy & Levis, 1988; Maxwell, Miller & Meyer, 1971) repeatedly showed that persistence of avoidance and escape patterns, even in the absence of danger, relates to a history of conditioning and intermittent contact with fearful stimuli. In a nutshell, then, avoidance and escape refer to response-producing changes that *terminate* some aversive event. *Termination* takes several forms. Responses may:

1. Delay the impending aversive event.
2. Alter the impending aversive event before it arrives.
3. Eliminate the impending aversive event before it arrives.
4. Interrupt the aversive event while it occurs.
5. Alter the aversive event while it occurs.
6. Eliminate the aversive event while it occurs.

Superstitious Behaviors

One common subclassification of avoidance and escape behaviors is *superstitious behaviors* (Ferster, Culbertson, & Boren, 1975; Hollis, 1973; Skinner, 1947; Timberlake & Lucas, 1985). Within the tradition of experimental analysis of behavior, Skinner (1948) first showed patterns of stereotyped responding by food-deprived pigeons given grain on fixed-time schedules of reinforcement. Pigeons developed behaviors not intended for the reinforcer, and accidentally these "strange" behaviors recurred every time that reinforcer was available. Skinner characterized the acquisition of this responding as a "sort of superstition," because responding followed a ritual and by accident received strength from the reinforcer (Ferster & Skinner, 1957). Superstitious behaviors have been found in humans for the same reasons (Bachrach, 1962; Ono, 2013). Of particular importance were pathological obsessions, compulsions, and phobias (e.g., Herrnstein, 1966; Zeiler, 1972).

Superstition patterns have unique topographical and functional properties. The topography consists of repetitive, ritualistic, or cyclical responses done in some sequential chain, from beginning to end. Outwardly the patterns vary from verbal self-statements to sporadic or slow body motions, all at varying speeds as the response chain progresses along. Time between each subresponse of the response-chain is very short, barely discernible, in that continuity is maintained with rare interruptions. Interdependence between each subresponse is very tight, with frequent overlap between responses as well as one response morphing into the next successive response.

Functionally, responses in a superstition chain are *sequential* or *concurrent*, both relieving a motivational operation. This motivational operation is called an *Establishing Operation* (EO) (Michael, 1982, 1988, 2000). EOs are setting events, whether biological or social, that increase the probability of some response occurring for a reinforcer. EOs are common, from urges for food and pain relief to escaping congested traffic, to finding misplaced keys when in a hurry. Individuals under an EO *want something very badly, want it immediately, and are likely to exert much effort in the achievement of that goal* (i.e., reward). EOs are the engine that ignites response chains in superstitious behaviors. A child fearing his mother's ferocious verbal temper when she sees his messy room is under an EO. He scurries to clean the room by picking up objects simultaneously (response concurrence) and neatly putting them in different drawers (response sequence); then he goes through each drawer, one by one, to make sure the piles are neat, and the shirts folded properly. Satisfaction of the EO occurs by the frantic immersion of repeated, ritualistic behaviors, the combination of which is reinforced when his mother *does not yell, or postpones her yelling.*

EOs compel initiation of the superstition chain of behavior. But EOs also keeps each response within the chain robustly interconnected in a rapidly uninterrupted flow. Like a domino effect, where one domino triggers a cascade of a multiple-domino trajectory, in superstition chains, each response component in the chain serves three functions. One function is to prompt or cue the next response component in the sequence. A second function is to "reinforce" the response component preceding it. Support for this two-process contingency and its intracacies appears extensively in experimental and applied research (DeLeon & Iwata, 1996; Jerome, Frantino, & Sturmey, 2007). A third function lies in the properties of cues that signal onset of the next response component in the sequence. The property is an EO. For example, with a compulsive house cleaner, thorough dusting and washing of the kitchen and bathroom do not just "prompt" the next step in the chain of cleaning the bedroom. Once the kitchen and bathroom are done, visceral arousal (fear) increases very quickly in anticipation of *what else needs to be done*. This physiological arousal is an EO, which can be relieved (removed) the moment cleaning efforts begin on the bedroom.

Rule-Governed Behaviors

Repetition of compulsive or superstitious rituals partly is motivated by actual EOs underlying the social situation. Motivation also comes from the behaver's recitation or verbal behavior about the entire constellation of EOs, response chain, and contextual factors (e.g., is mom home?). The verbal behaviors are self-statements describing *how and why the person should behave in certain ways*. Such self-statements are reminders of the content of the response chain and include language about *why the chain should occur*. Said aloud or privately, self-statements form a "rule" regarding the causal connection between the superstition response chain (compulsion) and its outcome (e.g., mom will not yell at me). That is, rules vividly identify how behavior produces certain consequences to convince an individual to engage in the behavior. This "convincing" means the rule, alone, can facilitate engagement in responses with or without other setting events being present. A child may tell himself how horrible the consequence is for having a messy room when his mother comes home. His rule, alone, prompts or *governs* mobilization of his entire superstitous chain of behavior of cleaning regardless of what time his mother actually comes home that night.

Translated operationally, these rules can be conceptualized as *rule-governed behavior* (Hayes, 1987; Hayes, Brownstein, Zettle, Rosenfarb, & Korn, 1986; Zettle & Hayes, 1982; Skinner, 1966; Torueke, Luciano, & Salas, 2008). Rules are set up like cues or discriminative stimuli that parents give to their children in the presence of the cue, such as "Don't touch that, it will burn you," or "Taste this, you'll like it." Most people follow rules specifying direct behaviors, be those behaviors proactive or avoidant. Rules prohibiting action such as "Don't do that!" originally gain support from direct-acting contingencies or experiences where the parent presents instances of right and wrong behavior followed by punishment. A parent may set up a training situation (deliberately or inadvertently) in which good or bad behavior verbally are described. For example, abusive parents might shout, "See, I told you, you don't know how to clean a room; it looks awful." Stated rules describing the child's actions and its consequences lay the initial foundation of language later echoed or recited by the child on his or her own, without that parent present.

How do rule-governed behaviors develop? In this respect, there are three ways that rule-governed behaviors develop. First, rules are set up like cues or discriminative stimuli that parents give to their children in the presence of the cue, such as "Don't touch that hot oven, it will burn you." Consequences follow those cues. Reinforced behaviors (not touching the hot oven) or punished behaviors (touching the oven) teach rule-following faster. Children learn relevant rules that relate exactly to the situation, such as the burning sensation of the hot oven when touched. But punished behaviors also teach *unintended or adventitious* rule-following (Bloom, Venard, Harden, & Seetharaman, 2007; Mellon, 2009). This occurs when the wrong rules are learned. Irrelevant rules (i.e., where relevant variables are missing) instruct a child on possible but not actual situations.

For example, this is what results from rules followed by punished behavior and learning irrelevant cues. A mother tells her child to clean the bathroom in the morning before going to school. But the child forgets to clean the bathroom before or after school, and is brutally scolded for this error. Relevant features of the rule here are "You better clean the bathroom before or after school." Irrelevant features of the rule are "cleaning the bathroom is most important over anything to avoid being yelled at." Two days later, in the morning, the child has last-minute homework to complete before going to school. He recites the irrelevant features about the rule to himself (i.e., obsesses over it), and cleans the bathroom instead of completing his homework. This decision backfires by his mother yelling at him for neglecting his homework.

To make matters worse, rules may vary randomly based on variations in the setting events, over which the child has no control. If he does not know when his mother may criticize him or how much bathroom cleaning may meet her satisfaction, his rule deliberations may consist of:

1. I should always clean the bathroom in the morning no matter what.

2. I should only clean the bathroom if and only if mom is home.
3. I should never complete my homework until I clean the bathroom. Homework is less important than household cleaning.

These rule-governed behaviors are forerunners to obsessive thoughts and later may become *values or principles of life about which the child adapts in decision making.*

A second way that rule-governed behaviors develop is after rules are instructed repeatedly by the parent. After hearing the rules so often, the child can imitate rules on his or her own. The parent fades out as the rule-trainer and a child reproduces the rule, vocalizing it to himself or herself using the same intonation or cadence heard when the parent stated it. Accuracy of rule replication will determine how persuasive the rule compels behavior. That is, if the child's imitation strongly sounds like or resembles (the relevant properties of) the parent's rule, the rule will feel like the parents' rule. The way the child reacted when hearing the parent's rule is also repeated when the child closely impersonates the rule. Fear, anxiety, guilt, and urgency to respond (EOs), among other properties, all emerge vividly when there is a point-to-point correspondence between child and parent rule-stating.

In this respect, rules are *self-generative* in two ways; rules produce behavior from *evocative effects* or *repertoire-altering* effects (Michael, 1983). Evocative effects are done without actual consequences. Rules trigger behavior almost exclusively from *self-statements* and *EOs*. A subtype of evocative rules is when self-statements are made about nonverbal or object-related environmental events. For example, when the boy says, "My room is really a mess today." Observational statements are *autoclitic tacts.* Such self-statements are only when the speaker doubles as listener to his or her statements. If the boy, instead, makes statements or rules hinting at an EO, and it compels him to immediately clean his room, that self-statement is called an *autoclitic mand.* Once he acts on the mand, and cleans his room, the EO disappears.

Repertoire-altering effects involve rules that specifically state the consequence for emitting certain behaviors. Self-rules identify reinforcers or punishers. "If I clean my room for two hours, just as mom comes home, she will compliment me." A reliable history of this rule coming true helps to verify the rule. The more reliable or truthful (predictable) the rule is, the greater chance the boy will state and comply with the rule.

A *third way* rules develop is when basic rules are insufficient to solve complex situations. This is especially when there are more irrelevant variables present and the risk of impending punishment is great. The rule may seem defective, unreliable, and unpredictable. The rule may need an addendum. That is where *Meta-rules* arise. Meta-rules consist of a pool of experiences between action and consequences (*contingencies*) that are retrieved (archived) as part of solving a problem on how to behave.

Retrieval of these meta-rules comes from our past history or *reactional biography* (Delprato, 1980; Kantor, 1929; Ruben, 1983). A reactional biography is the summation of total experiences in a person's life entirely from interactions and intra-actions. In this case, meta-rules draw upon idiosyncratic or unusual exceptions to the existing rule impacting decision-making of the individual. These exceptions call attention to *other conditions that may apply and should be noted.* Children develop meta-rules from observing *not just* the verbal and nonverbal behaviors or consequences of their parents, but also from witnessing the subtleties (or irrelevant properties) of these variables. Meta-rules supplement and may even supplant basic rules to help accommodate a perceived situation.

Here is an example of how rules (beliefs) become meta-rules:

AROUND MOTHER, *I should clean my room in the morning before I go to school,* but:
1. Not if mom is already angry; *then* skip cleaning my room and just go to school.
2. But if mom is quiet and walks past my room, *then* immediately start cleaning the room. If she says "Are you going to clean your room?," increase my speed of cleaning. If she says "room looks good," slow down my speed and get ready for school.

Rules and meta-rules form the hierarchy of self-statements and become core beliefs governing an individual's behavior. Individuals with obsessive-compulsive personality disorder use rules that are rigid, extreme, immutable, and consist of many meta-rules declaring "if and then" conditions. When rules intertwine with daily speech and thoughts, the length of the rule truncates and all of the reasons it evolved from are less important than the mantra of hearing an abbreviated version of the rule. Here are some examples of rules that emanated from extensive rules (long version), but are now succinct and just as evocative (short version):

Rule 1:	(long version)	"If I talk to Dad about problems, he gets angry at me, he tells me I am weak, and asks that I go to my room. I should keep my problem to myself."
	(short version)	It's not okay to talk about problems.
Rule 2:	(long version)	"Mom tells me I am stupid if I give up. I should always work extra hard to avoid her blaming me for giving up."
	(short version)	Strive for perfection.
Rule 3:	(long version)	"Dad told me to stop watching cartoons. It was selfish and I have chores to do. I should look for ways to help out in the house."
	(short version)	Don't be selfish

SELF-EVALUATORY, RULE-GOVERNED BEHAVIOR. One classic symptom of obsessive-compulsive personality disorder is incessant and severe self-criticism. Why is this? Reasons for self-criticism are twofold. First, as seen earlier, children either directly heard rules or observed contingencies from which rules were constructed. Second, some of these rules also included assignment of blame for failing to comply with rules or for related delinquencies affecting the contingencies. For example, a child already knows the rule, "You should clean your bedroom before going to school." If his parent also reprimanded and insulted the child for room neglect, the insult associates with the rule and becomes part of the rule. Here is how the child would recite the rule to himself,

"I should clean my room now, otherwise I am an idiot."

If the parent also warned the child of how conspicuous his error was in the eyes of other people, this is the slight variation on how the child's rule might sound:

"I should clean my room now, otherwise I am an idiot and everybody will know it."

Over time, distorted rules impose unrealistic standards of behavior, accompanied by negative self-judgments. These rules describe *why the person should have known to do better and how his incompetency once again proves how stupid he is, or will never amount to anything.* Such disturbing statements completely obliterate attempts to brainstorm solutions to problems. This is why many individuals with obsessive-compulsive personality disorder feel helpless, hopeless, depressed, and victimized by the irreparable chaos in their lives. They cannot "get over" their rule violations and prefer to self-flog, bemoan, and self-denigrate for under-achievements. Such individuals are pessimistic and feel undeserving of any praise, value, promotions, and privileges. They refuse any recognition until they rebound with energy and try to be *more perfect.*

Cluster C (Anxious or Fearful Disorders)- Obsessive-Compulsive Personality Disorder

1. Preoccupation with orderliness, perfectionism.
2. Rigid conformity to rules, hoarding, anxious, controlling.
3. Overpersonalizing of criticism, rejection, abandonment.
4. People-pleaser, with extreme effort.
5. Unforgiving of any self-mistakes
6. Over-explains, moralistic, and possibly has rituals (OCD)

Characters in Movies:
• Jack Nicholson's Melvin Udall in AS GOOD AS IT GETS
• Patrick Bergin's Martin Burney in SLEEPING WITH THE ENEMY
• Nicolas Cage's Roy Waller in MATCHSTICK MEN

Figure 1.16.

C'mon, remind me:
46. Obsessive-Compulsive Personality types are people _____.
47. They are _____ about any self-mistakes.
48. They over-explain and have _____.

Examples of *Obsessive-Compulsive* Personality Disorders depicted in characters in Hollywood movies might include Mary Tyler Moore's character in the family feud film, *Ordinary People.* Jack Nicholson was a classic obsessive-compulsive personality, with ritual compulsions, in *As Good As It Gets.*

Other Personality Disorders

Apart from the 10 prototypical personality disorders, the DSM 5 provides an eleventh category for pervasive patterns of adult behavior either related to medical issues or not found anywhere else. Three options exist in the diagnostic decision tree. The first is when known organic or medical conditions manifest some but not all of the symptoms definable under each of the personality disorders. Second, absent of medical conditions, there is recurrent disturbance in personality causing impairment in social, occupational, or other important areas of functioning. The predominate symptoms, although clinically significant, may not meet any criteria of the 10 personality disorders. Here, the classification of *Other Specific Personality Disorder* is used. Third, when there is a labyrinth of *ambiguous* symptoms randomly or recurrently present, and no identifiers exist to label the symptoms other than its functional impairment effects on the person, the classification used is *Unspecified Personality Disorder.*

On the first option, in the case of symptoms related to another medical condition, clear diagnostic criteria guide the logarithm of decision making. The five main criteria consist of the following:

1. A persistent disturbance that represents a change from the individual's previous personality pattern. In children, this change marks a difference from normal development, lasting at least one year.
2. Evidence from a physical examination or lab tests supports the personality disturbance is pathophysiological in origin or *iatrogenic, that is, a consequence of another medical condition.*
3. The disturbance is not better explained by another mental disorder.
4. The disturbance does not occur during the course of delirium (for example, postoperatively coming out anesthesia).
5. The disturbance causes clinically significant distress or impairment in social, occupational, or important areas of functioning.

The spectrum of symptoms can be narrowed down into eight sub-classifications. This division into classifications is an attempt to find common denominators or to operationalize the symptoms into clusters that are more causal. When redefined in operational language, the symptom are less ominous and more tangible and measurable to undertake steps for amelioration in therapy or with prescription of psychotropic medications. There are nine ways to subclassify these iatrogenic byproducts of medical conditions. These include: (1) Labile type, (2) Disinhibited type, (3) Aggressive type, (4) Apathetic type, (5) Paranoid type, (6) Other type, (7) Combined type, and (8) Unspecified type. Let us briefly consider each typology.

LABILE TYPE. Affective lability describes symptoms comporting with depression. The individual exhibits abrupt declines in energy, activity level, motivation, self-initiation, and socialization. Their flat affect pervades speech and psychomotor behaviors. Induced symptoms of depression or symptoms mimicking depression are common side-effects of many prescribed medicines. For example, the dermatologic drug Accutane, prescribed for acne, frequently creates lability. Other drugs potentiating transient depression include antibiotics, oral contraceptives, antihypertensives, and anticholesterol medicines. Interestingly, with many states legalizing use of marijuana for medical or recreational purposes, cases of depressed marijuana users will likely increase. Common side-effects of chronic cannabis use is constrictive affect, psychomotor retardation, social withdrawal, and general malaise.

DISINHIBITED TYPE. Disinhibited types refers to poor impulse control. Examples include unprecedented tendencies for sexual indiscretions, gambling, drug and alcohol abuse, reckless and endangering activities, or generally a flagrant attraction to at-risk behaviors. The assumption here is that the individual *never previously displayed such propensities for impulsivity to this extent.* Medical conditions likely to produce antithetical changes in people causing poor impulse control include (a) traumatic brain injury (e.g., prefrontal dorsolateral cortex injury), and (b) antiparkisonian drugs (i.e., hyperorality). In cases of premorbid impulsivity (before medical treatment), this category might also refer to exacerbation of pre-existing symptoms. For example, a cocaine-abusing drugdealer with a history of impulsivity, recently suffers prefrontal lobe damage in a motor vehicle accident. Postinjury impulsiveness intensifies in his accelerated desire for cocaine or other drugs or in frantically seeking immediate gratification. While his pathology of disinhibition may be better coded under Neurocogntiive disorders due to Traumatic Brain Injury, his condition is still applicable under this notation of *Other Personality Disorders.*

AGGRESSIVE TYPE. Unusual deviations in personality showing aggressive (verbal, nonverbal) behavior partly relate to disinhibition (see above), and partly relate to several other medical conditions. Traumatic brain injuries, for example, frequently correlate with escalation of aggression during early recovery periods. Prescribed medicines that may cause side-effects of aggression may include such anabolic steroids, antiepileptics (e.g., Keppra, velproic acid), and psychotropics (Depakote). The most frequent concomitant of aggression is pain. Pain-sufferers frequently will become agitated, irritable, sarcastic, and over-reactionary when pain levels exceed their tolerable thresholds. Pain-induced aggression is a well-known research phenomenon, exquisitely demonstrated experimentally and in applied settings (Ulrich, 1966; Berkowitz, 1993; Baenninger & Grossman, 1969; Ulrich & Azrin, 1962). Medicines for treating pain (antiinflammatories, opiate synthetics, antidepressants) may suppress neurotransmission activity (dull the senses), and concurrently suppress anger symptoms. Since pain relief is brief and users of high or regular doses of pain medicine develop tolerance to the medicine, drug-taking strategies also try to be pre-emptive; frequently the drug-taking regimen will specify for breakthough pain, or the pain arising in between dose schedules.

APATHETIC TYPE. Personalities dominated by indifference, dispondance, drowsiness and dysthymia may be an iatrogenic effect of antidepressants, pain medications (opiate synthetics), and many debilitating medical conditions (e.g., cancer, neuromuscular diseases). In recent years, recurrence of apathy from antidepressant medications (particularly from SSRIs) resulted in coining the syndrome *Antidepressant Apathy Syndrome* (Barnhart, Makela, & Latocha, 2004; Hoehn-Saric, Lipsey, & McLeod, 1990).

PARANOID TYPE. Acute suspicion, distrust, jealousy, and the litany of paranoid-like reactions may be very common symptoms from medical uses of marijuana. THC-induced anxiety arises more from episodic than continuous users, although the intensity of frantic fears experienced are identical. Current research has implicated the basolateral amygdala, located in the limbic system of the temporal lobe, a region responsible for emotional regulation. The basolateral amygdala is the nexus for paranoia in cannabis users (Huibing, Lauzon, Bishop, Chi, Bechard, & Laviolette, 2011). The study concluded that marijuana smoking actually is enhancing a *learning of fear. Fear-based learning* was possible to interrupt or even reverse by inactivating regions of the pre-frontal cortex, the brain function enabling executive reasoning. In other words, by analogy to human beings, if cannabis users could *realize their fears were irrational,* or use their executive functions, that might discourage the automatic suspicion-induced effects.

OTHER TYPE. This category permits a synthesis of any of the above typologies that may interlope at varying times without monopolizing the individual's personality.

COMBINED TYPE. In cases where two or more subtypes exist, although one subtype is temporarily more prominent, the *combined type* offers a diagnosis. Here, any number of medical-related problems can prevail. Caution is always advised to observe if combined presentations are actually transient mood swings invoked by normal medical circumstances. A normal circumstance would be postoperative discontinuation of taking a pain-medicine, or the interval of time in between completing one prescription and awaiting renewal of that prescription. Similarly, in the controlled use of the opiate deterrent methadone, interruption of daily doses may manifest acute mood alterations that disappear after the resumption of a regular drug-taking schedule.

UNSPECIFIED TYPE. Ostensible changes in personality not specified by the foregoing subtypes earn this designation.

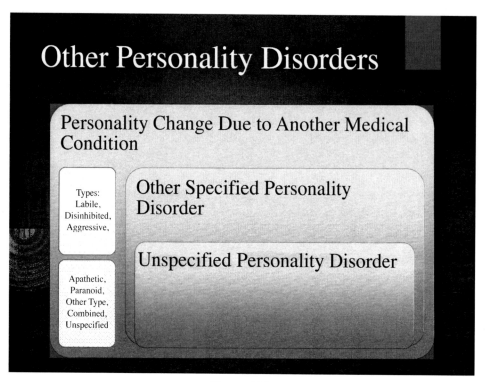

Figure 1.17.

C'mon, remind me:
49. Personality changes may relate to _____ reasons.
50. Sadness, depression exhibits the subtype of _____.
51. When two or more subtypes exist, use the _____ subtype classification.

Chapter 2

DSM-5 CHANGES IN OTHER DISORDERS COMORBID WITH PERSONALITY DISORDERS

Personality is an integrated interactional system. Personality disorders are disturbances in that system directly disrupting the entire behavioral segment (Kantor, 1959). In his simplification of Kantor's "behavioral segment," Pronko (1980) delineated between *operation behavior segments*, and *process behavior segments*. Operation behavior segments characterize the explicit contingencies confronting a person inside a situation. For example, Perry walks up to a soda machine, puts $1.50 in the slot, and expects to receive a beverage. The step-by-step process of Perry's contact with the soda machine, from start to finish, constitutes multiple segments flowing together, each with their own stimuli, responses, and media of contact enabling that interaction between Perry and the soda machine. Process behavior segments are not as palpable in the transaction between stimuli and behavior. Perry looks at the soda machine and *contemplates* whether to buy a soda. He abstractly draws upon several tangible and intangible stimuli and responses in these segments. Pronko, in this case, was trying to encapsulate the complications inherent when behavior is not simple, but is complex.

Personality disorders are examples of simple and complex behaviors permeating through operation and process behavior segments. When personality disorders pass through a behavioral unit or segment, there is no one specific or isolated behavior defining that personality, despite some conspicuous features. Avoidant personality disorders are a good example. Max avoids conflict situations and seems introversive at home with his wife; but at work, Max, the attorney, exhorts his opinions with authority when prosecuting a case in court. This bifurcation in behavior is not due to labeling him with the wrong personality disorder. He received the correct diagnosis that met criteria under DSM-5. But Max *demonstrates varying degrees of this personality differently across different segments of his behavioral field.* Since Max's disposition can be different at home compared to at work, he is bound to display *other or comorbid disorders with his diagnosed personality disorder.*

This chapter reviews changes made in DSM-5 of *other* disorders associated or comorbid with the 10 personality disorders discussed in Chapter 1. While many of these disorders appeared in DSM-IV and DSM-IV-TR, revisions in DSM-5 conceptually and operationally redefined the disorders to make better sense for practitioners (clinicians). Nine disorders are explored for their corollaries to personality. These include (1) neurodevelopmental disorders, (2) schizophrenia spectrum and other psychoses, (3) depressive disorders, (4) bipolar and related disorders, (5) obsessive-compulsive and related disorders, (6) sleep-wake disorders, (7) disruptive and impulsive control disorders, (8) substance-related addictive disorders, and (9) neurocognitive disorders.

Neurodevelopmental Disorders

Neurodevelopmental disorders share an onset period of early development. Disorders cover a wide range of deficits largely impeding social, academic, personal, or occupational functioning. Types of deficits consist of specific learning disabilities and global emotional-behavioral limitations such as Attention Deficit Hyperactivity Disorder (ADHD). In large part, neurodevelopmental disorders occur too early in childhood to coexist with personality disorders. Personality disorders, by tradition, are endemic to adult-, not child-psychopathology. In other words, a child diagnosed with a neurodevelopmental disorder is very unlikely to comorbidly receive a diagnosis of a personality disorder. However, many adult personality disorders trace to clear etiologies of pathology found in neurodevelopmental disorders. The most common of these disorders linked to adult personality disorders include (1) Autism Spectrum Disorder (ASD), (2) ADHD, and (3) Specific Learning Disorders (SLD) and (4) motor disorders.

AUTISM SPECTRUM DISORDER. DSM-5 revised this category of behaviors, eliminating distinctions between Asperger's Syndrome (AS),

Pervasive Developmental Disorder (PDD), and autism. In dropping the former, used instead is a rating scale along a continuum of severity, scored as *Level 1, Level 2,* and *Level 3.* This continuum of severity comprises the *autism spectrum.* Determination of levels depends on criteria being met of specific behaviors under the rubric of *Social Communication,* and *Restricted, Repetitive Behaviors.* Additionally, once levels are identified, qualifiers apply to the disorder, such as (a) with or without accompanying intellectual impairment, (b) with or without accompanying language impairment, (c) associated with another neurodevelopment, mental or behavior disorder, or (d) with catatonia.

Children diagnosed with autism generally lack social communication skills. They underdevelop awareness of interaction styles, social cues, and the flexibility with which to initiate or adapt into routine peer-based situations. They are introverts, isolated, disenfranchised from peers, emotionally indifferent, and fixate on objects, activities, or verbal topics (monologuing), where they lack reciprocity with the world around them. *Consequently, autism traits are frequently forerunners to Schizotypal and Avoidant Personality Disorders.* Schizotypal attributes consist of magical thinking, eccentric or bizarre habits, indifference and profound interpersonal deficits. Likewise, in avoidance personality, although the individual may be interpersonally mature in close partner relationships, they are fearful of conflict, prefer seclusion, and dislike crowds or socialization.

Schizophrenia Spectrum and Other Psychoses

Schizophrenia traditionally was a subset of psychosis disorders marked by (a) delusions, (b) hallucinations, (c) disorganized thinking, (d) odd motor behaviors, and (e) negative symptoms. In prior DSM coding systems, elucidation of these symptoms divided into subcategorical typologies of schizophrenia including disorganized, catatonic, paranoid, undifferentiated, and residual. Subtypes supposedly delineated the progressive deterioration in functional capacity and clustered together homogenous cognitive or psychomotor symptoms. In the DSM-5, in realizing symptoms of psychosis were heterogenous, revisions in the classification scheme eliminated the subtypologies and replaced them with a clinician-rated assessment of symptoms and related clinical phenomena in psychosis. This rating, similar operationally to the Autism Spectrum, surveys traits of psychosis across a continuum of severity. However, preserved in this continuum were general sub-types including (1) delusional disorder, (2) brief psychotic disorder, (3) schizophreniform disorder, (4) schizophrenia, (5) schizoaffective disorder, (6) substance/medication-induced psychotic disorder, and (7) psychotic disorders due to another medical condition. Among other psychotic disorders covered, catatonia is a separate category.

The comorbidity of a schizophrenia spectrum with personality disorders lies, specifically, with Schizotypal and Schizoid personality disorders. Both adult disorders presume a brief episode (1 to 6 months) of psychosis involving positive symptoms (hallucinations, disorganized thinking, delusions), and negative symptoms (alogia, avolution, anhedonia). In schizotypal and schizoid personality disorders, the pervasive pattern of detachment from social relationships and restricted range of emotions in interpersonal settings frequently associates with preoccupation with one's thoughts. Thought and perceptual distortions resulting from a solitary life insulated from social feedback may perpetuate as long as the individual regards these distortions as normal. Not surprisingly, individuals with these personality disorders exhibiting positive or negative signs of psychosis, or odd or eccentric motor movements, and who date nonpsychotic partners or begin employment in public settings, undergo a drastic change. They receive corrective feedback on their behaviors that quickly alter their outward actions. Verbal feedback differentially shaping culturally-appropriate behavior has been a powerful modifier in changing psychotic responses (cf. Allyon & Michael, 1959; Fuller, 1949; Gomes-Schwartz, 1979).

Depressive Disorders

Each of the ten personality disorders cover symptoms ranging from elation to depression. Depression signifies a decompensation from some measure of normal functionality, while also increasing susceptibility of the individual to cognitive and motor disturbances. Depression, then, already is an a priori comorbid pattern with personality disorders. However, in DSM-5, revisions in the subtypologies of depression provide a more operational understanding of depression proclivities and its link to the personality disorders. While subtypes of major depressive disorder always have been relevant, three particular subtypes repeatedly seen in Borderline, Histrionic, Avoidant, and Dependent personality disorders include (1) disruptive mood dysregulation disorder, (2) persistent depressive disorder (dysthymia), and (3) premenstrual dysphoric disorder.

DISRUPTIVE MOOD DYSREGULATION DISORDER. The core feature of disruptive mood dysregulation disorder is chronic irritability. Two prominent manifestations of irritability include frequent tantrum outbursts, and persistent angry moods. Onset of this disorder may begin in preschool years and persist over the course of adulthood. In adults, patterns of the angry episodes, albeit frequent, appear verbal, impulsive, and reactionary in mishandling daily stressors, in contrast to explosive tirades that threaten physical violence. The nonviolent temper reactor is consistent with individuals who have rapid mood oscillations (Borderline), get frantic aroused ("dramatic") over real or imagined circumstances (Histrionic), or passively suppress their frustrations until ventilation of them at grossly inappropriate times (Avoidant and Dependent).

PERSISTENT DEPRESSIVE DISORDER (DYSTHYMIA). Dysthymic disorder, its former name, remains largely the same denotation as it appeared in prior DSM guides. The prevailing feature is a constant sadness or depressed mood occurring most of the day for over two or more years. Symptom recurrence is now subdivided into specific criteria qualifying (a) accompanying features (e.g., anxious distress, melancholic features, peripartum onset), (b) level of remission, (c) onset period (late or early), (d) comorbidity with major depression, and (e) level of severity (mild, moderate, severe). Reasons for this enhanced precision of dysthymia was to consolidate many ambiguous features of typical or atypical depression falling outside the realm of major depression. Clarification also ended the misuse of dysthymia as a temporary or acute depressive reaction to some event (e.g. bereavement). In the personality disorder of borderline, dysthymia underlies the repeated theme of feeling empty, abandoned, insecure, and dissatisfied. In histrionic personality disorder, dysthymia describes the undercurrent or bedrock upon which escalation of emotional panic occurs. The pseudo-elation from catastrophic thinking often is a visceral self-medicator of depression; the individual "escapes" sadness by deliberately engaging in rage-and-rant-like behaviors arousing the sympathetic nervous system. In avoidant and dependent personality disorders, dysthymia is a safe refuge. Passively timid or submissive individuals quickly become sad or depressed when (a) they cannot avoid or escape form conflict, (b) they feel unvalued, and (c) they feel abandoned.

PREMENSTRUAL DYSPHORIC DISORDER. Unofficially, the lay public commercially diagnosed a woman's menstrual cycle as biologically engendering symptomatic depression. The short interval just before onset of menses typically has been called *Premenstrual Syndrome (PMS)*. Data supporting a rise in lability, irritability, and dysphoria as the cycle commences and remits as the menstrual period progresses has been significant and influential on the need for an *official diagnosis* of this phenomenon (Pincus, Schmidt, Palldino-Negro, & Rubinow, 2008; Richard, Rubinow, Daly, & Schmidt, 2006). In the DSM-5, this new subtype of Depressive Disorders requires a minimum of five symptoms present in the final weeks before menses. In particular are the symptoms classified under criteria "C," which include the following:

1. Decreased interest in usual activities.
2. Subjective difficulty in concentration.
3. Lethargy, easy fatigability, or marked lack of energy.
4. Marked changes in appetite; overeating or specific food cravings.
5. Hypersomnia or insomnia.
6. A sense of being overwhelmed or out of control.
7. Physical symptoms such as breast tenderness or swelling, joint or muscle pain, a sensation of "bloating" or weight gain.

All of these symptoms pose immediate distress or interfere in the individual's work, school, unusual social activities, or relationship with others. The caveat is that none of these symptoms are merely exacerbations of symptoms from other psychopathology or physiological (medical) problems. In clinical settings, high correlations may be found between premenstrual dysphoric disorder and Histrionic Personality Disorder. Gender-related significance is critical here. More women than men are diagnosed with Histrionic Personality Disorder. The same is true for more women diagnosed with Dependent Personality Disorder. In both personality disorders, elevations of the symptoms shown above may be concomitant with premenstrual cycles, or the symptoms may occur independent of the hormonal (biochemical) alterations endemic to menstruation. Since the risk of overlap remains clear, no matter the extent of the overlap, clinicians should anticipate concurrence of symptoms and possibly rule out the conclusion that it is a personality disorder.

Bipolar and Related Disorders

Bipolar disorder passes through a new stage of evolution with each version of the DSM. The revised DSM-5 devotes a separate category to Bipolar and Related disorders. It maintains and refines definitions of Bipolar I and Bipolar II, and enhances the specifiers for Cyclothymic Disorders. In clinical diagnostic cases lacking specific criteria for Bipolar Disorder, alternative coding categories include *Other Specified Bipolar Related Disorder*, and *Unspecified Bipolar and Related Disorder.* Bipolarity, for years, has been omnipresent in personality disorders. Profound mood swings is structurally part of Borderline Personality and frequently comorbid with Paranoid personality. In the former case, periods of hypomania, characterized by euphoria, invincibility, and impulsivity, often shift within hours to deflation, anhedonia, and self-loathing. The rapidity of mood transition frequently is adjunctive with *splitting,* the phenomenon of either idolizing or demonizing a target person. In Paranoid Personality, elevated ideas of grandeur, distrust, and persecution co-occur with spikes in mood (hypomania). Visceral intensity seems proportional with symptom severity, particular in the verbal enumeration of conspiracies. However, in calmer dispositions, individuals may still feel suspicious but are less creatively elaborative about conspiracy schemes or their own lives feeling in danger.

Less extreme mood swings, seen in Cyclothymic Disorders, may entail periods of anxious distress of mild and transitive sadness. This chronic, fluctuating mood disturbance, although chaotically disruptive in a person's life and unpredictable for onlookers, is *more controllable and less durable during each episode.* Comorbidity of a Cyclothymic Disorder is most prominent in Histrionic Personality Disorder, Narcissistic Personality Disorder, and Avoidant Personality Disorder. Individuals with Histrionic Personality Disorder spike into panic or catastrophe mode and level off their anxiety when receiving endorsement from other people. Individuals with Narcissistic Personality Disorder appear excitable, anxious, and hypomanic while pushing their egocentric agenda and incessantly and irrationally boasting their virtues. When they do not receive external praise or encounter roadblocks to self-fulfillment of their personal agenda, episodes of depression emerge lasting several days.

In individuals with Avoidant Personality, mood elevations consist mostly of anxiety. Engrossment in conflict or near-conflict situations spark profound anxiety (fear) and mobilization of many conflict-averting strategies that are tedious and exhaustive. For example, a man may engage in excessive compensatory behaviors to avoid conflict with his wife, such as buying her flowers, making dinner, cleaning the house, or giving her carte blanche for credit-card store purchases. Following his extravaganza of generosity (avoidance behaviors), he may outwardly show signs of fatigue, defeatism, sadness, and social withdrawal. Recurrence of this cycle remains infinite as long as it controls conflict.

Obsessive-Compulsive and Related Disorders

Much discussion on the behavioral etiology of Obsessive-Compulsive Personality Disorders occurred in Chapter 1. In the DSM-5, consolidation of many different compulsive behavior subsumes under one category. Additional ritualistic compulsions recognized include Hoarding Disorder, Trichotillomania, and Excoriation (skin-picking) Disorder. Hoarding Disorder is the persistent difficulty of parting with unneeded possessions leading to unsanitary accumulation or clutter of debris. Required specifiers go beyond the six criteria defining Hoarding, and ask if the individual demonstrates (a) excessive acquisition, (b) has good or fair insight, (c) has poor insight, and (d) has absent insight/delusional beliefs. Hoarding also associates with features of indecisiveness, perfectionism, avoidance, procrastination, difficulty planning or organizing tasks, and distractibility. For this reason, Hoarding is comorbid with Paranoid Personality, Schizoid and Schizotypal Personalities, and Avoidant Personalities.

In Paranoid Personality, individuals may barricade themselves in a self-made refuge from a mistrustful world. Retention and storage of useless papers, mounting in piles, may be idealized as protecting them from insidious threats on their lives. When dismantling of the debris commences, levels of anxiety spike in anticipation of eliminating this imaginary firewall from the public. In other words, mass accumulation occurs on a negative reinforcement contingency. The removal or avoidance of social contact and containment of fears *increases the future probability of more hoarding.*

In Schizoid or Schizotypal Personalities, hoarding appears the result of indifference to the surrounding physical environment. Detachment from social contact includes a comfort with burrowing into one's space. The individual "hides" in the grooves of their debris-piles, and is insensitive to social approval or disapproval about their congested quarters. Secondary to their despondence is their skill deficits. Individuals with Schizoid or Schizotypal Personalities lack development in self-care and house management skills. They may view their clutter as normal and dismiss any abnormality about the clutter, since they always had clutter in their lives, and their dysfunctionality is not any more significant than is already caused by symptoms of depersonalization.

Avoidant Personality Disorders also include comorbid tendencies of hoarding for different reasons. Avoidance and escape behaviors are not always so obvious *functionally*, or clearly traceable to relevant contingencies. The contingencies may seem obscure or remote due to rule-governed behaviors or short rules (see Chapter 1), that evoke a matrix of highly intricate avoidance/escape patterns. For example, a recently divorced woman who abhorred conflict and was embarrassed to appear socially indulged in a cacophony of excessive projects around the house. She tore apart wall paper from multiple rooms, piled up furniture, and lifted floor tiles to refinish floors. She shoved all of the debris mixed with household items into corner piles and navigated around the piles to complete her work. She worked persistently and simultaneously in each room, never completing tasks with any pre-planned criteria. Her house quickly grew into high pyramids of filth and collection, all tolerated as she rationalized the mess as part of her remodeling project. Her pillars of debris all became self-measures of her value in doing the projects. The projects also excused her from facing social duress. Her motivator (establishing operation) for remodeling each day was "I need to do this to feel important." The rule shotguns her into starting the tasks, whereas the mounting clutter positively reinforced persistence in the disorganized tasks.

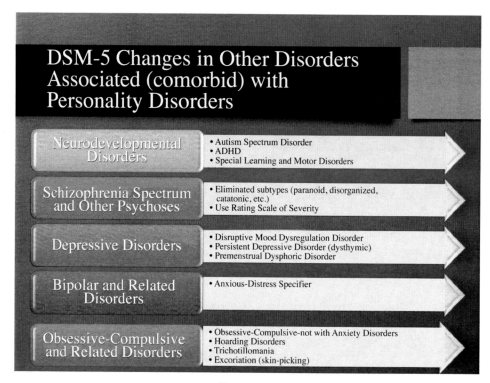

DSM-5 Changes in Other Disorders Associated (comorbid) with Personality Disorders

Neurodevelopmental Disorders	• Autism Spectrum Disorder • ADHD • Special Learning and Motor Disorders
Schizophrenia Spectrum and Other Psychoses	• Eliminated subtypes (paranoid, disorganized, catatonic, etc.) • Use Rating Scale of Severity
Depressive Disorders	• Disruptive Mood Dysregulation Disorder • Persistent Depressive Disorder (dysthymic) • Premenstrual Dysphoric Disorder
Bipolar and Related Disorders	• Anxious-Distress Specifier
Obsessive-Compulsive and Related Disorders	• Obsessive-Compulsive-not with Anxiety Disorders • Hoarding Disorders • Trichotillomania • Excoriation (skin-picking)

Figure 2.1.

C'mon, remind me:

52. Neurodevelopmental disorders deal with problems in _____.

53. In Schizophrenia Spectrum, eliminated where _____ like paranoid.

54. Bipolar Disorders request a specifier on Anxious _____.

Sleep-Wake Disorders

DSM-5 provides a separate heading called *Sleep-Wake Disorders*. This classification replaces and expands the *Sleep Disorder* classifications in prior DSM editions. The specific disorders most prominently comorbid with Personality Disorders include the (1) Breathing-related Disorders, in particular Circadian Rhythm Disorders; and (2) Rapid Eye Movement (REM) Sleep Behavior Disorder. While all of the sleep disorders listed (e.g., Obstructive Sleep, Cheyne-Stokes breathing, Sleep-related Hypoventilation) probably contribute idiopathically to Personality Disorders, the behavioral contingencies affecting mood alteration are more precise with the three explored herein.

CIRCADIAN RHYTHM DISORDER. This disorder is an example of a psychophysical condition resulting from disruption to the endogenous circadian rhythm and sleep-wake schedule. Homeostatic dysregulation occurs due to changes in the physical environment or social or professional schedule. In the military, for example, patrol guards shifting surveillance schedules from late night to early morning constantly adjust their sleep schedule. Likewise, plant assembly workers on alternating shifts of daytime and evening hours also require undue sleep adaptation. For this reason, variations of schedule impact on sleep-wake cycle require subclassifications for coding. The disorder is divided into *Delayed Sleep Phase type, Advanced Sleep Phase type, Irregular Sleep-Wake type, Non-24 Hour Sleep-Wake type, Shift-Work Sleep type,* and *Unspecified type.* Further specifiers qualify the conditions across a continuum of severity from *episodic,* to *persistent* and *recurrent.* Symptoms generated from these subtypologies range from insomnia, excessive sleepiness (hypersomnia), morning confusion, anxiety and mania (hypomania), to concomitant physical problems. These medical problems often include obstructive sleep apnea, and restless leg syndrome.

Examination of sleeping habits of reintegrated military personnel were most revealing of the short- and long-term impact of this disorder on the individual and family (Neylan, Marmar, Metzler, Weiss, Zatzick, Delucchi, & Schoenfeld, 1998; Peterson, Goodie, Satterfield, & Brim, 2008; Selig, Jacobson, Hooper, Boyko, Gackstetter, Gehrman, Macera, & Smith, 2010). Veterans reported high rates of insomnia attributable to (a) hypervigilance, (b) constant sleep interruption, (c) paucity of naps or compensatory sleep, (d) overuse of sleep medications or substitutive drugs, and (e) diminished exercise. Months after deployment and return to family, veterans found their uncorrected insomnia worsening into symptoms of mania, irritability, agitation, and low frustration tolerance. Not surprisingly, protracted sleeplessness was comorbid with traits of cyclical moods and pervasive emptiness arousing desperation for spousal reassurance, the absence of which made the veteran infuriated and stirred feelings of abandonment (i.e., Borderline Personality).

RAPID EYE MOVEMENT (REM) SLEEP BEHAVIOR DISORDER. Sleep phases typically pass through stages. Stage one (N1) lasts about five minutes, a transitional phase producing low arousal threshold. Stage two (N2), lasting 10 to 15 minutes, extends low arousal. Stages three and four (N3), or "delta" sleep is a slow wave sleep lasting 20 to 40 minutes. Twenty percent of sleep occurs with Rapid Eye Movement (REM), or during tonic hypotonic muscle relaxation. An abnormal condition during REM is frequent arousal (awakening) associated with vocalizations or complex motor behaviors. Arousal is usually abrupt in response to suddenly awakening from an action-filled or violent dream of being attacked or trying to escape from a threatening situation. Such "dream-enacting behaviors" may entail outward explosive rages of profanity, running, punching, thrusting, hitting, or kicking, all of which frighten another partner sharing the bed with the arouser.

Confusional states of awakening, following a frightening dream, may occur to any person asymptomatic of personality disorders. However, frequently these disruptions associate with individuals with Paranoid Personality disorders. Awake states are fraught with interminable obsessions about distrust that others may be harmful, exploitive, or deceptive. Perceived attacks on one's character or reputation seem real, and instantly invoke retaliatory responses or at least methodical strategizing on how retribution might occur. Individuals with this disorder typically see the world and other people as malevolent, and will bear grudges irrationally and incessantly, unwilling to show forgiveness, and with a ruthless sense of impunity.

Since dreaming, nearly always in REM states, can be viewed behaviorally (Dixon & Hayes, 1999), two interpretations are feasible to understand the generalization of paranoia into dream states. First, that dreaming is an example of seeing something without actually seeing it (cf. Skinner, 1969, p. 273). Here, punished activities through operant and respondent conditioning may reappear in vague (dream) images, but recall is mostly of physiologic sensations experienced during the real-life conditioning episodes. That is, dreams are less about what *one does in the dream than how one feels in the dream.* Second, dreaming is an implicit function (Kantor, 1926). Dreamers interact with fewer outside functions in their dreams (i.e., the setting events shrink), and more with affective (emotive or reflexive) functions implicit in the response itself. That is, the dreamer is more emotional and instinctive based on same or similar contexts in wakeful states. Together, these analyses explain that individuals with paranoid ideations reproduce feelings or misperceptions of distrust in dreaming tantamount to their histories while awake.

Disruptive and Impulsive Control Disorders

Different from its predecessors, the DSM-5 consolidated disruptive and impulse control disorders into a single category called *Disruptive, Impulse-Control, and Conduct Disorder.* Disorders covered here involve problems with self-control over emotions and behaviors, often manifested in rebelliousness or rights violations (e.g., Oppositional Defiant Disorder, Kleptomania, Pyromania, etc.). A preponderant impulse disorder found in both Borderline and Antisocial Personality disorders is *Intermittent Explosive Disorder.* The rapid onset of aggressive outbursts may seem spontaneous and unrelated to traceable antecedents. This lack of a prodromal period might implicate the outburst as involuntary or reactionary as opposed to premeditative. Outbursts also are more tame or nonviolent and consist largely of temper tantrums, tirades, verbal arguments, and debates without damage or physical injury to objects, people, or animals. In Borderline Personality, extreme shifts between happiness and unhappiness frequently accompany tirades of contempt. The frustrated individual faces stressful obstacles (i.e., an establishing operation) and hastily blames self or other people for obstructionism. Anger, here, is not a vehicle for intimidation or persuasion but a sign of underdeveloped skills in problem solving.

In the Antisocial Personality Disorder, just the opposite may be true. Intermittent outbursts are for leverage. Anger inflates an aura of superiority that bolsters the individual to bully, scare, or exert control over passive or unassertive subordinates. Anger is directive, methodical, and threatens physical violence on the surface. The aggressor is unfeeling, selfishly manipulative, and seeks to convince other people of his or her inarguable reasons. This is one type of aggression. Functionally, however, there are two other types of aggression. First, already discussed in Chapter 1, is *anticipatory aggression.* This is when anger ignites pre-emptively or when the individual expects imminent conflict. Anticipatory or "flashflood anger," is transient and entirely conditioned by a history of random delivery of aversive stimulation. Yellers project verbal assaults to avoid, avert, diminish, or escape from challengers. A second type of aggression is visceral gratification. This type occurs when visceral elevation literally *feels good.* The sensory gratification may (a) stimulate noraepinephrine (i.e., adrenaline) to reach manic or hypomanic states; (b) artificially stimulate confidence, control, or motivation in a person; and (c) compete with feelings of depression or helplessness.

Substance-Related and Addictive Disorders

Interrelations between mood swings, personality disorders, and substance abuse long have been established in empirical research (Hasin, Endicott, & Keller, 1989; Keller, Lavori, & Coryell, 1986; Schuckit & Raimo, 1998; Wilson & Lud, 2009). Influence of substances, historically, evolved either by the emotional (psychological) or physical (biochemical) effects produced in individuals over regular use of the drug. Psychological effects described the overuse of the substance for stimulant or depressant changes to offset unwanted feelings, stressors or biophysical conditions (e.g., pain). This was called *abuse*. As tissue absorption levels increase and more of the substance becomes necessary for effect replication, the drug-craving and risk of withdrawal without the drug was called *dependence*. This dichotomy between drug *abuse* and *dependence*, over years, was unclear. The terms were interchangeably used, and conceptually misrepresented by the professional and lay community (see Ruben, 2004). One solution to this confusing dichotomy was to eliminate it entirely and replace it with a continuum of severity of drug or alcohol abuse.

The DSM-5 presents a "spectrum" or a course of progression of the substance misuse along multi-dimensions of physical and psychological markers. The continuum represents the metamorphosis of drug tolerance effects, but it does not specify the functional etiology of substances. Simply understood, drugs and alcohol produce either stimulant (highs) or depressant (lows) effects, both being establishing operations (EOs) that depend on many factors for attainment of the favored sensation. These factors range from the individual's reactional biography (response and biological history, setting events (cues), and media of contact (resources enabling drug use), to the interactive and sequential field segments (response and stimulus patterns interrelated and predictive of use).

ABUSE-DEPENDENCE CONTINUUM. Revisions in the DSM-5 redefine 10 separate classes of drugs under *substance related and addictive disorders*. These include alcohol, caffeine, cannabis, hallucinogens (with separate categories for phencyclidine and other hallucinogens), inhalants, opioids, sedative-hypnotic-anxiolytic drugs, stimulated-related drugs, tobacco-related drugs, and other (or unknown) substances. Added to the DSM-5 was the nonsubstance-related disorder of gambling addiction. Further division of substance use exists between two subgroups:

Substance use disorders, and *substance-induced disorders*. The latter refers to iatrogenic side-effects of intoxication, withdrawal, or from concurrent use of other psychotropic or other medicines. For example, a *substance-use disorder* may result from overuse of cocaine. A *substance-induced disorder* may result from overuse of the psychostimulant Adderall; desired effects of hyperalertness, energy, and high rate of productivity may encourage drug-seeking of similar stimulant agents believed to generate similar or more agonist (accelerative) properties than Adderall. This titration frequently occurs, for example, among competitive high school or college students abusing stimulants to stay awake, study more, or "feel they can" digest more information to score perfectly on tests.

The continuum from abuse to dependence parallels the progressive impact effects of substances on cognitive, behavioral, and physiological states of the addict. This is how *pathology* is defined. *Pathology*, in this respect, is operationalized by four subcategories to determine severity of drug addiction. These include *impaired control*, *social impairment*, *risky use*, and *pharmacological criteria*. Impaired control addresses the absence of self-restraint in managing impulsive urges. Reversal of impaired control may occur voluntarily or involuntarily. For example, consider individuals with Antisocial Personality Disorder, who are repeated criminal offenders of Driving Under the Influence (DUI) of alcohol. They suddenly face two to three years of probation or parole, and must wear an ankle bracelet using alcohol monitoring systems (e.g., SCRAM). These addicts are under a "controlled environment" that coercively deters drinking. Violation of the controlled environment (i.e., court order) would result in revoking probation/parole and immediate incarceration.

The second subcategory is social impairment. Recurrent use of substances may decrease or greatly interfere with fulfillment of daily obligations at work, school, or home. Persistent overuse may arouse anger and agitation, increasing intrapartner domestic violence. Likewise, drug-consuming activities among parents may result in child neglect, household neglect, or failure in fiduciary responsibilities. High-risk individuals of social impairment include those with Avoidant Personality Disorder, Dependent Personality Disorder, and Borderline Personality Disorder. Avoidant Personality describes self-alienated individuals dislocated from mainstream activities. They may use substances to further disaffiliate without a conspicuous trace. Dependent Personality describes clingingly desperate attachments. Here, drinking or other drug use may alleviate fears of rejection and abandonment and possibly even increase their susceptibility (gullibility) to the host person onto whom they are parasitical. In Borderline Personality, substances functionally serve to equalize mood swings. However, despite the equilibrium gained, the individual with Borderline tendencies still may view life as chaotic, empty, and chronically stressful. Stress mismanagement proportionally increases as substance use increases. Such individuals become grossly unreliable and unpredictable in their job or family duties.

The third category is risky use. Risk patterns consist of thrill-seeking, impulsiveness, and recklessly daring behaviors frequently seen in Narcissistic Personality Disorder and Antisocial Personality Disorder. A Narcissistic Personality typifies hedonistic or egocentric indulgence without weighing the consequences of the chosen action. The impulsive decision for substance use is purely for self-gratification; moreover, the activities facilitated by substance use also are under egocentric establishing operations (EOs). For example, heroin users may thrive on the comatose-like sedation that allows escape, not just from fear of withdrawal symptoms, but also from the bombardment of stressors such as a failing business or impending breakup with a spouse. The setting of heroin use also provides a social connection with other partners. This often results in casual sexual encounters.

The individual with Antisocial Personality, while also motivated selfishly, operates under another set of conditions. His or her establishing operation is social defiance. The cocaine user may feel invincibly courageous to break into a house, or engage in carjacking. The stimulant sensation of cocaine, in other words, is only *one* setting event or a discriminative stimulus. It triggers *much* more desirable responses in the response-sequence (i.e., segments of behavioral fields); the paramount response is *risking a crime and getting away with it.* The risk arouses anticipatory arousal that is self-rewarding. The cocaine, in this example, only *sets the occasion for the anticipatory arousal (risk).* Fulfillment of the risk, by committing a crime, reinforces the entire response sequence. The addict will seek cocaine in the future as an antecedent to engaging in the risk. Similarly, shoplifting offenders may never need the objects stolen from stores. Their thrill comes from the same *anticipatory excitement of planning and navigating around a busy store, away from store detectives, until they can remove items unobtrusively.* They simply use cocaine or other stimulants to induce the phase of *anticipatory excitement.*

Pharmacological criteria pertain to the increasing dose of some drug due to physical tolerance level. Tolerance, and its obverse *withdrawal,* can be misleading. Variability occurs in both conditions due to over-lapping (or poly) substance use and individual differences in biology depending on their licit or illicit drug use history and tissue absorption rates. Chronic pain sufferers, for example, are accustomed to high use of narcotics often consisting of cocktails of Oxycodone, Demerol, and Fentanyl. Sufferers may show mild to moderate withdrawal symptoms if only one is discontinued if the other opiate synthetics in the cocktail remain unchanged. The other opioids absorbed in the blood stream and tissues remain constant, replenishing the absent dose. Similarly, *drug replenishment* occurs with a polysubstance addict of crack cocaine, alcohol, and skittling (i.e., OTC cough and cold medicines combined). Elimination of one drug, say, skittling, may only marginally disrupt the amphetamine-like sensations generated from the buffet of other stimu-lant drugs used. Here, coexisting drug use masks a withdrawal syn-drome and misrepresents the individual's true index of drug use sever-ity.

Idiographic differences in drug-tolerance can also account for wide variability among addicts and nonaddicts using identical or similar drugs. For example, fetal-alcohol (syndrome, FAS) offspring already possess a congenital predisposition for higher tissue absorption rates of ethanol. Ingestion levels of alcohol in their teens may profoundly differ from their non-FAS drinking peers. The FAS teen may drink five beers to his non-FAS friend's one beer per hour. A similar problem of high tolerance predisposition is found among chronic pain patients. Many experienced users of opiate synthetics cannot start a new opioid at a reasonably low dose. Lower doses of, say, Darvocet, will insufficiently anesthetize the pain whereas stronger doses are needed to achieve the desired effect. Physical tolerance to opiate synthetics is already high and does not reverse so quickly, even when an individual detoxifies from all opioids for one week to six months. For this reason, and to mit-igate the long-term detrimental effects of opioids on the physical sys-tem, nonopioid alternatives are becoming popular such as antidepres-sant medicine for pain management (Jackson & St. Onge, 2003; Jann & Slade, 2007; Sullivan & Robinson, 2006)

Problems with assessment of pharmacological criteria particularly are evident with individuals with Narcissistic Personality Disorder and

Antisocial Personality Disorders. While all of the personality disorders risk complications *to some extent* from cocktails of psychotropic medicine, individuals who seek selfish goals are more prone to polysubstance use. Both personality types prominently consist of impulsiveness, effusiveness (hypomania), and excitement arousing a feeling of invulnerability. Achievement of these physical and emotional states requires a constant supply of stimulants boosting artificial confidence. Whether it is alcohol, cocaine, OTC amphetamines, or meta-amphetamines, the stimulant effect activates adrenaline, *or sets an occasion* to respond euphorically, spontaneously, and without moral restraint. Such courage or tenacity consists of interconnected or sequential responses involving risk and opportunity-seeking, all occurring at high rates in a short period of time. Each of the interconnected responses is self-reinforcing. The latency between each response is very short, for example, as in the rapid-moving sequence of buying the cocaine, setting up drug paraphernalia to snort cocaine, snorting cocaine, finding a house to rob, and robbing the house. Each time interval between responses (IRT) may be as short as 30 seconds, but not longer than 30 minutes. The robbery is the last or terminal response in the response sequence. When the terminal response of the sequence occurs (e.g., house robbery), it reinforces repetition of all the responses preceding it. The sequence cycle looks like this:

R_1 = Buying the cocaine.
R_2 = Setting up drug paraphernalia.
R_3 = Snorting the cocaine.
R_4 = Finding a house to rob.
R_5 = Robbing the house.

Each response in the sequence is self-stimulating; it serves a dual function of (a) reinforcing the action preceding it and cuing the action after it to occur. Although it appears above that the responses are neatly linear in a consecutive order, the irony is that sequential responses may be *concurrent, convergent,* or *divergent.* Concurrent chained responses overlap or occur simultaneously. The addict, for example, may snort the cocaine while online checking for vacant homes found in real estate listings. Convergent chained responses intermingle with varying degrees and produce similar topography and function. Here, the addict may start snorting cocaine before completing the setup of paraphernalia; part of setup involves laying out the powder dust that is also done when snorting. Together, layout of powder dust and snorting generate self-stimulatory outcomes. Divergent response chains may begin as concurrent or convergent chains but subdivide into multiple response or *secondary response* patterns, all interdependent on functionally producing a desirable effect. *Secondary response patterns comprise the main or primary responses in a sequence.* Each secondary response entails its own contingencies impacting the probability of the primary responses in the sequence occurring or not occurring. An example of a divergent response chain appears below:

R_1 = Buying the cocaine.

    R_{1a} = Dealer not home, so call two other people.

    R_{1b} = Insufficient personal funds, so steal money from parents.

R_2 = Setting up drug paraphernalia.

    R_{2a} = lack snuffer tube, razor blade and snuff spoon; improvise or delay use.

    R_{2b} = call addict friends and borrow supplies; offer favors in return.

In this example, the primary responses in the chain included R_1 buying the cocaine, and R_2 setting up drug paraphernalia. Buying cocaine depends, of course, on (R_{1a}) the dealer's accessibility or whoever else is available to buy the drug from. Failure to reach a dealer means delay of the purchase, risk of psychological withdrawal, and increased visceral or emotional arousal. Likewise, lacking sufficient funds to buy cocaine (R_{1b}) may require drastic steps to steal money from parents to complete the purchase deal. In-house theft may backfire, in the user incurring angry reactions from his parents that delay or prevent the current or future purchase of cocaine. In R_2, setting up the paraphernalia depends on having the right equipment. If needed equipment is absent (R_{2a}), the addict may need to improvise, which may delude or improperly prepare the dose (depending on whether using crack or powder cocaine). For example, out of desperation, addicts who inject the cocaine (i.e., *injection drug users*) frequently risk dangers of destroying skin and blood vessel linings. If the injection drug user borrows a friend's syringe (R_{2b}), this increases the risk of contracting HIV, Hepatitis B or C, STDs, and blood and bone infections. Disruption from these biological events directly impedes transaction of subsequent responses in the drug-taking chain.

STIMULANT-DEPRESSANT EFFECTS. The role of substance abuse in personality disorders is largely to disguise untoward symptoms causally responsible for maladaptive responses. Impairments found in each personality cluster (A, B, C) either manifest from anxiety-inducing events, or depression-inducing events. A third causative pattern is rapid cycles of moods shifting from anxiety to depression. In anxiety states, fear arousal ascends quickly to near-panic levels, as life stressors or obstacles increase and confrontations with these obstacles become inescapable or unavoidable. In depression states, failure to overcome life's hurdles, particularly after a torrent of stressors, causes rapid deterioration in psychomotor, cognitive, and behavioral efforts. In prodromal stages of depression, decompensated responses may accompany verbal complaints, protests, or bereavement-like statements that sound pessimistic, skeptical, and embrace futility. One way to self-medicate anxiety, depression, or mood cyclicity is with alcohol or drug use. The functionality of self-medication is ubiquitous in each personality disorder. What is different, however, is the specific anxiety- or depression-related behavior patterns that disrupt the individual's life. Let us consider the prominent behavior patterns selected for self-medication in all three clusters.

CLUSTER A PERSONALITY DISORDERS. Cluster A, the "Awkward" personality disorders, consist of Paranoid, Schizoid, and Schizotypal. Common denominators among all three disorders include (a) underdeveloped social skills, (b) odd or distorted beliefs, (c) depersonalization, and (d) generalized or social anxiety. Underlying the common denominators is a basic failure to adjust to the *anxiety* of adult responsibilities in interpersonal, educational, or occupational capacities. There is a preference for avoidance and escape from these responsibilities and anxiety. For the Paranoid Personality, escape is from the anxiety of imagined conspiracies perceived as threatening to the individual. The individual wants a rapid way to stop obsessions about victimization and also to stop the fears of being persecuted. In Schizoid and Schizotypal personalities, avoidance and escape are from social anxiety around groups of people. They seek disconnection from mainstream interactions to reduce anxiety and feel artificially safe in the private sanctuary of their homes. Since *anxiety* is the main symptom, preference is for anxiety-decelerators such as depressants or sedative agents. Cannabis and opiate synthetics, in particular, are popular, since the effects produce calmness and dissociation. However, overuse of these agents may exaggerate these desired effects to a point of persistent constrictive affect, anhedonia, dysphoria, and derealization (bordering on psychosis).

A secondary problem with depressant-effect drugs is rebound anxiety. This is when the withdrawal symptoms mimic the original (baseline) symptoms prompting drug use. A heroin addict who abruptly abstains from daily use may notice within hours a spike in nervousness, excitability, restlessness, and racing obsessive thoughts. Anxiety symptoms may feel worse than when the heroin addict first used heroin to self-medicate symptoms, and consequently temptation for relapse remains very high. In Schizotypal Disorder, the spontaneous return of baseline anxiety symptoms is more than a nuisance. It completely engulfs the individual who already lacks strategic coping skills for interpersonal or other stressors. Frustration from poorly coping becomes intolerable, and in a panic, the individual regresses to heroin use. This vicious cycle of rebound (withdrawal) anxiety triggering readdiction has been the bane of many treatment interventions for opioids and benzodiazepines (Herman, Brotman, & Rosenbaum, 1987).

CLUSTER B PERSONALITY DISORDERS. Cluster B disorders include Antisocial, Borderline, Narcissistic, and Histrionic. Common threads running through the fabric of each disorder are cyclicity of moods, mood and response exaggeration, and unpredictability of responses. Volatile mood swings exhibited in individuals with Borderline and Histrionic disorder can vary in degree from moderately cyclothymic to severe bipolarity. In self-medicating, such individuals seek depressant or stimulant drugs for mood regulation. Cannabis, for example, may neutralize mood oscillation and suppress anxiety symptoms. On the obverse, crack cocaine or meta-amphetamines may springboard the individual out of depression. Symptoms of mood and panic exaggeration ostensibly occur in Histrionic, Borderline, and Narcissistic personality disorders. This panic exaggeration often is connoted as "overdramatization." Self-medicators for overdramatizers, such as alcohol (as depressant), may deflate excitability and reduce hypomania. Ingestion of alcohol as a stimulant may induce a bravado; it inflates confidence, invincibility, independence, and proportionally decreases fears of abandonment. For the Narcissistic type, ethanol may also numb or curtail angry feelings from denied attention, or from feeling deprived of entitled needs.

Response randomness or unpredictability is a frequent characteristic of the Antisocial and Borderline personalities. Both disorders feature impulsiveness or anxiety triggered by obvious or subtle establishing operations (EOs). Individuals with Antisocial personality, for example, may be sarcastic, sardonic, cynical, or outright aggressive for *no apparent reason.* Onlookers cannot fathom what situations precipitated this mean streak and are left clueless about the individual's anger. One answer is that spontaneous aggression is self-reinforcing. Aggres-sion can be self-stimulating and function as self-medication. For example, Mark exploded into a rage every time he felt anxious, intimidated, inferior, and uncertain how to handle situations. Sometimes his anxiety pertained to people around him, but most of the time these people were irrelevant or *not the cause per se.*

He deliberately aroused his sympathetic (visceral) nervous system by raising his voice and running around the house. This action achieved two goals. First, it scared his children and wife who stayed away from him. Second, he enjoyed the "rewarding" effects of the biochemical process. Release of hormones from the hypothalamus and pituitary glands (oxytocin, vasopressin, corticotropin, adrenocorticotropin) set off a chain reaction in the adrenal cortex. This hormonal transmission delayed (avoided) or suppressed (allowed escape from) his anxiety. Anger self-medicated his anxiety. Sadly, like drug tolerance, anger is also like a drug insofar as increasing the intensity and frequency of anger as Mark's body adjusts to it and the *anxiety requires more anger.*

CLUSTER C PERSONALITY DISORDERS. Cluster C or "cowardice" personality types consist of Avoidant, Dependent, and Obsessive-Compulsive. A common denominator underlying each disorder is *anxiety.* Anxiety varies in magnitude from specific or situational stressors (specific phobia, social anxiety) to multiple situations or broader-based stressors (e.g., generalized anxiety disorder). Curtailment of excessive fear and anxiety may entail prescribed anxiolytics (e.g., benzodiazepines, nonbenzodiazepines). Nonprescribed or illicitly taken drugs producing similar anxiety-reduction effects include alcohol (depressant), cannabis, and opioids. For example, Jason, an intravenous heroin abuser, abhorred any lapse of days without heroin since he felt endless anxiety for the simplest of daily routines and tasks. His legs shook, his hands tremored (non-Parkinsonian), and his tachycardia fooled him into thinking he might be having a myocardial infarction. He titrated to the prescriptive use of the antagonist Naloxone and Buprenorphine (i.e., Suboxone) but found his anxiety relapsing as the cocktail drug wore off or he took brief drug holidays suspending the administration of the cocktail. To supplement the cocktail, he borrowed his mother's prescriptions of Valium and Darvocet, both opiate synthetics that anesthetized his anxiety. Jason creatively used substitutive agents to replace the heroin for self-management of anxiety.

But there is a mistake in this thinking. The mistake addicts make in assuming the opioid will instantly relieve anxiety is that anxiety is a *not* unified or single symptom. Anxiety, like all behavior, consists of multiple responses interconnected like the cars of a train, from engine to caboose. *A response is extremely variable and a unique sequence of processes* (Kantor, 1921). Elimination of one response in the pattern, like eliminating only the caboose, does not automatically erase the remaining attached responses from (a) arousing similar anxiety; and (b) spontaneously generating a similar response, whose function resembles the one removed (caboose). Both events (a) and (b) are possible due to *spontaneous recovery*. In classical conditioning, spontaneous recovery refers to the re-emergence of a conditioned response after pairings cease between a conditioned and unconditioned stimulus. In operant conditioning, spontaneous recovery refers to re-emergence of a response after contingent extinction (withholding a consequence). In both cases, responses deliberately altered or that decrease suddenly regain strength. *The suddenly is not sudden at all.* Strength returns to the altered responses due to interresponse dependence (e.g., Kawashima, 2003). That is, the caboose only moves when pulled by the car in front of it, whose locomotion depends on the physics or force of cars preceding it.

Similarly, anxiety is a multicomponental and multisequential pattern involving muscular contractions, glandular secretions, and the resulting proprioceptive sensations. Intramuscular use of heroin may numb proprioceptive sensations generated from muscular and glandular changes but not retard or stop the somatic nervous system from ongoing activity. In the example of Jason above, illicit use of Valium and Darvocet may quickly eradiate noticeable headaches or abdominal aches (proprioceptive stimuli), but his legs may still be shaking, his hands may be slightly tremoring, and his heart rate remains abnormally high. Since constriction in these biological responses interdepends on the cranial and abdominal muscles, directly influencing them as part of the response pattern of field, Jason will probably notice his headache and stomachache return; he will conclude his anxiety is the same or worse than it was before taking the Valium and Darvocet.

GAMBLING DISORDER. A nonsubstance-related disorder added to the DSM-5, in response to the outcry of addicts of internet gaming and casino gambling (Ferentzy & Turner, 2013), was *gambling disorder.* Pathological gambling, like any addiction, predicates on loss of control. Helplessness is a symptom of (a) preoccupation with gambling; (b) overuse of nonexpendable resources (money); (c) engaging in gambling to relieve distress; (d) fabrication or lies to cover the extent of gambling; and (e) perils of gambling that reverberate in one's social, occupational, interpersonal, intrapartner, or family roles. Gambling disorder divides into two types: episodic and persistent. Episodic refers to pathologic gambling with at least several months in between each incident. Persistent refers to continuous diagnostic symptoms occurring over multiple years. When gambling is episodic but stretches of time of abstinence extend beyond several months (at least three), the individual may be in *partial remission*; abstinence beyond 12 months qualifies for *sustained remission.*

A frequent concomitant of casino gambling (not so much for internet gambling) is alcohol consumption. For many years, and still in selective casinos internationally, game players inside the casino received free liquor beverages. The incentive of free liquor, of course, was to lure uninterrupted playing on machines or tables. The other reason for serving free drinks was to exploit disinhibition while inebriated. Intoxicated players may lose track of their losses or inflate their chances of jackpots or outsmarting the card dealers.

Apart from this intentionality by casino owners, pathological gamblers shared three other common denominators. First, they enjoy the anticipatory thrill of any sizeable winnings. This viscerality is an establishing operation (EO) for which there exists some probability of reinforcement. Second, they enjoy and engage in superstitious behaviors associated with random reinforcement. Gamblers may go to the casino or online gaming sites *only on certain days, at certain times, or play certain games ritualistically due to accidental reinforcement for these rituals.* Third, gamblers exhibit impulsiveness relative to engaging in reckless behaviors contrary to any rules governing incompatible behaviors. The response effort to gain something of greater value is extensive, exhaustive, and produces more extinction (no reinforcers) than it does reinforcers. Consequently, promulgated rules have evolved warning gamblers of obvious fallacies, for example, that the "house usually wins," or "odds are against the gambler." Rules about unpredictable reinforcement schedules and the disaster of overspending money are widespread, mostly propagated by the platform of Gamblers Anonymous.

Despite the ubiquity of these rules, pathological gamblers persist with their egocentrically-consuming needs for pleasure. The personality disorders most likely predisposed to gambling disorders are (a) Antisocial personality, (b) Narcissistic personality, and (c) Borderline personality. Antisocial personality describes the social nonconformist and rule violator who is both self-serving and feels immune to punishment consequences. Narcissistic personality also characterizes self-importance, but the individual also operates on unreasonable expectations, attributes to self a high status of privileges, and is preoccupied with fantasies of unlimited success, power, brilliance, and beauty, all achievable by gambling. Such individuals may take advantage of other people, just as they would exploit *a system of machines or a casino.* Their sense of superiority blocks the recognition of the rule-caveats discussed above, that clearly expose the fraudulence in gambling. However, unlike Antisocial or Narcissistic personalities, the individual with Borderline personality disorder does not show credulity. They are very cognizant of and take serious the warnings of gambling and gaming. They are not necessarily and selfishly defying social rules. For them, the choice to gamble excessively is a self-medicator for (a) filling (reinforcing) the emptiness in their lives, (b) arousal of hypomania during bipolar episodes, (c) and avoidance or escape from oppressive stressors. In other words, individuals who are Narcissistic or Antisocial personalities gamble to bask in the pleasure. Borderline individuals gamble to avoid or escape troubles in their lives.

Neurocognitive Disorders

In recent years, extensive behavioral interest has been on the neurocognitive and neurobehavioral correlates of operant and respondent behaviors (Barrer & Ruben, 1985; Dworkin & Smith, 1989; Puente & Horton, 1986; Schmajuk, 2010). In fact, neuroscientific implications for personality theory follow this integrative trend toward a behavioral neuropsychology (Franzen & Getz, 2006; Horton & Wedding, 1984). Correlations are particularly curious between damaged neuroanatomical areas, as in Traumatic Brain Injury (TBI), and postinjury personality changes (Barratt, Stanford, Kent, & Felthous, 1997; Dolan & Park, 2002; Garcia, Mielke, Rosenberg, Bergey, & Rao, 2011). Neurocognitive sequelae of personality disorders are also visible in *delirium.* In the DSM-IV, neurocognitive disorders cormorbid with or causing behavior changes appeared under the classification of *Dementia, Delirium Amnestic,* and *Other Cognitive Disorders.* As clinical importance grew about these syndromes, many of which surfaced as presenting symptoms in private and agency practices, elaboration was necessary on the etiology and potential impediments of the syndromes. In the DSM-5, the new classification of *Neurocognitive Disorders* consolidates the most preponderant major and minor neurocognitive and neurobehavioral syndromes impacting child and adult behaviors. For our purposes, in affecting personality disorders, the categories of neurocognitive disorder most relevant include (a) delirium, and (b) Traumatic Brain Injury (TBI).

DELIRIUM. Delirium is a temporary disturbance in attention and awareness, often fluctuating during the day and directly impacting language, memory, and visuospatial ability. Causes of delirium typically are traceable to a physiological consequence of another medical condition, such as drug intoxication or withdrawal, medication underuse or overuse, exposure to toxins, TBI, postoperative recovery, or combinations thereof. Manifestation of delirium depends, in other words, on premorbid biophysical conditions. Does that mean any person, given unfortunate medical circumstances, might be susceptible to delirium? The answer is probably "yes." However, certain personality types may present higher propensities for iatrogenic delirium given a slower ability for resilience or pre-existing disorganized thinking. For example, Cluster A disorders, that of Paranoid, Schizoid, and Schizotypal personalities, largely consist of fragmented or confabulative reasoning, perceptual distortions, depersonalization, isolationism, and negative symptoms of psychosis (flattened affectivity, detachment, anhedonia, dysphoria, etc.). If a schizotypal client prescribed Seroquel walks in a daze, bumps into objects, seems inattentive to his surroundings, or lacks reality orientation, delirium is suspected but not as the major problem. Delirium is an exacerbation of the baseline prepsychotic features. A byproduct of possible mis-medication, delirium may be reversible by correcting the dose of Seroquel. This would restore a level of moderate dissociation (prepsychosis) in the person. The adjusted dose will not ameliorate the entire thought confusion or dissociation.

TRAUMATIC BRAIN INJURY (TBI). Postinjury trauma to the head is a devastating intrusion on the victim's world. Complete and abrupt cessation occurs in routines of work and school, coupled with profound difficulties in basic biophysical functions taken for granted, such as in expressive and receptive language, memory, reasoning, vision, hearing, and psychomotor coordination. The acuity of neurocognitive and neurobehavioral restrictions, in the days to months following the TBI, abound intolerably and unravel normalcy through predictable stages of severe personality maladjustment (Ruben, 1993c). Lundin (1987) described a similar transformation of such "defective personalities" as the "development of wrong behavioral equipment so that they (individuals) are unable to adjust to their natural and social surroundings" (p. 43). In explaining Kantor's personality typologies, Lundin defined "disintegrating personalities" (see Kantor, 1926) as behaviors held stable and normal up to a certain point until an abrupt breakdown. Disorganization of behaviors from TBI fits this "disintegrating" concept and helps to clarify the preponderant behaviors seen in TBI patients during early recovery.

Common behaviors seen in early stages of recovery include confusion and aggression. Confusion arises from postconcussive, postcomatose, or posthospital reorientation to a familiar (house) after a period of absence from it. Confusion is worse and adjustment is slower to unfamiliar settings, for example, to placements in an extended care rehabilitation facility. Acclimation to the surrounds depends entirely on the speed and operation of an individual's sensory modalities, thinking, reasoning, problem solving, or what Kantor called the *implicit interactions* (Maham, 1968; Pronko, 1980). Implicit interactions depend on the accessibility of stimuli, the availability of stimulus control, and the total field of interaction producing an effect. Skinner offered a more succinct account (1974), in explaining processes in problem solving. That a person suffers a problem when some condition might be reinforcing, but the person lacks the response to produce it (p. 123). The essence is that impaired implicit interactions brought on by, for example, a Diffused Axonal Injury (DAI), affecting the dorsolateral perfrontal cortex, will greatly limit production of responses for the accessibility to stimulus functions. Consequently, confusion persists until a point in recovery where the TBI individual can (a) *connect the stimulus-response contingencies within one or many new fields of interaction,* and (b) *memory permits continuity of responses from that one field (setting) to another field (setting).*

Anger, the other common response seen early and later in TBI recovery, is largely a function of defective responses. More than a response deficit, that is, a skill underdeveloped from unenriched life experience, a defective response instead lacks the componental parts (concurrent, sequential responses) to properly execute contingencies. A TBI impacting the left-hemispheral frontal lobe in Broca's area may prevent speech retrieval during oral discourse. Such motor aphasia disables structural completion of sentences and precludes the speaker to connect with stimulus objects. This is a more concrete etiology than blaming speech loss on inner causes (Ruben, 1986).

Memory loss can be explained just as easily (Fryling & Hayes, 2010). Despite the prefrontal cortex disturbance, a defective memory registration really means the (a) delay or obstruction of an individual's sensory contact with stimuli, and (b) a delay in spotting the discriminative qualities of some stimulus, with which to label the sensation. For example, if Johnny sees and touches the apple but cannot say "apple," this is traditionally called agnosia. But Johnny knows the word "apple," has plenty of experience of tactile and gustatory sensations with the object to call the object an "apple," and can discriminate the object from other types of fruit (e.g., "No, it's not a banana, I just cannot think of what it is"). Johnny *has all of the behavioral equipment to make the discrimination except for the medium of contact.* The medium of contact can be closely bound with the anatomical and physiological properties of the individual (cf. Delprato & Smith, 2009; Kantor, 1947). That is, damage to the prefrontal cortex disables contact medium with which Johnny can complete the labeling of "apple."

Johnny's incapacity to emit the word "apple" when touching an apple is frustrating. He may demonstrate frustration with angry words. Overuse of obscenities occurs in postinjury TBI individuals who may or may not have a past history (reactional biography) of profanity. Why is this? One partial reason is neurobiological. Disturbance to the medial orbitofrontal areas causes poor impulse control. Likewise, damage lateralized across the left and right temporal lobe affecting the limbic system, and injuring the amygdala, might cause aggressive behaviors. But emission of profanity goes beyond a neurobiological reason. Profanity has a unique response topography of aggression. It is frequently learned in respondent association with physical pain or stimulus conditions similar to physical pain. For example, Sheila shouts a profanity when she gets a paper cut and feels the skin surface nociceptors exposed to the air causing pain. By response generalization, she may also slide her finger against a thin, razor-sharp piece of paper and not get a paper-cut, but in anticipation of the paper-cut or *because it feels just like the paper-cut*, she shouts the profanity anyway. She experienced a physiological analogue or similarity of what caused pain, although the actual pain-evoker (antecedent) was absent.

Likewise, with a TBI, the individual *experiences analogue sensations evoking anger from the damaged amygdala.* These sensations may occur independent of any external environmental event, or be aggravated by the external events. TBI individuals may spontaneously get angry since they "feel inside the same sensations they typically would if something or somebody made them angry." However, there is no identifiable antecedent or consequent stimulus event triggering the anger-profanity response. However, what if there is an external event? If Johnny, to borrow an earlier example, cannot say "Apple" when he touches an apple, his propensity (i.e., establishing operation) for anger and using profanity will be *greater* from his failed labeling of apple. A similar behavior analysis was offered about neurobiological sensations *resembling* authentic contingencies, in the case of postpartum mothers who cried excessively absent of any "reason" for crying (Ruben & Ruben, 1985).

TBI is not specific to any personality disorder. Any individual, no matter his or her psychopathology, faces the risk of head injury from accident trauma. However, certain personality disorders consist of behavior patterns that might accentuate TBI disabilities and propensities for confusion and anger. Cluster C personality disorders include the anxiety-based typologies of Avoidant, Dependent, and Obsessive-Compulsive. Avoidant Personality entails behavior of conflict-avoidance, withdrawal, and guarded protectiveness of any vulnerability. Such individuals may hide, mask, or improperly compensate for defective response to prevent what is perceived as negative judgments about them. For example, before his TBI accident, Tony was a mild-mannered, docile teacher who was subordinate to his wife. One year after his vehicular accident, and after comprehensive speech and occupational therapy "to rebuild his skill," Tony outwardly reassured his therapy team and physiatrists that he was doing great and really felt his life restored. He returned to teaching, resumed his fitness routines, and went about his daily business seemingly routinely. On closer inspection, Tony never remembered by mid-day what he did that morning, and everyday seemed a blur. He also was horribly forgetful about promises made. When confronted by the team on this working memory loss, Tony embarrassingly admitted he has been "faking good" to make his team feel his rehabilitation was successful.

TBI in a Dependent Personality produces a slightly different picture. Dependent typologies (a) require excessive advice from other people about basic decisions, (b) resist initiating projects without strong alliance with other people, (c) go to extreme lengths to obtain nurturance and support from others, (d) replace one close relationship with another one to avoid loneliness, and (e) is preoccupied with fear about being left to care for self. Heidi, who suffered frontotemporal damage from a work-related accident, received strong rehabilitation team support for two years. She overcame anterograde amnesia, an interference in learning new information. She also had a premorbid (pre-existing) dependent personality. For two years, she met once or twice weekly with speech and occupational therapy and saw a behavioral psychologist. When learning of her team discharge, she panicked. She insisted her (a) skill achievement level remained far below the target goals, (b) that being entirely alone triggered flashbacks of the accident, and (c) her "confidence" for transition back to work was very low. She started to email and send phone texts to her therapy team members promising to do small favors for them such as baking a cake or babysitting their children. With a male rehabilitation assistant, she made flirtatious overtures to interest him to stay longer at her house beyond his assigned shift. Heidi went *overboard* in her indulgence to appease and assuage staff to support and nurture her, or at least to not discharge her. Her Dependent Personality features nearly sabotaged measurable gains in her rehabilitation.

In the case of Obsessive-Compulsive Personality, TBI individuals are less clingy and desperate as rehabilitation services end. The problem here lies in the rigidity for perfection during the fragile learning curve of restoring daily functional skills. Unlike persons suffering dementia, who many not be aware of their skill deterioration or imperfections, recovering TBI individuals reach phases of rehabilitation where they are cognizant of the difficulty in producing a pre-existing skill. Exceptions may exist, however, such as *anosognosia,* a condition resulting from lesions in the fronto-temporal-parietal area in the right hemisphere. This condition is when the individual is unaware of his or her disability not owing to denial or defensiveness, as in the foregoing case of Avoidant Personality. Other than this particular neurological pathology, hypersensitivity to mistakes during learning trials can have detrimental effects. For example, before his Motor Vehicle Accident (MVA), Matthew ran his life like a machine. It was orderly, methodical, synchronized with his family, and he poorly tolerated deviations in schedule or last-minute changes. Three months after the MVA, in overcoming right-sided temporal lobe disturbance affecting his auditory cortex, Matthew routinely received speech therapy focusing on receptive language ("auditory processing"). He could hear the words, and could tell you what each word meant, but did not follow the sequence of words when given an instruction. Each trial of relearning entailed dividing the sequence of words into smaller units, matched with his appropriate response and positive feedback. Although objectively and measurably, Matthew "aced" the early two-word, three-word, and four-word instructions, he struggled to discriminate proper responses to longer word combinations.

With each failed trial, Matthew became enraged, but not at the speech therapist or behavioral psychologist. Expulsion of anger at the staff *is a common phenomenon as described earlier.* Instead, Matthew exploded with abrasive self-critical remarks about his "stupidity" and "mediocrity" in repeatedly failing the task. He spiraled into a prophecy of pessimism about reaching a skill plateau and lacking the momentum for advanced progress. His premorbid features of Obsessive-Compulsive Personality threatened to sabotage the already tediously difficult steps of relearning to hear and understand the longer sentences. Delays in his successful rehabilitation were not due to lack of evidence-based gains or even unhealed bilateral temporal lobes. His obstruction to skill mastery lied with a propensity for perfectionism. In forcing himself to be overscrupulous with completing the learning tasks precisely and productively, he left no room for normal errors. In short, he viewed errors as anathema.

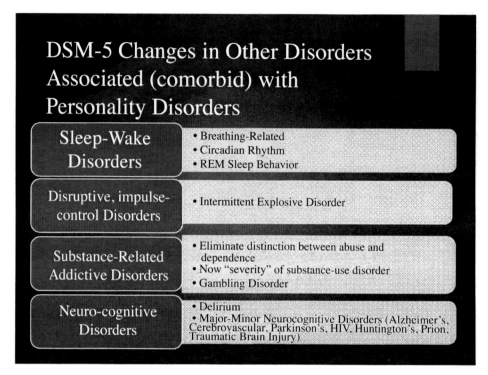

Figure 2.2.

C'mon, remind me:
55. One type of sleep-wake disorder deals with _____ rhythms.
56. Intermittent Explosive Disorder belongs to disruptive, impulsive-_____ disorders.
57. The most common neurocognitive disorders is Traumatic _____ _____.

Chapter 3

DECISION TREE FOR
PERSONALITY MANAGEMENT

Navigation around the maize of personality disorders requires a reliable compass. Nuances in overlapping response patterns and the behavioral contingencies under which these response patterns occur can seem daunting. Many personality disorders may even seem identical. For example, Schizotypal and Schizoid personalities share many relevant features of social awkwardness, depersonalization, and reality disorientation. Antisocial and Narcissistic personalities, as well, share defining features of egocentricity, hedonism, and disregard for social norms. With these common denominators, the risk is high of diagnosing a type-I error (false positive), misleading both the client-customer and treatment team, and then misformulating specific treatment interventions. One way to avoid this mistake is through a systematic decision tree that asks straightforward questions about the psychopathology. This chapter introduces a decision tree model for expedient conclusions about which personality clusters (A, B, or C) best matches the behavior dimensions in question.

The systematic steps of decisions in making a diagnosis of personality disorder is the first part of *personality management*. Personality management, *in toto*, consists of (a) a diagnostic (assessment) instrument, and (b) behavioral interventions. The assessment and intervention are equipped with the measurable sensitivity and evidence-based integrity to record and control integrative response patterns pervasive in a person's life. *Managing personality* is euphemistic for the *reductionism* of dissecting responses into their subproperties such as topography, intensity, magnitude, rate, duration, and function, and then interrelating these subproperties with known stimulus objects and functions. Such reductionism of response activity not only is consistent with natural science, but it is also fundamental to providing eventual behavior-change strategies to correct abnormalities in the personality response patterns.

A decision tree is the first roadmap along the course of *assessment* in personality management. In Figure 3.1, note the organization of a flow chart consisting of burst nodes (labeled in squares) that split into multiple decisions. These decisions offer a descriptive means of calculating *conditional probabilities* of response patterns in a personality that meet criteria under clusters A, B, or C. The tree is linearized into decision rules starting with the first question of:

Is the person oriented to reality?

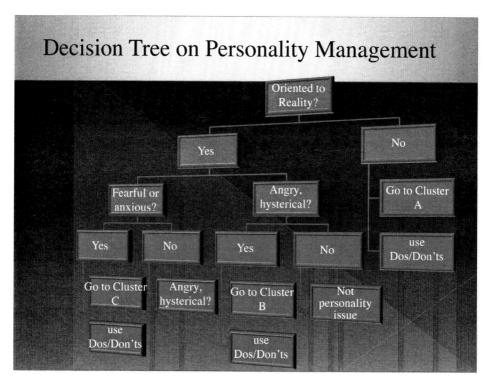

Figure 3.1.

Affirmative answers ("Yes") begins the algorithm to the left; a "No" response begins the algorithm to the right. On the left side, the first decision box asks if the person is:

Fearful or anxious?

If observed response patterns of the person confirm fear and anxiety ("Yes"), arrows flow to a processing step of diagnosing the typologies in Cluster C (Avoidant, Dependent, Obsessive-Compulsive). An additional branch guides the user to the "Dos and Don'ts when working with Cluster C (see Chapter 4). If observed response patterns of the person disconfirm fear and anxiety ("No"), the flow of control moves to a decision branch asking if the person is:

Angry or hysterical?

Affirmative answers ("Yes") flow back up to the branch that begins with "Angry-hysterical." Again, this decision step subdivides into branches of "Yes" and "No." If this answer is "Yes," that the person's response patterns depict anger or hysteria, consider diagnosis of the Cluster B personality disorders (Antisocial, Borderline, Histrionic, and Narcissistic). In addition, arrows flow underneath the processing reminder step to implement Dos and Don'ts with Cluster B personality types (see Chapter 4).

If the answer to the branch of "Anger-hysterical" is "No," this answer logically concludes the person (a) is oriented to reality, and (b) does not meet criteria for fear/anxiety or anger/hysteria. Ruling out these criteria, one probable outcome is that the person's response patterns do not qualify for personality disorders vis-a-vis DSM-5.

Now, let's return to the first decision node,

Oriented to reality?

Recorded occurrences of negative or positive symptoms of prepsychosis or psychosis would prompt the negative answer "No." This decision linearizes to two obvious processing branches: consider Cluster A for diagnosis (Paranoid, Schizoid, Schizotypal), and implement the "Dos and Don'ts" of working with Cluster C personality disorders (see Chapter 4).

Following this decision analysis map across clusters of personality disorders can bypass the morass of reified conceptual or theoretical issues often underlying diagnoses. For example, a common conceptual scheme in personality management derives from the psychodiagostic instrument called the Millon Clinical Multiaxial Inventory (MCMI) (see Divac-Jovanovic, Svrak, & Lecic-Toesvski, 1993). Here, personality disorders divide systematically into different classifications of deviant levels of functioning (i.e., normal, neurotic, and borderline), with a limited number of categories describing maladaptive behaviors. The advantage to this system, theoretically, is showing that classifications of personality can be orthogonal. However, as described earlier, personality patterns of behavior are not mutually exclusive. They consist of response patterns that are *interdependent and interactive* with stimulus conditions passing through multiple segments of the stimulus field.

Conceptual schemes, by contrast, like the classifications of deviant functioning in the MCMI-theory, can be problematic. These schemes invite elaboration of nonobservable dimensions of personality presumed to have cause-and-effect relationships. While, admittedly, many nonobservable events of personality are important for behavioral analysis (Ruben, 1988), conceptual schemes like the MCMI-theory are hyperboles of inferred capacities mudding the scientific waters for accurate diagnoses. By limiting personality management to observable, measureable, or operational relations, practitioners can remain on more solid ground in assessing response patterns.

Here are two examples of personality management using this decision tree.

Example 1: Timothy K. A 22-year-old, single male Caucasian in graduate school at a local university is referred to a clinic after a succession of delinquent course assignments and falling behind schedule on the first draft of his masters thesis. He reported the delinquencies related to procrastination, chronic social anxiety, and anticipation of harsh judgments from his committee chair about missing the thesis deadline dates. He described in precise detail the chronology of events leading up to his missed assignments, his guilt for the lateness, and gave a realistic account of impending (unwanted) consequences for continued improprieties.

On the decision tree (see Figure 3.2), first begin with the burst node or primary decision that splits off into two answers: Is Timothy K. oriented to reality? The answer is "Yes" (see white space in the figure), since he described in precise detail the chronology of events leading up to his missed assignments and gave an accurate portrayal of punishing consequences for his continued mishaps. Second, follow the branch arrow down to the first decision node: Is Timothy K. fearful or anxious? Again, the answer is affirmative ("Yes"), given his self-reported reasons for assignment delinquencies, including (a) chronic social anxiety, and (b) anticipation of harsh comments from his committee chair.

Social anxiety implicates underdevelopment of interpersonal or communication skills, and overuse of avoidance or escape as defective coping strategies. His anticipation of harsh comments, in fearing an imminent conflict, may suggest deficits in assertiveness and unwilling risks to expose other personal weaknesses (vulnerability).

In the first session or meeting with Timothy K., the interview may inquire about this extent of his skill impoverishment and seek other sources of pretherapy or baseline data supporting a reactional biography of anxiety. Most importantly is to rule out any congenital or adventitious physical (organic) conditions mimicking symptoms of anxiety (e.g., hyperglycemia, hyperthyroidism). Acceptance of self-report data is reasonable when the data corroborate with sample observations or artifacts from the individual's world. For example, such artifacts may include letters written about the client by his girlfriend, male friends, parents, teachers, clergy, or other therapists; or permanent products of his behavior include his original music compositions, details on Facebook, Linked-in, Twitter, and other electronic media. Collectively, baseline data may offer a provisional diagnosis of either Avoidant, Dependent, or Obsessive-Compulsive Personalities, all of which belong to Cluster C (next processing node).

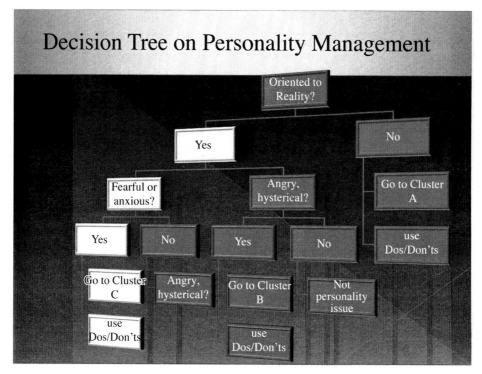

Figure 3.2.

Example 2: Heather S. Heather is a 45-year-old, divorced, African-American female self-referred to vocational rehabilitation services after being laid off from her job of 15 years in hospital administration. She reported a comorbid diagnosis of fibromyalgia and cervical herniated discs (C1 to C3), accounting for unrelenting neck pain. Intense neck pain restricts her head rotation, bending, or stooping, all of which, if done abruptly, cause vestibular imbalance; she gets dizzy and may faint. She provides medical documentation attesting to these illnesses and the work accommodations previously made at her office job. She also reported pain-related mood disturbance. A primary mood shift is her prodromal symptoms of depression including social withdrawal, self deprecation, agitation, anger, work tardiness and increased absenteeism, and appetite reduction. Presented with this litany of symptoms, Figure 3.3 guides the decision map to determine her proclivity for a personality disorder. The first decision node asks if she is oriented to reality. You answer "Yes" (see white space in the figure).

This branches into two decision nodes:

Fearful or anxious?
Or Angry and Hysterical?

You rule out "Fearful or anxious," since Heather S. never reported any history or currency of anxiety symptoms. Instead, her iatrogenic anger, a byproduct of unmanaged cervical pain, appears significant and directs the step to "Anger, hysterical." Upon further inquiry, when asking about her past episodes of anger, and tendencies for catastrophic-thinking, little evidence supports a pervasive course of these behaviors. An evolution of pathogenic anger and histrionics is necessary to provisionally conclude that Heather S. qualifies for Cluster B personality disorders (e.g., Antisocial. Borderline, Histrionic, Narcissistic). Since Heather S. does not meet this diagnostic criteria, the decision tree yields to the node of "Not (a) personality issue."

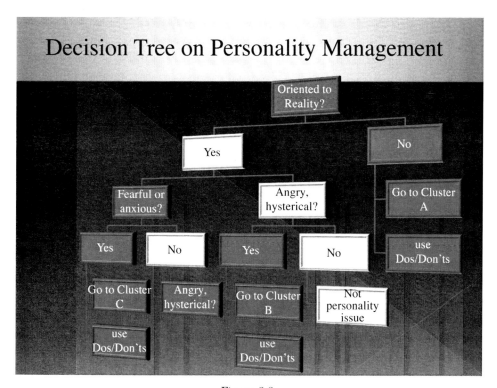

Figure 3.3.

In short, the objective of using the personality management decision tree is not to perfect clinical diagnostic skills. It is just the beginning step of behavioral triage. For therapists, assessment includes other corroborative data gathered during the first or second session of the mental health examination. This rich collection of data is computed into a larger picture of the person. The flow chart, specifically, is efficient to rule out invasive pathological factors affecting personality. For other service providers, who are not commonly diagnosticians but need a working knowledge of the diagnosis, the decision tree may support or question pre-existing diagnoses found in current or obsolete medical records. Discrepancies between diagnoses in current or obsolete medical records and the current observations from meeting the client in person, may raise a red flag; it may prompt referrals for an updated psychological examination. Results of that examination provide a very special yardstick of measure; results offer valid predictors of how the client or customer may *accept* or *reject* customized rehabilitation services. As we will see in the next chapter, the validity of this personality management instrument is only as good as the training and awareness of the service provider to use the instrument correctly and design behavioral goals based on its outcomes.

Chapter 4

DOS AND DON'TS OF PERSONALITY DISORDERS: APPLYING PERSONALITY MANAGEMENT

Skillful execution of personality management goes beyond the microscope of assessment. Analysis of response patterns may begin with direct mensurational records of baseline, or collection of anecdotal data. But once the data form a working definition of personality disorders, the second step in personality management is to strategically cope with the maladaptive behaviors of personality interfering with the provision of some service. In therapy, the service is *change-oriented, insofar as using systematic and methodical interventions to decrease or increase certain behaviors.* However, in most other service delivery systems, such as in vocational rehabilitation, speech therapy or occupational therapy, the goal is *not to change personality patterns*. Rather, the goals focus on correction of *collateral maladaptive behaviors* with which the individual ineffectively manages his or her environment. Collateral maladaptive behaviors describe the lack of response equipment that one needs to fulfill basic daily functions. For example, poor speech retrieval and receptive language obstructs communication. Speech pathologists address this maladaptivity. In occupational therapy, for another example, the goal may be to repair limited ambulation, weak physical manipulation of hands, or slow visual scanning with which to find clothing in one's closet.

In this chapter, discussion of personality management is not about the actual methods implemented by mental health therapists or therapists of allied health fields to correct personality disorders or collateral maladaptive behaviors. Important here is the behavioral guidelines used *during the process of employing correction strategies.* How does a provider *talk to a client with Borderline Personality without risking exacerbation of dysfunctional symptoms?* Is there a right and wrong way to give feedback to a person with *Antisocial Personality Disorder* without completely sabotaging the behavior management plan? These questions beg a more fundamental question: What are the "Dos and Don'ts of working with volatile, fragile, or otherwise precarious personality disorders? That's a good question.

This chapter supplies a guideline for practitioners in multidisciplinary health fields to navigate correctly around the sometimes turbulent, confusing, and seemingly unpredictable response patterns of personality disorders. The chapter divides into three sections. The first section addresses the Dos and Don'ts on dealing with Cluster A personality disorders. The second section addresses the Dos and Don'ts on dealing with Cluster B personality disorders. A third section finishes by addressing the Dos and Don'ts with Cluster C personality disorders.

Cluster A Personality Disorders

The predominant concern when dealing with Cluster A personality disorders is patience. While this simple therapist attribute seem ubiquitous, the exigency of daily office routines often compel busy schedules unsympathetic to unwanted interruptions. Office practices run efficiently when the pace and order of clients seen per day balances with replies to emails, telephone calls, agency requests, and completion of progress notes or reports. When snags arise in any of these time-pressured units of time, practitioners experience their own establishing operations (EOs), under which they are prone to misreact, misjudge, and outwardly appear impatient. With personality disorders such as Paranoid, Schizoid, and Schizotypal, the preponderant symptoms are hypersensitivity (fears) and poor social skills. Therapist impatience may unknowingly punish this hypersensitivity, worsening fears, and distancing the already self-alienated clients. Like patience, there are four more advisable strategies when first meeting or having ongoing interactions with Custer A personality disorders.

Dos with Cluster A Personality Disorders. The four additional strategies include (1) design motivators; (2) coach small steps, not large ones; (3) structure the program and keep client on task; and (4) show empathy. Design of motivators means employment of measurable and definable contingencies outlined at the outset of therapy or training that spell out the client's expected behaviors in return for specific service outcomes. In vocational rehabilitation, for example, a contingency may request weekly email correspondence or telephone calls made by the client to update job-searching efforts. In exchange, the counselor supplies a job coach per one to two hours a week to help the client in resume-writing and job-application completion and submission. Contingencies ostensibly instill motivation for productive response efforts and compete with maladaptive responses such as isolationism, anxiety, depersonalization, or preoccupation with paranoid thoughts.

Coaching small steps comes from a fundamental behavioral philosophy of teaching or shaping new skills. The philosophy is to *start where the behavior is at.* This means, in assessing baseline or prerequisite skills, evidence may clearly appear that the client lacks rudimentary responses to handle some situation normally considered to be part of an adult's social repertoire. In speech therapy, for instance, asking questions of a speaker when confused by the message sent, may seem an obvious step in clarification. However, Schizotypal and Schizoid personalities lack interpersonal skills and engage in chronic avoidance behaviors. They frequently would withhold such questions or *it would never occur to them to ask the question.* A small step approach to teaching message clarification, then, begins with what the client *can* do. The client *does* stand, listen, and looks at the speaker when spoken to. These response patterns are solid, consistent, or might always occur during an intraverbal transaction. In teaching clients to ask questions, then, the first step outlined in the behavior plan might include standing so close or far from the speaker while giving direct eye contact to the speaker. Methods of small-step learning borrow from a litany of evidence-based research on the use of successive approximations (Brown & Jenkins, 1968; Miltenberger, 2012).

Structure the program and keep client on task. Program development for prospective clients typically tailors to individualized outcome goals. For example, if teaching a stroke-recovering elderly person how to tie her shoe, the goal is regaining strength in the contralateral side of her body affected by the stroke or to use adaptive devices guiding shoe-tying. But, shoe-tying may be not be possible unless contingencies also are set for *staying on task.* On-task contingencies, at first, might involve both concentration on tying the shoes and reducing distractibility.

Schizoid and Schizotypal personality disorders involve similar distractions in the form of disconnection or derealization. This means the person drifts off into other thoughts unrelated to the task. With Paranoid personality, off-task drifting involves verbal tangents about elaborately irrelevant topics that may engage the provider, such as about current news events. One way to remain on-task is to define the unit or length of a discrete learning trial and contingencies before training begins. For example, "Sally, we will work for 30 minutes on tying your shoe with this device, then give you a five-minute break." Sally, who has Schizotypal personality, is already fearful of making mistakes, of somebody talking to her, and cannot stay focused for more than 40 minutes. Clarity of these contingencies helps her to discriminate cues for immediate responses and resist incompatible drifting or off-task behaviors.

Show empathy. Empathy defined here is a bit different from its denotation in most clinical and training applications (cf. Ruben, 1986b). Empathy does not mean a vicarious identification of the client's feelings, or showing compassion for a client's life predicament. Instead, empathy serves a distinct reinforcing effect in praising any successive approximations toward the target behavior goals. Empathy is like descriptive feedback in content, but it goes beyond the function of mirroring the task observed. It includes praise of the *behavior, person, and the situation.* For example, when James called his vocational counselor punctually to report three job searches done that day, the counselor used empathy by saying,

"James, I am so glad you called on time, that you are really caring about your job search, and you're doing a great job at managing your day so far."

Why are these factors in the feedback so important to Cluster A personality disorders? The reasons are threefold. First, feedback of any sort, as described above, is a discriminative gauge or stimulus allowing the person to *know what to do and when to do it.* Without direction, the client quickly gets lost, distracted, or preoccupied in their disorganized thoughts. The second reason is that empathy identified *all of the behaviors important in the task, not just the target or ostensible task of calling punctually.* While the empathy statement is brief and does not cover in detail each small step in the total response pattern of job searching, it makes reference to it. However, in cases of TBI, where receptive or abstractive reasoning skills are still disturbed, a clearer and more detailed empathy statement might be needed. For example,

"James, I am so glad you called at 3 PM today. You're great for calling on three jobs today and submitting the applications. It is fantastic you got up early and spent so much on your job search and prioritized your goals for the entire day."

A third reason why empathy feedback is so essential is for *safety*. Cluster A personality typologies distrust the world. They are chronically fearful of reality-based interactions and learned from childhood the safety of isolationism or viewing people as arch-enemies. An empathic statement *does not make the client feel good about himself or herself*. This is a misnomer. Individuals with Schizotypal and Schizoid personality disorders are anhedonic and dysphoric. They are unfeeling, indifferent to praise, and most certainly will not perceive the empathic provider as somebody who "cares for them." Such perceptions of caring are nonexistent and probably inconceivable from the client's reactional biography. Instead, *safety* means the practitioner does not appear frightening or aversive; the provider is approachable and allows the client to make mistakes without repercussions. In this way, the provider *mands or enjoins the client to respond in anticipation of reinforcing (not punishing) conditions, increasing risk-approach behaviors.*

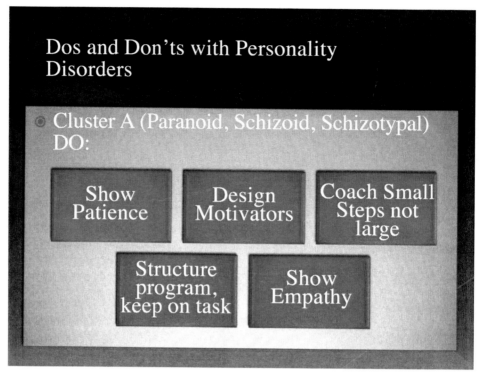

Figure 4.1.

C'mon, remind me:
58. Important is to show _____ with Cluster A personality Disorders.
59. Coach _____ steps, not large steps in teaching Cluster A.
60. Empathy is to convey _____, not to show you care.

DON'TS WITH CLUSTER A PERSONALITY DISORDERS. Delicately balancing empathy with direct contingency management is the strategy advised for proactive interactions with Cluster A personality disorders. Attainment of goals is easier, faster, entails less cumbersome obstacles, and maintains a positive client-provider rapport, which is paramount to building trust in highly distrustful clients. As straightforward as this advice sounds, the "interbehavioral field" reminds us of the essential spoiler that undermines implementation of effective behavioral management. First, segments of the field interrelate and casual occurrences in one segment specifically and broadly impact successive segments. Second, and most important, within the field segment itself, interactions between organism and stimuli are reciprocal and not unicausal (Kantor, 1959, pp. 92–95). This bidirectional (nonlinear) relationship between, say, therapist and client, better explains the multiple cause-and-effect outcomes expected during a given session or meeting. For example, as important as it is to know about Frank's magical thinking, paranoid thoughts, and weak social responses, so it is for the therapist to be cognizant of his or her own establishing operations and personal reactional biography. Both are idiographic factors predisposing providers to properly or improperly handle the deluge of Cluster A behavior patterns in clients.

Mistakes likely to unravel the therapeutic milieu and stonewall progress on goals may stem from the therapist's existing life strategies to handle normal or routine conflicts, both at home or at work. But many of these seemingly common-sensical strategies are contraindicated with Cluster A personality typologies. Among the most pronounced mistakes or "Don'ts" include (1) argue, defend, and demand; (2) accuse, threaten, or set ultimatums; (3) tease, use idioms or use profanity; (4) allow excuses or excessive autonomy; and (5) overinstruct or give large tasks. Let us consider each of these mistakes separately

Argue, defend, and demand. Temptations for conflict are usually uncommon in provider-client relationships. However, with the Paranoid Personality, the individual can be hyperbolic in launching intellectual or philosophical arguments proving their convictions. While their logic is faulty and is built on syllogisms (e.g., $A = B$, $B = C$, *ergo* $A = C$), their language in articulating the argument can sound surprisingly sophisticated. Consequently, an easy mistake is to misinterpret their insightfully-sounding comments as a worthy challenge for dispute. Such intraverbal exchanges, however, will not dismantle the irrationality of the client's thoughts or persuade acceptance of healthy beliefs. *What is really occurring is the reinforcement of the client's defective verbal behavior and accompanying disorganized thoughts.* From the earliest-documented behavioral research with psychosis (e.g., Allyon & Azrin, 1964; Allyon & Michaels, 1959; Greenspoon, 1955) to more contemporary studies on altering relevancy of verbal behavior (Ruben, 1983b; Sundberg & Partington, 2010), evidence strongly supports the careful and selective use of reinforcers on verbal content. Applying the methods prudently, providers are encouraged to overlook excessive soliloquies of paranoid grandeur, and differentially attend to on-task statements about the therapy or rehabilitation goals.

Accuse, threaten and set ultimatums. Prolongation of unmet goals is very frustrating to providers and clients. Providers invest time and effort in skill-building to mobilize productive changes in a client's life. When these changes are slow, inconsistent, or never made, a common mistake is to blame the client for failure to *try to achieve the behavior goals.* Blame may consist of accusing the client of deliberate or inadvertent sabotage, failure to practice the skills, or looking for excuses and diversions from the learning trials. Annoyed by this seemingly endless futility, providers might mistakenly exert pressure on the client to work harder and show more interest in learning. Ultimatums are put into place as soft or harsh threats to compel completion of tasks. However, with Schizoid and Schizotypal personality disorders, such individuals already are hypersensitive to verbal harshness and reprimands. They abhor confrontation and lack any functional skills in properly interpreting and responding to adversity. The anger "messages" communicated by the provider will frighten, suppress, and nearly guarantee the client's attrition from the program.

Tease, use idioms or use profanity. On the obverse, providers may feel value in showing levity. To make the stressful client feel at ease, providers may "dumb-down" language or use idiomatic expressions as mands for relevant dialogue about goal-related tasks. The downside of such casual demeanor has to do with social skills deficits in Schizotypal and Schizoid personality disorders. First, profanity may seem *offensive* no matter its calming or playful contexts. The client simply may not differentiate *good from bad profanity.* The situational or verbal cues distinguishing *good from bad profanity* may be unclear and lack any linguistic reference (symbolism) for the client (see Kantor, 1929b). Given their history of profanity associated with punishment, it is more likely clients will misinterpret profanity cues as signals of impending aggression. To make matters worse, idiomatic or colloquial expressions may sound like a foreign language to clients. Such expressions require advanced abstractive reasoning that extracts metaphorical or metonymical properties that are meaningful to the client. These properties presume a certain experiential background in social communication in diverse settings, and on complicated topics. By contrast, individuals with Schizoid and Schizotypal personality disorders are poor communicators, lack exposure to an enriched socialization, and would be clueless to the underlying meaning of such phrases and innuendos.

Allow excuses or excessive autonomy. Delivery of therapy or rehabilitation services predicates on patience, understanding, and flexibility. That latter attribute, that of flexibility, appears a type of discretion used when one of two conditions exist. First, evidence supports the client's observable progress on goals and there are normal obstacles interfering with progress, the removal of which may require some latitude of time to achieve. A second condition is when, regardless of measurable progress, the client elaborates reasons for delays in progress of goals and asks for more time or exceptions to supposedly work on the goals. The flexibility of honoring the client's request is not the issue here. The issue is the believability of excuses. Excuses, functionally, may be disguises for avoidance and escape behavior. With Cluster A personality types, unfamiliar tasks of any sort impose a risk of behavior failure. Individuals with Paranoid personality disorder may be suspicious of punishment looming in the future and rationalize many excuse for "needing more time." Individuals with Schizoid or Schizotypal personalities may simply forget to work on tasks and then justify their forgetfulness by saying the provider's directives were confusing. Granting such individuals more time will reinforce avoidance/escape response patterns, that is, it will encourage apathy, complacency, and lack of task-initiative.

Overinstruct or give large task. On the other hand, when there is a glimmer of progress from the client's conformity to procedure and task completion, providers get very motivated to add more tasks onto the client's slate. Assignment of new or more complex task may seem a natural step in promoting healthy behavioral growth and to keep up the momentum of interest. With individuals who are Schizoid and Schizotypal personality disorder, progress and task conformity may be evident but for different reasons than the *client wanting to get better or be more healthy.* High spikes in behavior may (a) appear unstable, (b) occur under the stimulus control of only one environment (behavioral field), (c) involve maladaptive behaviors, and (d) respond to the wrong establishing operations (EOs).

For example, Samantha, who has Schizotypal Personality Disorder, emailed her vocational counselor every day at 9 AM and explained her vocational efforts. However, (a) she only wrote about her resume two days of the week, (b) she only emailed her vocational counselor, (c) her explanations tangentially went beyond resume-building and talked about her supernatural powers, and (d) she wrote and sent emails even when she did not fix her resume or did anything vocationally. In the latter case, her EOs pertained to *the anticipatory reinforcing value of the provider responding back to her email.* That is the *wrong* establishing operation expected for writing the email. The provider *presumed* the establishing operation referred to Samantha's excitement about sharing her resume-activities.

When progress seems visible, but the reasons for progress are uncertain, the best strategy is to maintain the course of short instructions and giving small tasks. A streak of consecutive days mastering a simpler set of instructions is beneficial for several reasons. First, smaller units of task completion are more measurable and verifiable with or without self-reports. There is a clear beginning and end to the task. The client can bring in samples or make corrections on the sample more frequently. Second, smaller tasks enable a repetition of the task. Cluster A personality typologies consist of very ritualistic, or habit-forming behaviors; the client may repeat it by rote without frequent reminders (probes). Third, it is easier to generalize a smaller unit of progress than a larger unit of progress. The client may find it facile to show his or her resume to other adults, or even a prospective employer, when the resume *is the only task worked on and mastered.*

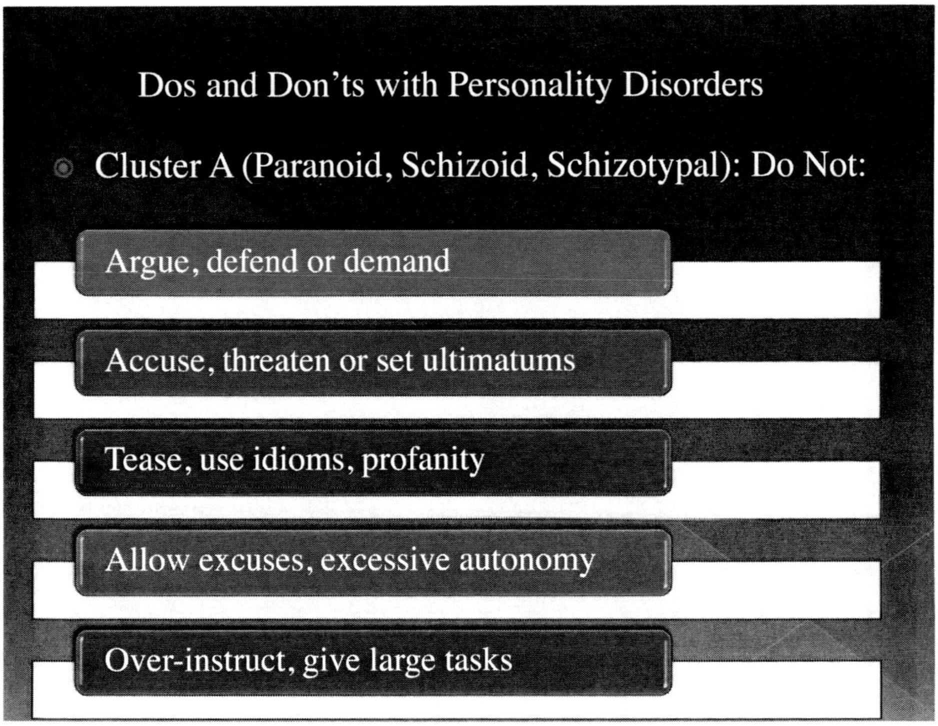

Dos and Don'ts with Personality Disorders

◉ Cluster A (Paranoid, Schizoid, Schizotypal): Do Not:

- Argue, defend or demand
- Accuse, threaten or set ultimatums
- Tease, use idioms, profanity
- Allow excuses, excessive autonomy
- Over-instruct, give large tasks

Figure 4.2.

C'mon, remind me:
61. It is inadvisable to defend or _____ of Cluster A individuals.
62. Idioms are not always _____ by Schizoid and Schizotypal personalities.
63. Rarely allow _____ or grant excessive _____ to prevent avoidance/escape.

Cluster B Personality Disorders

Wisdom is a cumulative record of trials and errors underscored by the humility of realizing and correcting these errors. In working with Cluster B personality disorders, wisdom sprouts from many trials and errors in the management of several difficult behaviors or *response patterns*. First, difficult response patterns are "over-the-top" or excessive and spark proportionally labor-intensive reactions from providers. Second, response patterns are aversive (punishing), and may intimidate or challenge providers to a point of defensiveness. Third, verbal response patterns may seem deliberate, retaliatory, malevolent, provocative, overcontrolling; it appears the client does not want a provider's help. This is opposite to the victim-centered helplessness that typically welcomes a provider's compassion and services. Fourth, a common thread interwoven in Cluster B personality disorders is unpredictability. Response patterns are impulsive, random, illogical, and often lack congruence with social norms. Faced with this cacophony of disruptive and hostile behaviors, it is easy to misjudge a clinical situation and overreact passively or aggressively. How can providers overcome these mistakes?

Dos with Cluster B Personality Disorders. Here we discuss two main approaches to assist with Cluster B personality disorders. The first approach is to give constant positive feedback. This divides into (a) design a structure and incentive system, and (b) offer intersession support. A second approach is keep specific goals on task. Task organization divides into (a) be "matter of fact" (objective), (b) show patience, (c) define boundaries, and (d) watch for countertransference.

Constant Positive Feedback

Design a structure and incentive system. Prolific use of positive feedback is common in most applications of behavioral and nonbehavioral clinical interventions. Corrective and specific details about responses in a task can build more reliable practices of that task. In most cases, reinforcement-centered feedback approaches can even streamline errorless learning to optimize the speed and mastery of nearly any complex verbal or nonverbal set of skills (Cipani & Madigan, 1986; Terrace, 1963). However, in the case of Cluster B personality disorders, reinforcing feedback alone is insufficient. Placement of the feedback is just as important as what the feedback consists of. Is feedback valuable only when it is given during training? Or what about feedback provided in between training sessions?

Offer intersession support. Intersession feedback is not a new concept (Ruben & Ruben, 1985b, 1987). It was revived lately amid the development and dissemination of Linehan's pioneering Dialectical Behavior Therapy (DBT). In principle, DBT may have much to offer therapeutically, but research on its efficacy has been controversial (Bankoff, Karpell, Forbes, & Pantalone, 2012; Scheel, 2000). DBT typically consists of three fundamentals: cognitive behavior therapy, validation, and dialectics. The latter, dialectics, addresses three underlying assumptions pervasive during every stepwise intervention. These assumptions include (1) all things are interconnected, (2) change is constant and inevitable, and (3) opposites can be integrated to form a closer approximation of the truth. The assumptions, particularly about interconnections and constancy of change, bare an uncanny and unmistakable resemblance to earlier postulates of Kantor's interbehavioral psychology (Kantor, 1959). One special component in Linehan's DBT framework is very different from traditional clinical practices while it is very consistent with the interventions used in applied behavior analysis (Linehan, Schmidt, Dimeff, Craft, Kanter, & Comtois, 1999). This is the component of *intersession* support.

Intersession support provides continuity of *implemented procedures* or *behavior changes* across settings, from therapy session to the natural environment. Clients update their progress or may ask questions of the therapist via skype, email, texting, or phone calls, all to prevent regression on unwanted symptoms in between training or therapy sessions. The advantage of inter-session support with Cluster B Personality disorders is to provide ongoing feedback for control over high-risk or severe behaviors. For example, an individual with Histrionic Personality Disorder may want validation (i.e., answers) on self-image questions to prevent overdrinking or acting promiscuous. A person with Borderline Personality, on the cusp of threatening suicide, may need refresher feedback on his positive qualities to restore confidence and end suicidal thoughts. Granting this brief intersession contact may interrupt a disastrous trajectory of maladaptive behaviors or reverse deterioration of behaviors to baseline levels.

While benefits of intersession feedback sound socially valid, the downside of this feedback is obvious. *It positively reinforces dependence and resurgence of problem behavior in between meetings or sessions.* For example, a recreational therapist found that she planned and executed social outings on Mondays and Fridays for a frontal-lobe injured patient, with Borderline Personality Disorder. On Tuesdays and Wednesdays, she received a torrent of emails from the patient inquiring about details in preparation for the Friday outings. At first she regarded this inquiry as normal and believed it was a healthy sign of restored executive functions. That is, the client exhibited problem solving, judgment, prioritization, and planning skills. However, the ritualism of Tuesday and

Wednesday emails seemed causally connected to how *angry or happy the client appeared on Friday during the outing.* When the Recreational therapist responded efficiently to the deluge of emails, the patient greeted her on Fridays with energy and enthusiasm. When the Recreational therapist did not respond to the emails or responded only to a paucity of emails, the client was rude, sarcastic, and blamed the Recreational therapist for a bad social activity. The therapist's responsiveness to the emails was not a therapeutic benefit since it accelerated the Borderline individual's splitting symptoms. It reinforced and maintained a cycle of splitting and undermined the client's self-regulation.

The answer on how to conduct intersession feedback, then, lies with balance and boundaries. As will be seen below, clearly defining the frequency and content of intersession contact can eliminate abuse of the system and uphold its value as an external conduit of therapy. Providers can specify in advance (a) how many times contact is acceptable, (b) what is acceptable and unacceptable content, and (c) the time distance or intervals in between each correspondence.

Keep Specific Goals on Task

Matter of fact. A matter-of-fact approach speaks to the heart of scientific or evidence-based interventions. Language used in communication with clients needs to clearly reference aspects of the target behavior and not tangential aspects of the target behavior. With Cluster B Personality Disorders, individuals overanalyze and overdiscuss irrelevant and tangential matters to divert attention (escape) from the unpleasantness of confronting problem behaviors. Such individuals abhor confrontation, despite their bravado in debating with others when minor or major conflicts arise. But the altercations are decoys, guarding against vulnerability. Histrionics exhibit guardedness by overdramatization. Individuals with Borderline Personality Disorder show guardedness by panic and clinginess. Individuals with Antisocial Personality Disorders show guardedness through aggression, intimidation, and rule violations. Individuals with Narcissistic Personality Disorder show guardedness through self-grandiosity and self-absorption. One way around these decoys of guardedness is to be *matter-of-fact.* This means, when giving instructions, focus the requests (mands) on exactly *what you want the client to do, how to do it, when to do it, and the contingencies for its proper or improper execution.*

Show patience. Professional ethics dictate an empathic, patient, and understanding approach to rehabilitation. Ethical guidelines may vary for different allied health professionals, but are largely uniform in the edict of a harassment-free interaction. For example, code 1.05(e) for Behavior Analysts, explicitly states that "behavior analysts do not knowingly engage in behavior that is harassing or demeaning to persons with whom they interact in their work based on factors such as those persons' age, gender, culture, ethnicity, national origin, religion, sexual orientation, disability, language, or socioeconomic status, in accordance with law (BACB, 2014, p. 5; cf. Bailey & Burch, 2011). Parameters of nonharassment, however, go beyond demographic features of the client. It also includes *the client's behavior excesses or deficits about which the practitioner may find offensive or beyond the level of expertise of that practitioner.*

Phyllis, a well-respected speech pathologist, met twice weekly with Carmen, a traumatically-brain-injured adolescent with left frontal lobe damage affecting Broca's area. Carmen also was diagnosed with Antisocial Personality Disorder before her head-injury accident. Carmen's speech was dysfluent and she struggled to retrieve words in any conversation. When delays of retrieval exceeded 15 seconds, Carmen became frustrated, sputtered obscenities, and accused Phyllis of pushing her beyond her limits during training. Phyllis, a morally conservative individual, took offense at the obscenities and defended her training strategy while threatening to terminate future services. Was Phyllis within her rights to protect herself and put Carmen on notice?

From an ethical standpoint, Phyllis did not violate any code insofar as mistreating Carmen due to biases of age, gender, culture, ethnicity, national origin, religion, sexual orientation, disability, language, or socioeconomic status. However, Phyllis was intolerant with a common behavior excess of profanity abuse in closed-head injured individuals; Phyllis did not objectify the situation, forgoing her moral beliefs or personal assumptions that Carmen's profanities were ill-willed. Although there are ethical codes qualifying when, for example, *psychologists* can terminate therapy when threatened or endangered by clients (APA, 2010), the degree of *threat or endangerment remains interpreted subjectively by the practitioner.* In this case, Phyllis' was probably not under any threat of danger or harm given the client's premorbid diagnosis of Antisocial Personality, and potentiation of the symptoms from the closed-head injury. Phyllis needed to depersonalize from the situation and be patient with or understand the client's outbursts.

Define boundaries. As suggested earlier, the downfall of excessive intersession client contact lies in the failure to have clear boundaries. Boundaries, operationally speaking, consist of precise time intervals and contingencies under which behaviors are expected or forbidden, with little wiggle room for interpretation. With individuals having Histrionic Personality Disorder, time intervals may restrict contact between certain hours of the day, and designate the reasonable latency from client contact to the provider's response (if there is even a response needed). Boundaries are *contingencies* that define the exact type (topography), number or limit (frequency) of responses acceptable in a given contact, and the consequences implemented if responses violate or comply with the contingencies. These contingencies are outlined in a contract mutually reviewed and agreed upon by both provider and client. For example, a contingency restricted Megan, a client, to write only a 250-word email on a job-related question. If Megan overwrote an email that exceeded the 250-word limit by 1000 words, plus she detailed the catastrophe of her broken marriage, the provider already had in writing the policy of nonresponsiveness to these emails.

Watch for countertransference. A corollary to defining patience and boundaries is developing an inappropriate emotional reaction to the client. When feelings build for or against the client, ranging from romantic interest to aversion, that redirection of feelings is traditionally called *countertransference*. It differs from *transference*, the phenomenon of clients attaching emotions onto the provider. Countertransference occurs during every dyadic between provider and client. Clients may display behaviors or physically appear in ways that enjoin or evoke responses in providers retrieved from their personal and professional segments of the provider's life. For instance, a client may wear a *Tommy Bahama (brand)* shirt, similar to the style of clothing worn by the provider; the provider is thus more likely to respond favorably to the client. Another client may speak about visiting *Sandals*, a vacation resort in the Caribbean, coincidentally also enjoyed recently by the provider. These similarities draw on a repertoire of familiar verbal comments from the provider about these events, since the provider and client *shared similar experiences but separately.* To share similar experiences means the provider listens to and responds to statements as if somebody else, not the client, said the statements to the provider. This is known as stimulus generalization. The provider *generalized familiar verbal behavior to other speakers (clients) engaging in a familiar topic (i.e., metaphorical extension).*

Is this bad? No. It is not bad. Providers are human. They respond to properties of a stimulus, in this case the stimulus is a client, and the properties are verbal or nonverbal cues. Providers respond with more intensity or less intensity depending on a past history of conditioning with these verbal or nonverbal cues, and especially when the cues tap pleasurable memories (*memorial* behavior, see Kantor, 1925, p. 85). Kantor underscores this point by saying, memorial behavior "involves very close connections between specific responses and the particular stimuli coordinated with them" (p. 87) The "close connection," in this example, is when the provider responds affably to a client talking about Tommy Bahama clothing or Sandals vacation resort. The provider's proclivity to talk elaborately and energetically is a form of *countertransference*, of sharing memorial experiences, but it is not a pathological form of countertransference.

Pathological countertransference occurs when generalization of responses *crosses the line from shared experiences to behaviors frequently associated with or evoked from shared experiences.* Verbal behavior is more than words. When providers share verbal behavior on familiar topics, it evokes an autoclitic function (cue, mand, tact); this occurs when a provider's own verbal behavior serves as a (discriminative) cue or establishing operation for the speaker to engage in more verbal or nonverbal behavior. Here is how the learning history works. Providers who talked about personal matters, for example, about taking a Sandals vacation, only did this historically *with an intimate partner.* That discussion associated with *feelings of tenderness and love.* When a similar discussion arises in therapy or rehabilitation, the client's verbal stimuli may first evoke several comments from the provider (from autoclitic cues and mands). As the provider responds, it also evokes *a warm and tender feeling inside the provider (autoclitic tact).* The provider may misinterpret these inner feelings with the wrong belief that *the warm and tender feelings are meant for the client.* Countertransference, in short, is a *misjudgment* of the provider's own verbal and nonverbal responses, triggered by the provider's (a) history of memorial behavior, and (b) an improper generalization to the client verbal stimuli (cues)

The reason for operationalizing the phenomenon of countertransference is to show its ubiquity in cognitive behavior therapy and rehabilitation (Prasko, Diveky, Grambal, Kamaradova, Mozny, Sigmundova, Slepecky, & Vyskocilova, 2010). A nonpathological form of countertransference is expected in the form of empathy. In many allied health fields, particularly the ones focusing on scientific practice, students and recent graduates are mistakenly more attuned to changing the client than caring for the process by which change occurs. The neophyte provider may outwardly appear mechanical, cold, insensitive, and intolerant to maturation, history, or other confounding effects naturally interfering with the internal validity of treatment and behavior change outcomes. For years, this accusation of heartlessness pertained to behavioral psychologists (applied behavior analysts) who expected rapid correction of behavior in human clients as quickly as seen in their infrahuman lab subjects (cf. Iwata Wong Riordan, Dorsey, & Lau, 1982). For example, this author vividly recalls an incident 35 years ago, then an intern in an outpatient clinic, of witnessing another behavioral psychologist scold an obese woman for her neglected charting of daily caloric intake. Although this author, inexcusably, was equally infused in a scientific mode, the rudeness simply seemed *wrong.*

Since empathy, caring, and general exchanges of feelings are preferential in building the therapist-client trust, as well as in facilitating behavior changes, the risk of countertransference always remains high. The solution lies with *limits on empathy, limits on disclosure, and specificity of reinforcement.* First, limits on empathy means a deliberate restriction of making one or two statements that vicariously identify with the client to build bond and comfort. Overuse of empathy is contraindicated, a position contradictory to the humanistic perspective (Rogers, 1961, Wann, 1965). Instead of building more confidence in clients, excessive empathy may only build dependent-confidence. The client may grow dependent emotionally or otherwise on the provider, increasing the probability of countertranserence. Second, limits on disclosure mean a tightening on how much providers share about their personal lives. Oversharing traps the provider in a familiar or intimate exchange, triggering the cascade of autoclitic tacts, mands, and cues discussed earlier, and the resultant faulty beliefs causing countertransference. Third, specificity of reinforcement is matching the positive feedback with measurable and observable progress in target behaviors. For example, to compliment the client for any approximation of calling-in job leads is more concrete than a broad compliment about their motivation and "optimistic attitude."

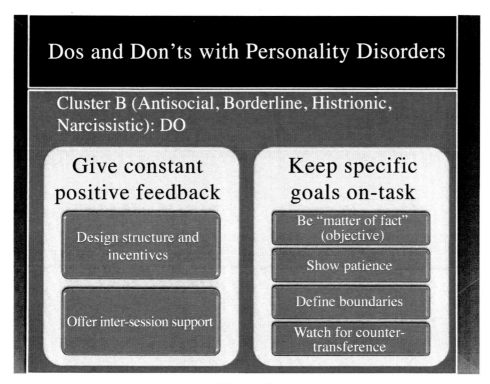

Figure 4.3.

C'mon, remind me:
64. For Cluster B, it is advisable to design structure and _____.

65. Providers should show _____ and define _____.
66. A common mistake is counter-_____.

DON'TS WITH CLUSTER B PERSONALITY DISORDERS. The nexus of therapy and rehabilitation is *behavior change*. Individual therapists or collaborative teams of therapists design elaborate programs aimed at replacing maladaptive responses with healthy, productive, and alternative functional responses to life's obstacles. The behaviors chosen as "healthy, productive, and functional" or adaptive behaviors, however, may or may not match the client or consumer's concept of what is adaptive. In Cluster B Personality Disorders, excessive reactions are the norm. Excitability, aggression, selfishness, and panic all have been coping mechanisms from childhood to adulthood and form an extensive reactional biography. The sudden threat of these response patterns being removed through therapy or rehabilitation poses an emotional liability for the individual. Clients may adamantly resist the change process. When providers witness this resistance, temptation is very strong to avoid confrontations, switch to a different target behavior more acceptable to the client, or agree with the client's reason and excuses to delay the therapy or rehabilitation.

Consequently, the two common mistakes committed when dealing with Type B Cluster Personality Disorders are (1) delay or procrastination of the change process and then quickly expecting the client to hastily adjust to last-minute changes, and (2) being fooled by false promises. Under each mistake, subproblems abound that not only disrupt the learning process, but act as agonists in exacerbating symptoms of the personality disorder. Let us consider each mistake more thoroughly.

Procrastinate and last-minute changes. Organizational systems are not always conducive to idealistic therapy and rehabilitation goals. Physical therapists need to see so many clients per day under contracts with a hospital, nursing home, or even in private practice. Their pace is faster and attention to details possibly compromised. Speech pathologists and occupational therapists may travel in hazardous conditions across rural or city areas to squeeze in three or four clients per day. Recreational therapists may only complete one or possibly two activities per day simply due to the sheer time-consumption of the activities, and other obstacles such as unfavorable weather (e.g., baseball game), or client's physical limitations (e.g., the flu, sprained ankle). Faced with this labyrinth of roadblocks, it is very easy to delay or put off a procedure due to natural reasons. Another reason to put off a procedure is if it unpleasantly challenges long-term behaviors in the client. Then, days or weeks later, facing some immutable deadline, the provider pulls rank and insists the procedure for the unwanted behavior must occur now and changes in the unwanted behavior must follow immediately.

Megan encountered the nightmare of this challenge. An occupational therapist for 20 years, Megan's finesse with client resistance was, by and large, exceptional. She regularly navigated around client refusals and complaints, and could turn negative situations into highly positive and enjoyable situations. Her client was a 45-year-old female diagnosed with Parkinson's disease who suffered hand tremors and needed adaptive devices for daily living skills such as self-clothing and self-eating. She was also comorbidly diagnosed with Histrionic Personality Disorder. For every new device introduced to aid her self-care skills, the client found legitimately-sounding excuses for not using it. Megan recognized this resistance and even discussed the client's stonewalling behavior as a problem in rehabilitation. Despite their amiable and insightful conversation, device-avoidance behaviors persisted.

Megan decided, in the best interests of rehabilitation and to preserve positive therapist-client relations, that she would postpone introduction of devices and instead focus on other aspects of daily living adjustment. But as time passed, pressure increased on Megan to teach the adaptive devices. The collaborative rehabilitation team inquired on the progress on the devices; the physiatrist, in particular, sent emails reminding Megan of this priority. Megan promised the team and physician she would alter her current agenda and reimplement device training. That is when Megan committed the major mistakes.

When Megan informed the client of plans to reimplement use of adaptive devices, she received a torrent of defensive comments. Defensiveness quickly escalated into mild panic or hysteria, accusing the therapist of betrayal, deception, and unethically imposing hardships; the client claimed she was already stressed beyond conceivable thresholds. Megan *blamed the client for these mistakes.* She criticized the client for (a) taking on too many activities, (b) overimmersion in activities, and (c) inflexibility in the learning process. She also criticized the client's overall lifestyle as chaotic, self-defeating, impulsive, and counterproductive – traits that Megan predicted would be detriments to whatever therapies the client undertook in the future. In lambasting the client, Megan unknowingly also (a) *fed into the client's panic-mode,* and (b) *fed into the client's mood swings.*

Panic-mode. All four Cluster B Personality Disorders intensify or deintensify based on improperly managed establishing operations (EOs). Anger spikes over minor disruptions, anxiety spikes over any ambiguity or abrupt (last-minute) changes, and depression typically follows each spike for a brief or prolonged period to escape the amalgam of perplexing problems. The crescendo of reactions spiral to panic-mode as the client feels *helpless, abandoned, rejected, or unvalued and lacks any resourceful way to self-decompress.*

Mood swings. When a cycle of unmet establishing operations (EOs) spins out of control, it effects most people the same way; we feel uneasy, confused, and even resentful. For example, awakening from postoperative anesthesia leaves many hospital patients "dopy," disoriented, and uncomfortably vulnerable. With Cluster B Personality Disorders, imagine the same postanesthetic effects multiplied by 100. Individuals with Antisocial Personality will react aggressively; individuals with Histrionic Personality will overdramatize helplessness and be clingy; individuals with Borderline Personality will threaten suicide or demonize the provider; and individuals with Narcissistic Personality will outright blame the provider for maliciously disrupting the client's peaceful life. Aggravation of mood swings is thus triggered by provider's mistakenly (a) blaming the client for mistakes, (b) feeding into panic, (c) feeding into mood swings, and (d) criticism of the client's lifestyle.

Being fooled by false promises. The other easy mistake to make is flowing with the client's hollow promises. Cluster B Personality Disorders share the common denominator of avoidance and escape, a pattern also found in Cluster C Personality Disorders. Under avoidance, the natural tendency is to delay or postpone some perceived adversity for eternity, but most likely for days, weeks, or months. Outwardly the client is unlikely to disclose fears about trying a new skill, or may not possibly know why the skill is aversive in the first place. Avoidance (and escape) only partly pertains to the difficulty-related fears of skill learning. The more paramount reason for avoidance and escape is *change itself. Change represents a high probability of failure, risk of vulnerability exposure, and the devastation of negative judgments incurred from failure and exposure.* At the mere suggestion of plans to alter a person's life, panic arises over the perils of an anticipated calamity and its aftermath causing unmerciful embarrassment. Terrified of this calamity, individuals with Cluster B Personality Disorders make excuses that sound rational, even negotiable, about postponement of the unwanted tasks. They promise to embark on and complete the tasks at some later date, all with alacrity, and most often with the provider's naïve blessings.

The habit of unfulfilled promises becomes very conspicuous and interruptive to the logical process of therapy or rehabilitation. After months of tolerating excuses and impatiently waiting for undelivered skills, providers may revert to a hierarchical series of tactics believed to overcome the tedious delays and motivate the client to comply. This hierarchy, while possibly effective to mobilize individuals with nonpersonality disorders, is disastrous with individuals with Cluster B Personality Disorders. The hierarchy consists of (a) micromanagement, (b) repeating yourself, (c) threatening termination (of services), and (d) showing too much empathy.

Micromanagement. Overconcern for training perfection during the course of skill learning is the first sign of micromanagement. In business and industry, micromanagement describes a supervisor who monitors and controls nearly every movement or task performed by subordinates. The advantage, theoretically, is that overattention to details assures subordinate conformity and relieves the supervisor of adverse effects from defective work products under his or her command. The disadvantage of micromanagement is fostering intragroup complacency and resentment among subordinates. That is why, for example, micromanaged or vertically-dictated management systems largely have been replaced by participative management systems (see Ruben, 1989; Ruben & Such, 1993). In participative management, employees and employers mutually contribute to training goals and take responsibility for fulfillment of individual objectives. In education, similar trends emerged during the 1960s and 1970s when pedagogy shifted from teacher-instructed to student-centered learning methods (e.g., Keller, 1968; Skinner, 1968). Both the shifts in industry and education were revolutionary approaches to increasing more learning trials to the independent learner, and decreasing learner-dependence on the manager or teacher.

Similarly, in delivery of therapy and rehabilitation, focus shifts from exclusively provider-directive methods to the client taking on more autonomous duties. The client may receive instructions from a physical therapist on how to stretch the tendon differently in self-exercising tennis-elbow syndrome. However, the client is the person practicing this exercise at home. Therapy may even cross over into the natural environment, as suggested earlier, with intersession spot-checks or actual visits to the client's home. Although the practice of intersession monitoring has its advantages, one of the disadvantages of continuous therapist surveillance is when therapists dictate and control every instance of the client's efforts. Such micromanagement with Cluster B Personality Disorders is disastrous. Individuals with Antisocial Personality Disorder will rebel with verbal aggression and violation of program policies or rules. Individuals with Histrionic Personality Disorder will spiral into a rage of anxiety and theatricality under the stress of constant policing; they will complain of being suffocated, trapped, victimized, and distrusted. Borderline individuals either will be rebellious or help-lessly submissive. They act passive-aggressively in withholding their personal opinions to avoid conflict. Individuals with Narcissistic Personality Disorder may act ruthlessly rebellious and condemn the provider for usurping their abilities to achieve some skill independent-ly. In all, exacerbation of the personality disorders disturbingly inter-feres with the goals of therapy and rehabilitation.

Repeating yourself. In observing poor client compliance on simple or complex tasks, providers often believe a valuable solution is to repeat the instruction. Repeating instructions, by truncating longer sentences and using succinct or "key" phrases, seems consistent with behavioral methods of employing probes and prompts (e.g., Olenick & Pear, 1980). The disadvantage of prompts and probes with Cluster B Person-ality Disorders is how it *sounds to the listener-client.* Clients may complain that the provider sounds condescending or patronizing, as if to say, "You are talking to me like a child." The misinterpreted "sound" of prompts and probes traces to a very specific set of aversive experiences in a client's reactional biography. The history likely entailed random verbal and nonverbal punishment. Children exposed to parents (or other guardians) who were yellers, fault-finders, and rigid disciplinari-ans for varying transgressions, most of which the child never under-stood or could predict, developed anticipatory fears about any new behavior they attempted, not only in childhood, but in adulthood. The same individuals also learned that any correction given to them for faulty behavior in childhood was an aversive cue for anticipatory fear. The cues aroused alertness to some impending criticism from another person (i.e., the parent). Over time, both the cues and anticipatory fears paired with self-denigrative statements such as "I cannot do this right. I am no good at anything." Consequently, when a provider repeats instructions in therapy, no matter how politely intended, the words *mand or evoke the cues of anticipatory fear and self-denigration from the listen-er-client.*

Threatening termination. Out of desperation, providers may reluctant-ly threaten termination of services if the client does not comply with some or all of the agreed-upon program requirements. As seen earlier, judgments about termination may be ethical when clients are danger-ous to the provider or exhibit increased symptom severity. Nondangerous situations involving, for example, administrative noncompliance, such as neglecting to practice home-based foot-stretch exercises, are a different category of violation. Here, clients' failure to practice or complete promised recovery skills is perceived as an infraction. Providers may conclude the noncompliance is a hindrance to progress and any effective amelioration requires a strong incentive for the client to get back on track. Ultimatums or threats to discontinue a program or services may seem like a logical warning to reactivate client motivation. And, for those clients comfortably operating under punishment contingencies or who learn to change by rules, perhaps this stringent approach yields positive results. However, with Cluster B Personality Disorders, threats of service termination are cues of *abandonment and rejection.* Such individuals have a profound antipathy to perceived disengagement and will rapidly escalate symptoms to self-protect from appearing vulnerable. Individuals with Borderline and Histrionic Personality Disorders are particularly susceptible, viewing any disconnection as a merciless demoralization. They panic with fears of having caused irrevocable harm to the provider and rapidly solicit ways to mend the broken situation and redeem their credibility. Examples include voluminous emails, excessive phone calls and texting, and elaborately grandiose promises to make permanent behavior changes to assure retention of therapy or rehabilitation services.

Showing too much empathy. As described above, overuse of empathy is an accidental precursor to countertransference. Providers unknowingly disclose too much personal information or vicariously identify with the client to the point of confusing boundaries and perceiving the client as they do a personal or intimate friend. On the one hand, empathy can be strategic. It can be a reinforcer whose calculated use includes the systematic and selective attention to certain behaviors, a procedure known as differential *reinforcement* (see Deitz & Repp, 1983; Piazza, Moes, & Fisher, 1996; Ruben, 2002). However, even differential reinforcement can misidentify the wrong behavior for attention and thereby shape maladaptive instead of adaptive responses.

Individuals with Cluster B Personality Disorders are insatiably hungry for empathy or any attention. Received for correct behavior, individuals may respond feverishly and with surpassing efforts to comply with homework assignments and other program requirements. But empathy (reinforcers) also shapes adjunctive patterns of behavior – patterns concurrent or synchronous with the target (desired) behaviors –

that increase and sabotage target behaviors and possibly can ruin the provider-client working relationship. For example, with Borderline Personality Disorders, overdependence on caretakers is very common. When providers give excessive empathy, Cluster B individuals will regard empathy as *signs of deeply caring for them, and inviting their absorbing attachment.* With Antisocial Personality Disorders, such individuals are rule-violators and exploit perceived weaknesses or vulnerabilities in other people, particularly persons in authority. Overuse of empathy may miscommunicate the provider is *unconditionally forgiving, tolerant, weak, and susceptible to manipulation.* Unknowingly, providers may *reinforce more of the client's infractions of policies and agreements,* since the client acts with a sense of impunity.

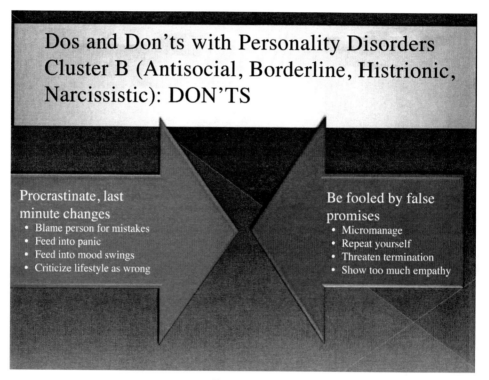

Figure 4.4.

C'mon, remind me:
67. For Cluster B, it is not advisable to _____ the person for mistakes.
68. Be careful not to _____ into mood swings.
69. Showing too much _____ can backfire and build dependence.

Cluster C Personality Disorders

Fear is a pervasive variable in Cluster C Personality Disorders. It is a psychophysiological phenomenon. Kantor (1947) reminded us that fear or "the visceral, muscular, and, in general, organic events, are participating factors in a complex field" (p. 201). Fear, like all emotions, is not benignly psychic states (like pain, hunger) correlated with body conditions and actions. Fear develops "meaning" after ostensibly integrated with response and stimulus functions. We label as fear the arousal of physiological (muscular, glandular, vascular) sensations, collectively grouped as the autonomic (sympathetic) nervous system. When people make a qualitative discrimination between the excitation of the sympathetic nervous system and deceleration of the sympathetic nervous system, verbal labels connote the former as fear and latter as relaxed. Both labels do not describe a single class of responses or single set of operations, but rather a fluid or a cumulative progression of interactive events for which the contingencies either are ambiguous or very clear (cf. Skinner, 1953, pp. 165–167). Ambiguous contingencies typically are punishment. Clear contingencies typically are reinforcement.

In Cluster C Personality Disorders, contingencies inside the segments of many behavioral fields are profoundly and chronically ambiguous. Since unclear contingencies foster constant fear, the client's response patterns typically revolve around avoidance behavior. *They want to avoid (or escape from) fear.* In Cluster C, each personality disorder marks a distinct typology of avoidance and escape behaviors. For obsessive-compulsive personality disorder, individuals avoid mistakes, imperfections, or violating some rule rigidly governing their routines and life beliefs. For avoidant personality disorders, individuals avoid conflict, varying degrees of interpersonal interaction, and fear undertaking projects perceived to invoke ridicule or critical judgments by other people. For dependent personality disorders, individuals avoid *rejection and abandonment.* Fear interferes with nearly any autonomous or independent decisions or risk-actions, unless the individual first gets approval from a revered source before acting on the decision or risk. Considering the magnitude that fear contributes to avoidance and escape behaviors, providers walk gently and precariously around the land mines of Cluster C personality disorders.

DOS WITH CLUSTER C PERSONALITY DISORDERS. The natural or "instinctive" therapeutic approach to take with Cluster C Personality Disorders might be to directly confront the fear and overcome avoidance and escape. Such a desensitization approach, theoretically, does build courage, tolerance, and greatly dismantles fear responses. On the downside, desensitization, if done too quickly, has the disadvantage of causing unpleasant flooding effects, no matter the systematic or gradual pace at which exposure steps are taught (Chambless & Ollendick, 2001; van Minnen, Harned, Zoellner, & Mills 2012). *Flooding, or the rapid exposure to fear-induced stimuli,* is contraindicated when there are comorbidities such as major depression, suicidal ideation, high recidivism of substance abuse, chronic anxiety, and suicidal ideations. These polymorbid conditions are frequently present among the Cluster C Personality Disorders. Taking prudent precautions, the alternative strategies to communicate interventions with Cluster C personality disorders can include (a) structure and specificity; (b) solicitation if customer/client needs help; (c) praise excessively but privately; (d) encourage nonstaff coaches; (e) focus on what is right, not wrong; and (f) encourage small risk-steps.

Structure and specificity. Fear and ambiguity remain preponderant causes of avoidance and escape behaviors. Fear derives from predominately punishment contingencies that weakened or suppressed independent risk behaviors and shaped a repertoire of docile, passive, unassertive, and people-dependent survival skills. These interpersonal deficits are salient roadblocks to effectively function in social or vocational settings. Ambiguity is also a side effect of punishment, derived from the *random schedule of punishment contingencies.* Randomness sparks confusion, disorganization, and paradoxical cues alerting the individual to when it is appropriate or inappropriate to respond. As the labyrinth of indiscriminate cues generalizes from one setting to multiple settings in the person's life, the capacity to predict and control one's environment shrinks rapidly. Loss of predictability and control means there is a distrust among the cues, arousing constant apprehension, helplessness, and overdependence on people or other resources.

One solution to fear and ambiguity is the installation of structure (Ruben, 1986c). Providers can outline very precise goals, objectives, and subobjectives, with detailed steps on how to execute target behaviors. In some cases, task descriptions can follow a format called a *task analysis*, which is a step-by-step sequence of the exact responses in a hierarchy from difficult or easy or based on the duration of the tasks accomplished (cf. Kirwan & Ainsworth, 1992). Task analyses provide a clear and predictable pathway from onset to termination of a task, and may include collateral (supplemental) steps enabling the uninterrupted flow of the desired task.

Jaszmine received this very recipe of a task analysis from her vocational counselor. Jasmine suffered comorbid panic attacks and social anxiety for two years since reacting negatively to withdrawal effects of Percocet, prescribed by her dentist during oral surgery. Shortly after her surgery, she misconstrued her body's stimulatory sensations (i.e., coming down from the Percocet) as anxiety and immediately fled the store she was in. Subsequently she avoided going into stores to prevent recurrence of the anxiety. She generalized her avoidance to *anybody or anything* (i.e., multiple segments of her life field) that may trigger anxiety including encounters with interpersonal conflict. Her diagnosis of Avoidant Personality Disorder combined with a history of childhood exposure to random punishment. Cheryl, her vocational counselor, assembled a list of top-priority tasks, and described one task per page. Each page divided a priority task into smaller, achievable steps, the length expected by the step, and the positive (reinforcing) outcome likely generated by the step. Substeps entailed responses that paralleled Jasmine's current level of skills to boost errorless learning or reduce a scaffolding of obstacles. With the task analysis format, Jasmine proceeded through each task at her own pace, and found her performance followed an order, had parameters, and clear feedback on whether her responses were accurate or inaccurate.

Solicitation if customer/client needs help. Fear is a skill-immobilizer. The customer or client is reticent to ask questions, venture opinions, or talk spontaneously due to inhibitions conditioned over years of punishment contingencies. Response suppression is chronically intact in their reactional biography and very unlikely to miraculously change due to insight alone. Since individuals with Cluster C Personality Disorders are notoriously nonresponsive and guarded, providers are encouraged to ask pointed questions about what the client does or does not know. Ironically, earlier we admonished such overhelping and overuse of empathy as deterrents to effective provider-client relationships; the caveat included that oversolicitation might even sound "condescending." However, with avoidant typologies, inquiries *are advisable, will not be viewed as condescending, and will penetrate the fortress of client silence.*

The type of questions asked should pertain to the tasks assigned or already performed. Meredith, a social worker at a short-term medical rehabilitation facility, met with 35-year-old Gloria, who was recovering from a total left-knee replacement surgery. Gloria already spent one week at the hospital before transfer to the medical facility for physical therapy and extended recuperation. Gloria was indignant that she *must have physical therapy three times a day and perform brilliantly at it.* Meredith observed that Gloria understood the goals, knew exactly the sequence of subgoals and subtasks, and could perform the tasks with relative difficulty as the agility in her left knee slowly improved. But in each physical therapy session, Gloria was impatient with her mistakes, cried excessively, and blamed herself for being a weakling. Meredith asked Gloria *what is it she expected to do at each physical therapy session? Is that expectation realistic?* These simple questions unleashed a maelstrom of anxiety-related complaints, mostly catastrophizing her circumstances and the perceived futility of any healthy recovery. Gloria was comorbidly diagnosed with Obsessive-Compulsive Personality Disorder, and, in her perspective, formed idealistic and unobtainable daily standards for leg-movement progress. Once Meredith solicited these faulty criteria, and corrected them, Gloria approached her physical therapy with more optimism and less self-deprecation.

Praise excessively but privately. Feedback is a natural therapeutic device for many obvious reasons. First, it gives an independent observation of some response occurrence. That is, it conveys key information about the topography, frequency, magnitude, intensity, duration, or other response properties relevant at the time. Second, feedback encourages repetition of the correct occurrences and revises or discourages incorrect occurrences. Learners refine their discrimination of right and wrong responses with precise details on how the right response produces desired consequences and the wrong response produces undesired or no consequences. Third, feedback provides samplers. A sampler is a demonstration of the important aspects of the response for the learner to imitate immediately. As the imitator more closely matches the model, behavior precision increases and the learner now practices the skill without the model as a reference. Use of this feedback system has been normative in many applied rehabilitation and industrial settings (Johnston, Foxx, Jacobson, Green, & Mulick, 2006; Ruben,1984; Ruben & Ruben, 1985b).

For its many laudable advantages, the downside of positive behavior support is its adverse impact on individuals who are hypersensitive to any feedback drawing attention to them. Recall that child victims of random punishment often associate the pain and confusion from punishment with verbal statements made by the punisher-parents. The verbal statements alone subsequently invoke fear. Abrasive insults that demean a child, for example, when the child is uncertain *what and why they did something wrong,* will teach the child to dislike and avoid *any remarks centrally focused on them.* That explains why individuals with Cluster C Personality Disorders *abhor compliments, deny or diminish the compliment, or reverse the compliment onto the speaker.* In therapy or rehabilitation, it is thus imperative to strategically use praise for concrete client behaviors and only when alone with the client. Public displays of compliments, by contrast, will excite anxiety in the client who feels he or she is under a spotlight or microscope, just waiting to be riddled senseless with criticism.

Fran was an administrative secretary for a mid-sized company and recently on medical disability leave following her right-sided temporal stroke that affected short-term memory and her auditory cortex. She heard but did not understand sentences or instructions of other people. She also easily forgot the topic of discussion engaged in two or three hours earlier, unless she labored to reconstruct the conversation in small pieces. Adding to her misery was a contralateral left-sided paresis along her arm and legs, causing a major hindrance as a left-handed writer. She previously was diagnosed Dependent Personality Disorder, despite the fact that, at work, she excelled in *independently executing a myriad of decisions when planning staff conferences and in-house programs.* However, in her interpersonal life, she was fearful to take any initiative for herself without the affirmation and permission of her husband William. During Fran's occupational therapy sessions at her house, she used strength exercises for her left-arm and hands in grasping objects or reaching elevated heights for objects. Her progress was measurably evident since the stroke but had not returned to baseline (premorbid) levels. Garrett, her occupational therapist, showed her exactly what new exercises were applied correctly and the positive effects it had on her hand and arm. "Great use of the object-reaching skill," he would say, "notice how your two-step approach of lift, turn, and grasp, made it easier to get the dish from the cupboard."

Garrett was very careful to focus attention on the tasks parameters instead of making a general laudatory remark, such as "Great job, Fran, you are fantastic at this task." He used specific feedback to minimize her confusion from disturbance of the auditory cortex. In other words, Garrett used descriptive feedback that matched her exact actions, for which she could immediately perform or modify, both offering her autoclitic tact's (cues) to strengthen her short-term memory of Garrett's instructions. More importantly, by emphasizing just the task components and not Fran in general, Garret spared Fan anxiety arousal. Had Garrett mistakenly praised Fran generically, Fran's reaction would be anxious and anticipatory. She would become "emotionally paralyzed," view him with wide-eye panic, be speechless, physically immobilized, and incapable of benefiting from his teaching trials.

Encourage nonstaff coaches. The calibrated use of nonstaff or naturalistic trainers in a client's integrative field of life has had a long tradition within applied behavior analysis as well as in other allied health fields (Ruben, 1993d; Tharp & Wetzel, 1969). Naturalistic trainers serve the multiple role of observers, behavioral engineers, and coaches in daily or incidental (i.e., noncontrived) situations during which the client is most *likely to engage in the target behavior free of formal structure.* The informality and intimacy of being at home, coached by a trusted or significant other, not only is less stressful, but also it is more inherently reinforcing. The naturalistic coach already developed a history of reinforcement with the client and *is automatically reinforcing without preparatory steps of conditioning.* Verbal and nonverbal subtleties in the natural coach are tasted (spotted) as positive affirmations, whereas the repertoire for a provider's reinforcement may be limited to verbal behavior. Most importantly, for Cluster C Personality Disorders, customers are hypersensitive to public exposure of failure and conspicuous risks of incurring punishment. A home-based coach is perceived as *safer (risk-free),* around whom to engage in imperfect behaviors, and who is not likely to censor the client for their mistakes.

Marcus was a 50-year-old divorced male living in his 21-year-old daughter's house. He was on a portable oxygen tank for Chronic Obstructive Pulmonary Disease (COPD) and receiving home health care nurse visits twice daily to monitor oxygen concentration levels and lung capacity using a spirometer. Exercises prescribed to increase lung capacity included breathing (relaxation), using a candle and breathing through a tube, and short breaths with arm movements. Before his medical problems worsened, Marcus was diagnosed with Dependent Personality Disorder. Around the nurses, Marcus seized the occasion to overwork his exercises and impress the nurses with his quantum rates of improvement. The nurses, most of whom were different during each visit, and outwardly impersonal and clinical, offered mediocre or listless feedback for Marcus' herculean efforts. He subsequently performed poorly on the exercises in their presence and began to view his COPD as more debilitative and incurable. One nurse suggested that Marcus's daughter, Nancy, be his home-based coach when he practiced the exercise.

Marcus and Nancy agreed to the arrangement and the frequency of nurse visits reduced to once daily. Nancy prompted Marcus, just as the nurse did, to commence the exercises, but she joked around with him, and used her playfully sarcastic style where she rolled her eyes when he made a mistake. Historically, this innuendo always invoked laughter between father and daughter, and made any laboring situation more tolerable. Within a week, Marcus's motivation to retry the exercises doubled; he also performed the exercises with uncanny perfection, and extensively drew from the lifeline of his daughter's enchanting remarks to repeat his daily exercise routines.

Dependent personality disorders include symptoms of neediness, elicitation of care-taking, overexertion of efforts to please an approver, and submissiveness to the doctrines or demands of a trusted authority. Marcus personified his daughter Nancy with this authority and put forth excessive effort in his exercises to appease her expectations of him. While, technically, some professionals may argue that his incentive for skill practice was more benevolent than authentically selfish, and thereby his improvement may only endure as long as Nancy or *somebody* is there dominating him, *the functional issue is this: Marcus did acquire* and *retain* a skill that ameliorated his medical condition within his natural environment, *despite debilitative response patterns of his personality.*

The function of responses in Marcus's Dependent Personality are to *enjoin other people to shoulder his burdens, navigate his decisions, and offset his self-despicable remarks.* Marcus, in all probability, will generalize his penchant to find saviors across different settings, from home and workplace to community activities. His daughter Nancy may be one of many naturalistic trainers sought, chosen, and admired as the gatekeeper of feedback for his practice of lung-capacity exercises. That Marcus does not perform the skill exclusively alone or purely for himself, without recruitment of other people perceived as more powerful than he, *is not a detriment to learning. But it can be a detriment if a provider improperly sets as a goal that Marcus can only master the exercise when he does it alone.*

Focus on what is right, not wrong. The colloquial expression "Catch 'Em when they're good!" gained wide popularity in the late 1960s early 1970s amid the liberal revolution in parenting research to focus more on what children do right than wrong. As parenting technology gained a scientific status, using Applied Behavior Analysis (ABA), codified procedures and methods mainstreamed into households, schools, and daycares with the same distinct message: "reinforce good behavior, not bad behavior." Teachers, parents, child care workers, and health service professionals shifted away from just labeling behavior (negatively) as psychopathology with diagnostic codes, a tradition in mental health, to quantifying the misbehavior as *excesses and deficits.* The gauge of behavior severity no longer was based on social abnormality but more on *social functioning.* Deficits meant the behaver (child, adult) *underperformed* according to social standards. Excess meant the behaver (child, adult) *overperformed* according to social standards. Moreover, social standards varied from one verbal community to the next, allowing for dissimilarity in definitions among behavior excesses and deficits across different cultural matrices. In one culture, a behavior deficit or excess may be the norm, whereas in another culture, deficit and excesses may deviate from the norm.

In today's practice of therapy and rehabilitation, recognition of cultural diversity and community practices is more conscious. When providers praise "what is right" in clients having Cluster C Personality Disorders, awareness is equally important of the subcultures of the clients, whether it be race, ethnicity, religion, or geographical locations. One particular subculture pertains to "child victims." Child victims of one type were discussed earlier as *Adult Children of Alcoholics or Dysfunc-*

tional Families. But other subcultures exist. The child who suffered repeated abandonment and rejection may manifest symptoms of "separation anxiety" in adulthood.

While historically a pediatric pathology, separation anxiety is a recurrent excessive distress when anticipating or experiencing separation from home or some attachment figures. Many adults with separation anxiety disorder (i.e., dependent personality disorder) may be overconcerned about their offspring and spouses and exhibit marked discomfort when separated from them. They are particularly emotionally reactive to feedback. When given feedback on "what is wrong" about their behavior, adults may respond to these verbal cues with heightened anxiety and compensatory behavior to prevent the misperception of being abandoned. They may tearfully plead for forgiveness, threaten self-injury if the threat persists, or even make grandiose promises for reform to defuse the feeling of chronic loss. Criticism is their nemesis and it always triggers a sense of foreboding.

This does not mean a client with Cluster C Personality Disorder can *never receive negative feedback.* As shown earlier, feedback focused on concrete aspects of the target behavior (for example, in a task analysis) is more acceptable and does not implicate an existential threat of desertion. Matthew, a Board Certified Behavior Analyst, learned the advantage of positive-behavior attention in teaching anger management skills to a physically disabled adult. He took a baseline period of nonviolent angry episodes erupted as the client experienced mistakes while cooking. He then introduced a habit-reversal method modified for anger control involving (a) alertness to prodromal phases of early visceral arousal and (b) competing behaviors (relaxation, sitting down), when anger escalated. In the first four days, the client's frustration with the procedure conspicuously threatened to sabotage the positive effects of the procedure. This tempted Matthew to interject with caveats about the sabotage. Instead, Matthew forewent the negative feedback about the client's mistakes and looked for some redemptive *and measurable aspects of the client's progress worth sharing.* Just from hearing the praise for positive on-task behavior, the client ceased his denouncement of the procedure and tried to repeat the exact behaviors that Matthew observed.

Encourage small risk-steps. The method of successive approximations or "shaping" was extolled earlier as the harbinger of reliable learning for sizeable tasks. Each step along the response hierarchy builds a progression of skill competence until the entire chain or sequence of responses is consistent and generalizable. A variation of this procedure is less concerned with the piece-by-piece connectedness of responses to form a complete task, and more concerned with the *risk potential of each target or adjunctive response emitted by the client*. Risk potential refers to a behavior historically associated with punishment and thus is aversive to engage in; that punishment may involve:

    a. Actual sensory or musculoskeletal pain in the behavior itself (e.g., playing racquetball after knee surgery).
    b. Adjunctive behaviors accompanying the risk behaviors that are unpleasant (e.g., to give a party – the risk – one has to email all of the cousins and order the food – the adjunctive behaviors).
    c. Expected outcomes (consequences) that are aversive.
    d. Underdeveloped or deficient behaviors.
    e. Overdeveloped or excessive behaviors.

The "risk" refers to arousal of anxiety from reluctantly engaging in these behaviors when the individual is under a strong establishing operation (EO) to avoid or escape from the risk behaviors. In Cluster C Personality Disorders, risk potential behaviors are robust and preponderant. Risk behaviors are like any concurrent or multiple response pattern; for every one target (desirable) response, there are two or three (or more) coexisting (adjunctive, risk) responses possibly interfering with the occurrence or duration of the target response. Jacquelyn, for example, was instructed to file three job applications at retail clothing stores in a local mall. She concurred with the task and gave every impression of its compliance. While visiting the stores and asking about jobs, she felt nervous (anxious) about the mall's congestion of shoppers and its deafening noise level. She feared her anxiety might intensify uncontrollably and embarrass her while completing the job application or talking to a store manager. Moments after she felt anxious, she aborted the task assigned by the vocational coach and left the mall.

Here, Jacquelyn's social phobia manifested concurrently with her attempted entry in the mall and filing job applications. Fear of open places, in other words, was an adjunctive (undesirable) behavior that blocked or impaired her simultaneous desirable behaviors. The adjunctive behaviors became, not *topographically incompatible, but functionally incompatible with the desired behaviors* – she could physically perform both behaviors at once, but the anxiety immobilized or competed with completing the applications. Cluster C Personality Disorders consist of infinitely complex matrices of anxiety-related behaviors that are risk potentials. When a method of successive approximation is considered to teach a choice behavior, remember to identify the coexisting risk behaviors. Slowly and safely working through both skills, with concise reinforcers available for minor success, can preserve the new skills for much longer periods of time.

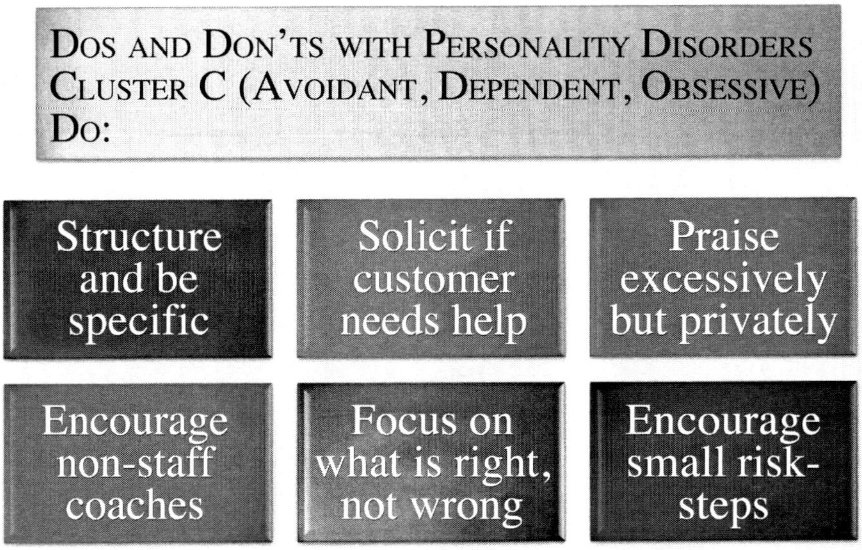

DOS AND DON'TS WITH PERSONALITY DISORDERS
CLUSTER C (AVOIDANT, DEPENDENT, OBSESSIVE)
DO:

Structure and be specific	Solicit if customer needs help	Praise excessively but privately
Encourage non-staff coaches	Focus on what is right, not wrong	Encourage small risk-steps

Figure 4.5.

C'mon, remind me:
70. For Cluster C, you should _____ if customers' need _____.
71. Always focus on what is _____, not _____.
72. In teaching new skills, encourage small _____ steps.

DON'TS WITH CLUSTER C PERSONALITY DISORDERS. The calibrative strategies applied with Cluster C Personality Disorders to optimize client learning and progress are not without drawbacks. For every energy of steps forward, customers or clients can be self-sabotaging and unravel weeks and months of arduous efforts. As observer and intervener on progression and regression, allied health providers enjoy the unique privilege of seeing this bigger-picture or *gestalt* and communicating ways to stay on target. Softly polite reminders, patience with coaching the learner through a maze of confusion and fear, and pacing the movement slowly and in small units of change, all comprise the treatment of Cluster C with kid-gloves. But in the course of treatment, especially over a prolonged duration, six procedural mistakes are inevitable no matter the provider's talents or years of expertise. These mistakes, mostly all innocently committed, erode quickly at the already precarious foundation of client or customer's self-confidence.

The most common mistakes made in service delivery include the following: (1) change case managers often; (2) criticize the client for mistakes (or blame); (3) a caretaker/enabling/overhelping; (4) make exceptions, accommodations; (5) be overlogical and debative; and (6) give large tasks, or have high expectations.

Change case managers often. Attachment to case manager is one of the inevitable casualties of working with Cluster C Personality Disorders. Individuals with Dependent and Avoidant Disorders may be conspicuously clingy, personifying the provider as a parental authority or entrusted friend, both regarded as inseparable to the client's life. When, in the course of agency business, providers transfer to another office, advance, resign, retire, or for other reasons have caseloads reallocated to other providers, the impact effect on loyal clients may be intense. Transition is undesirable and immediately invokes a threat of abandonment and rejection. The client misinfers underlying agendas for why a new provider took over. The inferences always center on self-condemnation and infusion of guilt over the false belief that the client *caused grief to the provider who left him or her.*

While the turnover of case managers, therapists, and other providers is likely unavoidable, preparation for this likelihood can mitigate the depth of symptomatic depression that follows. First, providers in clinics or agencies involving high staff fluidity can tell the client or customer up front, as part of service debriefing, of possible caseload reassignments. Second, when learning of this administrative policy in advance, providers can introduce the new case manager or therapist in joint meetings. This display of two providers together effectively portrays a collective team unit *concerned about the client*, not disregard for the client. Third, providers give a report-card to the client shortly before the staff reshuffling that lists the progress or achievement of certain goals and positive feedback reassuring a strong prognosis on the client's behalf. Such praise and descriptive feedback are enjoiners or minds that entice the client-listener to hear more about their positive qualities. As they hear more, the provider explains how the replacement provider plans to be a supplier of more feedback reinforcing similar client virtues and behavior progress.

This method is similar to promoting generalization of positive behaviors across trainers. In its simplest application, the familiar provider requests clients to demonstrate comfortable (mastered) behaviors in front of the replacement provider. For example, requests may be of the client briefly describing highlights of his other biography, or the recent achievement of some skill. Clients are encouraged to verbalize this information with identical intonation, semantics, or general enthusiasm shown previously in front of the familiar provider. The *generalization* occurs in transferring verbal behavior patterns from familiar to unfamiliar provider and receiving nearly identical attention for the verbal patterns.

Another method to assure effective generalization among trainers borrows from the protocol of activity-based instruction, also prolifically referred to as *Individualized Curriculum Sequencing (ICS) Model* (Holvoet, Guess, Mulligan, & Brown, 1980). Here, training is tailor-made or individualized to clients to facilitate acquisition and generalization of skills. Different applications combine *intersequentially and intrasequentially* to embed training into regular routines of a child or adult. Training components are like a buffet, either chosen at the learner's discretion, or pre-arranged for the learner to follow more logically and routinely. The main ideas underlying this technology are simple: to strengthen cognitive, affective, motor, social, communicative and intellectual skill within the relevance of the learner's natural environment (Brown, Holvoet, Guess, & Mulligan, 1980; Mulligan, Guess, Holvoet, & Brown, 1980). In transitioning one trainer to the next, the ICS model *already is in place with the learner (client, customer), and shifts nonchalantly to a different observer-monitor.*

Criticize the client for mistakes (or blame). A preventable mistake causing apocalyptic outcomes is criticism to the consumer or client for making mistakes. Fault-identification offers, at times, therapeutic value but is very limited due to its punishment effects. A fault-correction may point out a simple clerical or procedural error such as calling the wrong number to reach the provider; or reminders to check posted office hours on the webpage or front door of the facility. *Errors of facts* are palpable and can facilitate the learner's independent completion of some objective. It provides the missing piece of information with which the task now makes sense. Whereas *errors of judgment* are interpretable, subjective, and impose a moral or ethical value onto the learner, who may feel inanely incompetent for the delinquency. In both types of fault-identification, but mostly with errors of judgments, individuals with Cluster C personality types may react with severe anxiety and intensification of clinginess (attachment).

Avoidant, dependent, and obsessive-compulsive personalities share dynamics of (a) aversion to conflict, (b) desperation for acceptance, (c) hypersensitivity to character-judgments, (d) overanalysis of self-mistakes, and (e) instant mobilization to ameliorate or profusely apologize for the mistakes. For this reason, the "value" of criticism is lost from the moment words leave the provider's lips. All the consumer or patient sees and hears is a provider dissatisfied and angry with *something wrong the client did.*

Alternatively, providers can present errors of fact by showing, not telling, in concrete form how the error occurred and how to correct it. A speech therapist, for example, who demonstrates a new way to navigate through luminosity (a webpage for cognitive skills rehearsal) is correcting mistakes without blaming the consumer for misapplication of the website or software program.

A caretaker, enabler, overhelper. Overresponsible providers who clearly see the trajectory of grief and mistakes likely encountered by their patients are tempted to prevent this trajectory. They empathize with the physical, emotional, or behavioral obstacles undermining a patient's progress and feel their ethical duties are met when going that extra yard to be helpful. Helpfulness is an asset at times, but can unknowingly sabotage self-motivation and efforts in Cluster C Personality typologies. Helpfulness spans a continuum from *coaching with prompts and primes to enabling.* Coaching with prompts and primes is a fundamental technique of physical or verbal assistance. The technique is to facilitate acquisition of successive approximations to some task (Billingsly & Romer, 1983; McClannahan, MacDuff, & Krantz, 2002). Used in training are reminder cues teaching closer steps to a desired behavior. These cues include:

1. Verbal prompts
2. Gestural prompts
3. Demonstration/modeling prompts
4. Physical (touch) prompts
5. Physical (manual) guidance

Prompts are delivered continuously at first to lay out the learning trial and familiarize the learner (patient, consumer) with options on how to perform a task. Some selected prompts may work best; for example, verbal prompts may teach a skill faster than gestural or physical prompts, particularly if the learner suffered posttraumatic effects of childhood punishment and is reticent to be touched. As recurrent use of effective prompts guides the task, the next step is to gradually fade out prompts while building independent performance of the task. Procedures used for this fade-out approach vary widely but largely consist of:

1. Least-to-Most Prompting
2. Most-to-Least Prompting
3. Graduated Guidance
4. Delayed Prompting
5. Fading procedures

Least-to-most prompting is when learning trials begin with the least or fewest prompts and increase the number of prompts as task difficulty increases. The idea is for the learner to begin the task independently and borrow help from the prompter when tasks gets complex. Most-to-least prompting is just the opposite. Overuse of prompts begins the trials and shrinks as the task sequentially continues to more complex or repetitive tasks. Graduated guidance is like most-to-least prompting except for one difference; every trial has the trainer fade assistance. The amount of effort given is less and less per skill trial, with the learner more responsible for the task from beginning to end. Delayed prompting is postponing a prompt after giving an instruction. While used mostly in teaching receptive and expressive language, applications are widespread for any task already established at some minimum level. For example, in physical therapy, Bernice's arm lifting above her shoulder is slow and sometimes needs physical guidance. The physical therapist says, "Bernice, go ahead and lift your arm." A delay of one to three seconds may pass before the physical therapist guides the upward motion of the arm. Delay intervals grow longer between verbal and physical prompts as trials are repeated and the patient lifts the arm on his or her own.

Fading procedures represent the last step in prompt-teaching of systematically eliminating the prompts. The goal is not to stop *any helpfulness with prompts, but to replace artificial prompts with natural prompts that are generalizable and more permanent in the learner's environment.* Fading entails many different steps, from changing the locality of the prompter, to using the home-caretaker instead of provider, to shadowing the learner without any touch or verbal guidance. Most importantly, learners find naturalistic replacements for prompts, such as leaning against a bed for support in lifting up their torso, or using Google calendars or Facebook as task-reminders for the day.

With Cluster C personality types, prompting and fading procedures maintain an objective mode of helpfulness without the consumer feeling coerced or pampered. The learner is still in control, moves at a comfortable pace, executes the skill in varying degrees of accuracy, and is reinforced by the therapist/provider. The consumer never feels the prompter is impatient and doing everything for the learner. *There is no caretaking or enabling that occurs.*

Make exceptions, accommodations. For every quantum leap of new learning comes the inevitable setbacks faced when the learner's environment does not fit the learning scheme. This is very common in clinical therapy or home interventions of applied behavior analysis. Maxwell, a young adult with autism spectrum disorder, for example, learned the protocol of asking questions, giving good eye contact, waiting for responses from the speaker, and not repeating himself. The BCBA teaching these skills built in several natural cues for Maxwell to pace himself, spot when to ask and not ask questions, and discriminate a time for waiting. Despite this excellent topography of behaviors, Maxwell met resistance when his parents and sister, also living in the house, ignored him entirely and told him to walk away. This is a classic example of family resistance. It occurs when a consumer's problem-behaviors dominated the family so long, that any improvement, no matter how desirable, is *too late and too little.* That is, there appears little naturalistic reinforcement to generate family recovery to help with Maxwell's program.

One common mistake providers make with this family resistance is to make exceptions and accommodate the problem. For example, the BCBA may mistakenly have Maxwell practice his new skills outside of the house, away from the neglectful family, in a more receptive environment (e.g., at his sheltered workshop). Or, the BCBA may work longer hours at the house acting as family-surrogate to practice with Maxwell. In both cases, with Cluster C personality types, the provider builds a codependence with the emotionally-clingy consumer. These exceptions seem like a viable alternative in teaching a skill, but the teaching technology is lost when the consumer emotionally adopts the provider as supplier of compassion and attention – the variables that need to come from a naturalistic family. Instead, as difficult as it seems, the solution lies with troubleshooting the family resistance. It involves teaching the family, along with Maxwell, mutual goals to reunite their communication.

Be overlogical and debative. Providers are intelligent and highly educated professionals, equipped with an extensive arsenal of practical techniques. They know why these techniques work and can see the future value of the techniques improving the health and welfare of a consumer's life. The trouble arises when this idealism of using techniques conflicts with the reality of nonuse or refusal to use the techniques. Horatio, a respiratory therapist in home-health care, came to give Sarah a nebulizer (breathing) treatment. He showed her how to operate the equipment, check the medicine, administer the airflow, and clean up the equipment when completed. Sarah, an Avoidant personality, never told Horatio the errors that *she* commonly made in assembling the equipment, or her failure to breathe normally throughout the process.

Horatio spotted her misapplications and equipment errors and repeated emphatically the *reasons she must do it right. He gave many reasons, in slightly higher tones, and made sure his words were logical.*

Overprecision in stating a method or rehashing the method sounds like *punishment.* The analytical-details intended to clarify the procedure of using the breathing treatment apparatus may backfire when the consumer hears, *not the exactness, but instead the annoyance about the consumer not completing the task correctly.* The consumer feels guilty for failing to meet some expected criteria and is suddenly fearful of abandonment.

As logical overexplanations abound, consumers who are Cluster C personality may self-destruct. They may decompensate into a helplessness and worthlessness from being judged. They feel inferior and irredeemable. Horatio's plan might be better served by complimenting Sarah for what she did correctly and walking through the machine setup, operation, and cleanup; at each point along the walk-through, he can prompt her to describe different steps and paraphrase her wording, with one or two other phrases that clarify proper application of the steps.

Give large tasks or have high expectations. The lure of high production in rehabilitation is often a confusing predictor of progress. Providers are eager to build or repair foundations of skills with which a consumer or patient can increase exponentially to a point of proficiency and self-sufficiency. The higher volume of skills, the more skills seemingly in the foundation or repertoire to retrieve and build confidence with. The belief is this: a patient demonstrating more skills can outlast patients with less skills. While this premise is valid in some respects, that is, a larger behavioral repertoire does offer more generality and endurance of skills, the downsides of larger repertoires developing too quickly are just as bad. First, larger does not mean better. Second, formation of larger repertories, with certain Cluster C personality types, is a plan spelling disaster from the outset.

In Obsessive-Compulsive Personality, for example, where perfectionism rigidly steers the perception of tasks being right or wrong, or good or bad, the large size of tasks given can falsely signify that large meets criteria and small does not meet criteria. In consumer's preoccupied with reaching large criteria, the momentum kicks in immediately to overachieve at (a) high rates, (b) high intensities, (c) high frequencies, and (c) expecting high outcomes that are positive (reinforcing). This establishing operation to overexert skills, with incredible force, may produce seriously untoward effects. These may include:

1. Rapid deterioration of efforts after multiple failed trials.
2. Rapid deterioration of any other establishing operations, i.e., apathy, precluding initiation of new trials to produce the skills.
3. Increased generalized avoidance of any tasks resembling or specifically about the desired response.
4. Avoidance and escape from the trainer, provider, teacher associated with helping with development of the skill.

In other words, assignment of a large task for any of the Cluster C personality types, but particularly for the Obsessive-Compulsive Personality Disorder, sparks an initial burst of energy to complete the task. But, at first encounter of a hurdle; once that hurdle remains noncircumvented, passion for the task diminishes rapidly to a point of consumer idleness and depression.

Amy did not realize this. She was a vision therapist under the supervision of an optometrist. She worked with 34-year-old Zeena, who suffered visual tracking defects after sustaining an intracranial hematoma along the parieto-occipital region. Amy found Zeena a highly motivated and compliant learner, almost zealous about trying and achieving new techniques. Inspired by Zeena's devotion to rehabilitation, Amy designed a series of complex steps using computer software for divergence training to improve eye coordination and shifting focus. Zeena welcomed the challenge with unprecedented optimism and indulged in the exercises at home. Within 10 minutes, Zeena found herself get dizzy, feel the onset of a headache, and could not complete the tracking sequence. She became frustrated, angry at herself, and aborted the task, with self-effacing feelings that she was really inadequate to compete at the level Amy wanted her to.

Zeena's obsessive-compulsive personality *forbid* her from seeing the bigger picture. She did not see that a tougher exercise was discretionary and not compulsory. She did not allow flexibility in the slowness with which she approached the tough skills, and did not tolerate mistakes incurred during the rigorous learning. Zeena is not unusual. Zeena's failure at the task *is not because the task itself was hard or she lacked a repertoire to perform it.* Zeena failed from starting too high, too quickly, and expecting outcome success instantly.

DOS AND DON'TS WITH PERSONALITY DISORDERS
CLUSTER C (AVOIDANT, DEPENDENT, OBSESSIVE)
DON'T:

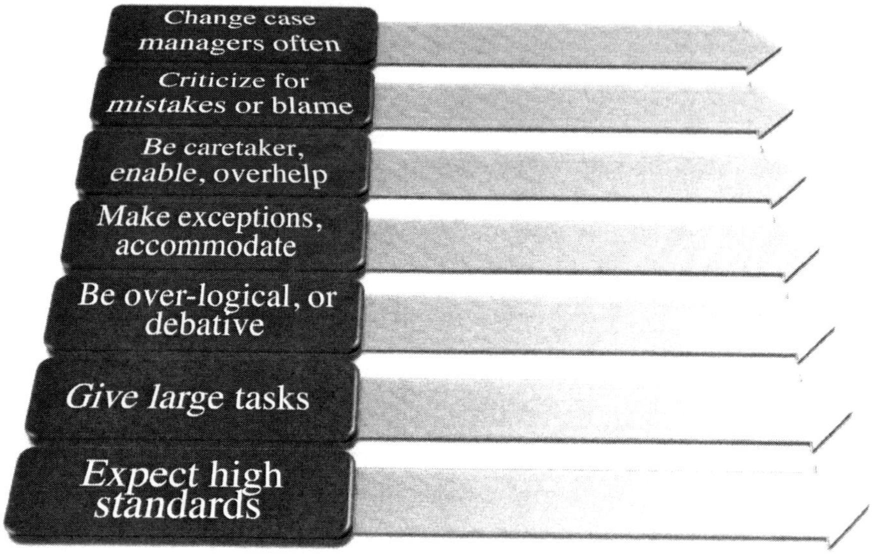

Change case managers often

Criticize for *mistakes* or blame

Be caretaker, *enable*, overhelp

Make exceptions, accommodate

Be over-logical, or debative

Give large tasks

Expect high standards

Figure 4.6.

C'mon, remind me:
73. For Cluster C, it is not advised to change case _____.
74. Providers should be careful to avoid over-logical explanations or being _____.
75. Giving a large task can quickly _____ the effort and motivation of clients.

Chapter 5

PREDICTORS OF PERSONALITY FOR SPECIFIC VOCATIONAL, THERAPY, AND REHABILITATION OUTCOMES

Personality Disorders consist of many infinitely diverse behaviors integrated by biosocial variables along a continuum of human development. At any given time, space, or environment, providing this continuum flows evenly, samples of the diverse behaviors can be extracted as predictors of future behaviors. This probabilistic sampling is the methodology used in experimental research. The integrity or "power" of that sample depends on the validity and reliability of that sample relative to a larger population (on the continuum), about which the sample represents. In stating behavioral probabilities or predictions, sample behaviors are more than snapshots of an individual's action at the moment. Imagine if that snapshot captured a calculated map of past and current behavioral contingencies, of how the individual responds appropriately and inappropriately, and likely conditions increasing and deceasing susceptibility to either choice of responses. The sample is more like a behavioral-DNA, comprised of cumulative responses to varying stimuli (i.e., reactional biography). These cumulative responses provide estimates of future behavior, or *behavior potentials*. Behavior potentials identify probability of response-occurrence should an individual face same, similar, or different circumstances in the future.

This behavioral-DNA that comprises the three clusters of personality disorders can be a prognosticator of many rehabilitation behaviors. Based on histories and current behavioral contingencies, predictions are possible of how rapidly or slowly a consumer may progress and adapt under challenging conditions imposed on them at different phases of their therapeutic program. This chapter discusses such predictors, or behavior potentials, to determine which cluster of personalities is most functional along 10 different domains. The domains are often considered the measures of rehabilitation outcome success. These 10 domains include:

1. Program Attrition
2. Absenteeism
3. Motivation
4. History of Transient Jobs
5. Coworker Relations
6. Supervisor Relations
7. Substance Abuse
8. Violence
9. Office Crime
10. Program Compliances

Program Attrition

Program attrition is a gauge of drop-out rates Consumers driven with energy and ambition at the outset of any baseline or intervention may be *strongly motivated by (i.e., under the establishing operations of)* powerful contingencies: economic, court-ordered, physical, and familial. No matter the exigencies, motivation may dwindle to apathy and disillusionment for several reasons, resulting in early self-termination of a program.

Absenteeism

Punctuality and regularity of attendance are the bedrock for cumulative learning and rehabilitative growth. Consumers receive upfront, or some time in the outset of training, a polite speech about the value of routines as the harbinger of strong and reliable skill development. Routines make it possible to observe, in a week's time, the power of a learning curve in shaping *major changes over baseline measures.* But, despite this convincing evidence, consumers may be absent frequently from training sessions. On the one hand, absences may be valid. Loss of a driver's license, exacerbation of pain, loss of medical insurance or unemployment all can derail the best of intentions. However, like program attrition, factors such as loss of control, hopelessness, apathy, and complacency are more common dynamics that account for absenteeism.

Motivation

Motivation pertains to three conditions. First, the establishing operation for entry into training must remain in effect despite amelioration of the problem. Motivators may decrease as therapy relieves the pathology that produced a strong desire for therapy in the first place. However, repercussions of fixing the pathology, or lingering pathologic effects, *must be present to sustain the establishing operation.* For example, a patient is motivated to begin physical therapy for postoperative knee pain; the goal is to reduce the swelling, stiffness, and immobility of the leg. But even as pain diminishes from routine physical therapy, *some pain remains and motivates continued use of* muscle-strength exercises. Second, progress must be observable during skill development. The consumer must see measurable improvement in some target behaviors. If the opposite occurs, that training hits a plateau and is not moving forward, motivation will deteriorate quickly. Third, social or other contingencies in the consumer's life, directly affected by therapy, and providing motivation for therapy, remain in effect despite positive changes in therapy. For example, a couple in marriage therapy improve their mutual communication style. But going to therapy per se *provides an opportunity for going out on a date together. The date out together serves as the motivator to continue therapy.* This matrix of social contingencies, then, that provides multiple establishing operations in other field segments of one's life, even peripherally, is called *ancillary contingencies.*

History of Transient Jobs

Job transience refers to a high job turnover rate. Frequent migration among jobs occurs for many reasons, from terminations and layoffs to geographic relocations, and voluntarily separating from a job for self-advancement. Terminations or "being fired' is an ambiguous area, and frequently is the outcome of the consumer or employee's deliberate disregard for the employer's best interests. However, operationally, the *real reasons* for discharge often overlap with five reasons: (1) poor performance rates or quality, (2) coworker communication problems, (3) supervisor communication problems, (4) customer-service problems, or (5) attendance.

Coworker Relations

High job perfomers may have poor social skills. Deficits in their interpersonal communication can limit awareness of verbal and nonverbal cues in coworker behavior, resulting in clumsy (underresponsive) or excessive (overresponsive) reactions. Underresponsive reactions appear as shyness, guardedness, withdrawal, isolationism, introversion, and social avoidance. These individuals are anxious around coworkers and minimize contact fearing disapproval. They avoid closeness to prevent exposure of personal information. Overresponsive reactions are defensive, aggressive, sarcastic, and cynical. Employees maintain distance from coworkers by artificially using decoys of bravado (e.g., outwardly looking confident), while masking underlying social fears. Both underresponsive and overresponsive individuals sabotage coworker relations by lacking appropriate and comfortable repertoires for daily routine sharing and conversations.

Jerrald, for example, worked in an assembly-line factory producing military uniforms. He observed coworkers using heavy slang and profanity as the main source of social conversation. Jerrald was more conservative, uncomfortable using vulgarity in innuendoes and jokes, and at first avoided the pods of coworker exchanges. Within a month, trying to assimilate instead of appearing odd, he mimicked the speech content and patterns of coworkers, thinking his words may sound like their words. Within a week of Jerrald's chameleon efforts, complaints were filed with Jerrald's supervisor about Jerrald's offensive language and harassment. Jerrald could not understand how his imitated version of coworker conversations backfired, whereas his coworkers seemed unoffended by similar comments shared among themselves. In this case, Jerrald's underresponsive (deficient) behaviors lacked many relevant verbal and nonverbal properties found within the peer exchanges. The profound differences in Jerrald's speech patterns not only were conspicuous, the differences were conspicuously awkward, forced, callus, and appeared condescending and insulting.

Supervisor Relations

High or low job performers may be socially competent. But they can be intolerant to supervisors who are authority figures, mistakenly perceived as controllers and manipulators instead of as mentors. Employees with a "grudge" against male or female supervisors likely had a history in childhood or adulthood of coercive subordination to other adults; demands for conformity often accompanied random punishment. As child victims, they either never knew when punishment might appear (arbitrary) or the reasons for the punishment (capricious). Under these adventitious schedules, uncertainty manifests helplessness, resentment, and eventually an unrelenting hatred for any person "in charge" whose demeanor or modus operandi of feedback resembles the original "adult" punisher, no matter how many years ago the punishment occurred.

Substance Abuse

The widespread and legal availability of alcohol and, in many states, marijuana, presents a continuous threat of job safety risks. Prospective and current employees with an extensive history of smoking marijuana or drinking, or even taking prescribed medicines, presume the employer will recognize these liberal laws and accept the employee's drug-use habits. But just the opposite is true. For example, a Federal Department of Transportation mandate prohibits any workers in safety-sensitive positions (e.g., operating a vehicle, installing electrical equipment, etc.) to score positively for any drugs or alcohol on drug screening tests, despite the state's legalization of marijuana or employee's possession of a medical marijuana card. Positive detection of a drug during a random drug screening *instantly triggers an assessment with an addictions specialist who determines the fate of that employee for job suspension and treatment before the employee gets released back to work.*

Misuse of drugs interfering with work duties is not a new issue, and most workplace policies are very explicit about the prohibition of alcohol or drugs related to work performance. However, a less clear-cut policy exists for long-term medication users. Employees claiming chronic anxiety, depression, or pain may be on a cocktail of medicine for over five or 10 years; by now drugs are deeply embedded in the bloodstream and that facilitates work productivity and social functioning. Interruption of the prescribed medicines not only would cause serious physical withdrawal effects, but also cause spontaneous regeneration of symptoms impeding social and occupational performance. Consequently, the balance between allowing *certain medicines to be used (e.g., Adderall for ADHD, Vicodin for pain), while banning other medicines (cannabis for pain)*, represents the turbulent controversy of drug-tolerance policies.

Gary, a 25-year electrical installer for a local utility company, had a perfect attendance record and was regarded by his coworkers as reliable, competent, and meticulously concerned about on-the-job safety. Gary scored positive for opioids on a random drug screening, prompting the protocol of meeting with a substance abuse specialist during a mandatory 10-day job suspension. The assessment showed Gary wore a prescribed Butrans skin patch, used to treat moderate to chronic pain around the clock; the medicine offset pain from his degenerative discs in the lumbar vertebrae. Gary presumed the medical prescription of Butrans covered him legally and would be acceptable to his employers, who observed no impediments in his job performance. However, considering it was a narcotic – a drug forbidden in employees while operating safety-sensitive tasks – Gary was mistaken about its approval and had to detox from the medicine or titrate to antidepressant medicines, also used for analgesic purposes, to satisfy conditions for work return.

Violence

Over the last 20 years, workplace violence statistically jumped to alarming rates of fatal and nonfatal incidents. The magnitude of job-related homicides was over 14,000 between 1992 and 2012, with a promising reduction of only 468 homicides reported in 2011 (US Department of Justice, 2011). Nonfatal attacks also showed decline, although the type of crimes committed became more diverse (e.g., rape/sexual assault, robbery, aggravated and simple assault). Trends showed that bartenders, security officers, and law enforcement officers had the highest rate of nonfatal workplace violence, with 17 percent of victims coming from protective service fields. At-risk jobs depended on the degree of (a) daily confrontations, (b) complexity of establishing operations interrupted, (c) demands for skill competency with an unskilled labor force, and (d) randomness of punishment toward workers despite good or bad performance outcome.

For example, Judy was an unemployment analyst answering the phones for jobless people who wanted to open claims for unemployment compensation. Judy earned an Associates Degree in English but never took classes or was trained properly in customer service. She had 15 minutes to field and solve each call, with 50 calls received per day, and over 300,000 calls received in the state system per day. Judy's 15-minute criteria was monitored closely and she worked feverishly to fulfill this quota. Under this establishing operation, Judy was less patient, more terse, formidable, and had no time to show empathy. She also increased her rate of error due to expediting claims incorrectly. However, the caller waited one to two hours online before being connected to Judy, typically faced a period of three to four weeks of severe financial hardship (foreclosure), and desperately needed to talk to somebody to secure funds. In many cases, the caller's establishing operations also included receiving a bill to repay twice or four-times the money received on unemployment due to suspected fraud. Between Judy's and the caller's establishing operations, both magnified by limited time to solve the problems, the probability of on-the-phone violence or even in-person violence exponentially increased.

Office Crime

Office crime has multiple typologies. There is white-collar crime, or financially-motivated nonviolent crime committed by business and government workers. Criminal acts include, among other things, fraud, bribery, embezzlement, cyber-crime, copyright infringement, money laundering, identity theft, and forgery. In Florida, for example, pharmacists owning a drug-store retail chain resold returned prescription drugs to street drug dealers for a high profit. The perpetration of Ponzi schemes is most popular, the most notorious case being financial advisor Bernard Madoff who unsuccessfully engaged in fraudulent investment operations.

On the other end of the office-crime spectrum are less legally invasive infractions commonly called *crimes of the cubicle* (Dugan, 2013). Here the beguiled nine to five worker, chained to the tiny personal working space of a cubicle, seeks freedom by creatively violating company policies. For example, Max worked for a state office of treasury confined to inputting numbers in his computer for eight hours a day. In his 30 square foot cubicle, he barely had room for his personal belongings amid the cluttered piles of data entry files, his phone, and computer equipment. Under these claustrophobic circumstances, Max gained some relief by (a) taking home paper-clips, pencils, and staplers; and (b) leaving his light on in the cubicle to mislead coworkers into thinking he was there when actually he left the building. Max was an offender of cubicle crimes that made his tediously mundane job more tolerable.

Program Compliance

The main litmus test of rehabilitation or treatment outcome success begins with program compliance. Consumers motivated for self-change may be very amenable to guidance, interventions, and regimens, with very minor or no evidence of misanthropy or imperturbability. Misanthropy is hatred or disdain for human beings, a symptom of excessive resentment and workplace rebelliousness. Likewise, imperturbability, a second predictor of program compliance, is a sanguine, nonchalant, and self-composed person. Unruffled self-assurance may, undesirably, mean the consumer is impersonal, apathetic, detached, uncaring, and aloof to some issues. A compliant consumer lacks misanthropy and imperturbability, whereas noncompliant consumers are nefariously devious, distrustful of people, and cold and calculated. They feel bitter and angry, and frequently find faults in the provider or a program, both of which fulfill the consumer's self-fulfilling prophecy that the program was doomed to fail.

These ten domains of rehabilitation adjustment *may vary enormously*, according to the consumer or client's diagnosed personality disorder. In the following, we re-examine each of the domains under the three clusters of personality to determine two points. First, we look at the degree of risk in relationship to the personality typology. Second, we look at options available to providers to minimize these risks.

Cluster A Personality Disorders (Paranoid, Schizoid, Schizotypal)

1. PROGRAM ATTRITION (HIGH). Three defining characteristics of the Cluster A personality disorders are (a) distrust, (b) distorted beliefs, and (c) underdeveloped (deficient) interpersonal skills. In jobs or rehabilitation programs demanding the rigor of high pace performance, self-discipline, or high expectations of social participation, Cluster A

individuals decline the fastest. High performance tasks require intense energy, endurance, persistence, and perseverance, all of which are poor or absent. Paranoid types may invest initial high rates of effort but be mistrustful. Schizoid and Schizotypal types function at generally slower paces, require repetition of instructions, and may get very confused when forced to move quickly. Self-discipline is an area of difficulty for all three typologies. Paranoid, Schizoid, and Schizotypal types frequently are preoccupied with disorganized thoughts and beliefs, distracting them from the concentration needed to self-regulate a task.

When they feel expectations are steep, the Cluster A consumer quits; the enormity of interpersonal deficits disable efforts and make it nearly impossible to reach expectations. Likewise, individuals with paranoid personality are either hypertalkative (about logical fallacies) or peculiarly quiet while they overanalyze other people or the provider. With Schizoid or Schizotypal, social deficits are so profound that communication is brief, tangential, irrational, odd, or scares the listener.

Considering the high risk of program attrition, it is incumbent on providers to engineer the therapeutic interventions with (a) slow paced-responses, (b) high latitude for mistakes, (c) physical or verbal guidance (coaching) in slowly approximating self-regulated (self-disciplined) tasks, and (d) more *independent* than *socially-dependent* opportunities for social learning. Slow-paced responses means the rate is slow, intensity is low, the time between responses is long, and magnitude produced by the response can be low. Latitude for mistakes involves a generous amnesty for repeated errors and guided encouragement for slower steps toward partial goals. The method resembles *Motivational Interviewing*, the effective approach originally conceived of to prevent repeated alcohol recidivism (Miller, 1983; Miller & Rollnick, 2012). It is a goal-directed approach of influencing the learner to overcome ambivalence about engaging in some task (e.g., not drinking, not practicing a social skill, etc.). Providers are nonjudgmental, nonconfrontational, and nonadversarial, but more objectively warm, empathic, understanding, and considerate of the pros and cons underlying the ambivalence. On the downside, this approach does rely on advanced verbal behavior on the part of both provider and consumer, a possible problem for cluster A typology. Paranoid types may seize the occasion for excessive verbal behavior tangential to the central issue of ambivalence. Schizoid and Schizotypal typologies may be *hypo*verbal or talking in thought fragments or distortions also irrelevant to the subject matter.

In Motivational Interviewing, physical and verbal guidance (coaching) involves direct feedback for small approximations of progress. Carefully worded praise for any favorable efforts displayed in a single session or across sessions can keep the consumer focused on task. Likewise, use of socially-independent opportunities enhances focus on tasks by eliminating the confounding variables from poor socialization. Tasks can be designed for solo, or more exclusionary practice of skills, with possibly one or two familiar people or family members nearby. To broaden training, simulations or *analogues* can be used inside the consumer's house to reproduce some but not all of the naturalistic features of the world outside the house (Ruben, 1983c). For example, Renee, a schizotypal personality, practiced her resume writing using Microsoft Word templates; she then uploaded her resume onto a database and invited two people in a chat room (simulation to real world) to give feedback on her resume. She never needed to meet the "chat-people" in person or socialize with them beyond thanking them for the resume review.

2. ABSENTEEISM (HIGH). Tardiness and failure to show up for work are common problems found in Cluster A personality types. The reasons are fourfold. First, a chaotic lifestyle and absence or deficiency in time-management greatly reduces follow-through on routine activities. Second, distractibility and impulsiveness create unintentional disregard for time-based structures. Third, risk of derealization (prepsychotic or psychotic episodes) may eliminate awareness of time-and-reality-based schedules. Fourth, aversion toward any part of the intervention, no matter how discrete, may quickly foster avoidance behaviors; avoidance behaviors also occurs from a dearth of interpersonal coping skills to directly confront or solve the aversion.

Take Karen, for example. She met once weekly with a counselor from Community Mental Health (CMH) to check on her coping skills. Karen always forgot the appointment time, and frequently forgot to call (CMH) to remind her of the appointment. On the appointment day, although uniformly scheduled the same day and time every week, Karen always felt compelled to do other tasks. She procrastinated her laundry until one hour before the appointment time and rarely finished the laundry with enough time to drive to CMH. On appointment days she did not do laundry, Karen was daydreaming about her mother visiting her from Guatemala, although Karen, a native of Michigan, and her mother, born in New York, never visited nor resided in Guatemala.

To make matters worse, Karen always felt nervous around the counselor, when asked questions that Karen could not answer or that required her to do tasks beyond her skills. Karen felt odd, indifferent, and just did not like the counselor. She never told the counselor about her antipathy. She thought the counselor would "figure it out" when Karen arrived late or never showed up for sessions.

Alternatively, attendance is a function of comfort and safety. Cluster A personality types are indifferent to praise, reassurance, empathy, or most humanistic tools to garner their support. But such individuals will respond favorably to a nonpressured or relaxed environment, in which they can freely express general (sometimes, odd or eccentric) statements, and discover aspects of skills learning more freely than under a rigid structure. Ironically, consumers diagnosed with Cluster A personality types are perfect candidates for an adult-version of Montessori-curriculum training. In the Montessori concept *for children*, the curriculum proceeds with (a) uninterrupted blocks of time, (b) independence, (c) freedom with minor limits, (d) guided choice of work activity, and (e) resources arranged meticulously and available for use at any time (Bagby, Wells, Edmondson, & Thompson, 2014). Borrowing from this pedagogy, the architecture of training programs for Cluster A personality types should optimize the freedom of movement and time in an aesthetically pleasing and unencumbered environment. The safety and serenity felt in this training environment would greatly prevent absenteeism.

3. MOTIVATION (MODERATE TO LOW). Hope and trust are two variables essential to cluster A personality types to maintain motivation. Hope means a point-to-point correspondence between a promise for change and observations of these measurable changes in the consumer's behaviors. If consumers see this connection, in a short time, they can be said to have *hope*. But when this connection falters, with little parallel between expectations for behavior change and actual changes made, the consumer feels instantly *hopeless. Motivation disappears immediately.* Trust is exactly the same but pertains to the provider. Consumers trust the provider to supply, show, and follow through on skill-training to enable completion of some goal. Fulfillment of that training, no matter the degree of progress in skill learning, verifies the trust and reflects positively on the provider. Lack of goal fulfillment has the opposite effect. It devours the trust and catapults the consumer into a purgatory-like state of immobility, where the consumer distrusts

everybody and withdraws into hiding.

Carl, diagnosed with paranoid personality disorder, was already dubious about having a job and did not trust his vocational counselor. At first, the counselor walked through all of the possible training opportunities in culinary arts, Carl's favorite subject. He showed how working in the food industry was possible by taking some classes toward a food-health certificate. The vocational counselor also spoke about the quickness with which Carl could track his learning progress and see the applications picked up by prospective employers. Carl was persuaded at first. After two weeks of in-class training in food-hygiene preparation, Carl felt the skills were knowledge he already had. He did not observe any measurable progress in his own food-management skills. He also learned the job market for food interns was very bleak. Carl's motivation deteriorated as he grew suspicious the counselor was deceptive and that the entire culinary arts training program was a fraud.

Carl, like many cluster A personality types, needed verification (reinforcers) much sooner than he received them. In programs that promise very specific outcomes, the skills comprising this outcome are divided into measurable and observable units of progress. Progress occurs *only when the consumer can see and confirm real-time efforts materialize.* The provider's role is to construct realistic units of skills based on the consumer's current (not future) abilities. The next step is to incorporate a regular system of self-monitoring to prove (support evidence that) these skills can achieve a reasonable standard. When the consumer can detect progress, see skills meeting criteria, and this progress matches the provider's predictions at the outset of training, the correspondence between words-and-actions can generate and sustain motivation.

4. HISTORY OF TRANSIENT JOBS (HIGH). Stabilization of jobs or, for that matter, of program participation, is an Achilles heel for individuals diagnosed with cluster A personality disorders. This weakness perpetuates as the individual withdraws and depersonalizes from perceived stressors. They abandon any programs or projects with indifference. This apathy lingers for days or weeks until another project or job peaks the consumer's interest and is seized. Self-terminating a job or program is also typically spontaneous; it is loosely connected to abstract and irrational reasons for disillusionment. Dispassion occurs for many vague reasons: boredom, confusion, fatigue, anger, impoliteness of the provider or clerical support staff, and dissatisfaction with the quality and quantity of service training received. Despite the reasons cited,

turnover is *not a calculated move*. Consumers with Schizoid and Schizotypal personality disorders make snap decisions on the flicker of any
unusual stimulus event that is metaphorical or metonymical in origin.
That is, with metaphorical events, the stimuli may bare some but not
all of the relevant properties found in the training events. For example,
take the consumer who hates the color yellow. The provider wears a
yellow sweater, and the consumer hates yellow sweaters, largely because this traces to a violently punitive parent who wore a yellow shirt
and trousers, but never sweaters. The hue of "yellow" is the vague
property supporting a conditioned avoidance response.

But now let us suppose the consumer reacts adversely to the color of
yellow when there was no obvious "yellow" in the consumer's childhood house or family. Or was there? Metonymical events (extension),
recalled from an earlier discussion, is when none of the relevant properties of a training stimulus appear in some new stimulus. But many
irrelevant properties exist, and seem to evoke the consumer's responses
as if the properties were relevant. Yellow was significant, for example,
but it was the color of a house adjacent to the house in which the consumer was raised. It was the neighbor's house the consumer ran to and
hid under when an abusive parent threatened to spank the consumer.
The color "Yellow" appeared nowhere in the consumer's house. The
irony is that, no matter how irrelevant or distant the color "yellow" was
from the relevant stimulus conditions controlling avoidance behavior
(i.e., punishment in the house), it still paired with the relevant events
and by itself can trigger *some* avoidance or escape responses today.
These avoidance and escape responses are responsible for the consumer quitting a program or job.

One way to solve the labyrinth of improper stimulus generalization
and produce longer job or program duration is to teach new discriminative control. "Discriminative control" involves a structure of (a) new
cues signaling on-task behavior, (b) new cues signaling healthy establishing operations, and (c) new cues signaling when to engage in proper avoidance and escape. In physical therapy sessions, for example,
teach a consumer with cluster A typology how to "know" when to
begin the first exercise. The provider's verbal greeting of "Hi Jake,"
may be a perfect onset (antecedent) cue. Next, teach the consumer how
to gauge the length of a response before starting a new response, and
identify a terminal reinforcer. Gauges, for example, may be the number of arm or leg rotations or orderly sequence of fitness equipment

used. As this gauge is in effect, the consumer also establishes an operation of wanting the terminal reinforcer (e.g., drinking Gatorade), and
thus paces his or her exercise consistently or routinely based on how
thirsty the consumer gets. At first, without perspiring and not feeling
thirsty, pace of exercise may be slow. As the consumer gets more
parched, exercise rate may increase and the consumer goes through the
sequence faster. After exercise, when the consumer quenches his or her
thirst by drinking Gatorade, this also allows for *escape from the deprivation (establishing operation) of thirst*. This is an example of proper avoidance or escape behaviors.

   5. COWORKER RELATIONS (POOR). Forging healthy coworker relationships requires a minimal social repertoire. This repertoire typically
involves (1) recognition and comprehension of verbal and nonverbal
cues (i.e., speech pragmatics); (2) use of nonverbal behaviors (e.g., eye
contact, expressions, body posture, and gestures); (3) formation of peer-
age-level friends; (4) spontaneous seeking to share enjoyment, interests,
or achievements of people; and (5) social and emotional reciprocity. An
impoverished repertoire may significantly lack these qualities. In addition, cluster A personality typically exhibits marked impairments in (a)
alternative modes of communication (e.g., talking to oneself), (b)
stereotyped or repetitive and idiosyncratic use of language, and (c)
stereotyped or repetitive motor mannerisms. Not surprisingly, the
aforementioned list (1-4) not only characterizes schizoid and schizotypal individuals, but it is also the qualifying definition for Autism
Spectrum Disorder (ASD) (APA, 2013). Many children exhibiting ASD
are asocial and risk the epigenesis of adult Cluster A personalities
(Barneveld, Pieterse, de Sonneville, van Rijnm, Lahuis, van Engeland,
& Swaab, 2011). They grow up detached, socially clumsy, and missing
important interpersonal cues from people. At work, underdeveloped
social repertoires greatly restrict opportunities for coworker relations
and, should opportunities for comingling exist, the skill deficits prevent
a normal and productive interchange for any duration.

   One remedy to facilitate coworker relations among individuals with
Cluster A personality disorders is to integrate their therapy or job into
a social context. Nancy, a hospital dietician, met with recovering heart
surgery patients before their discharge to review nutritional meal planning. She met with Tonya, diagnosed with Schizoid Personality
Disorder, and during their one-on-one sessions could convey logistics
about meal planning. However, Tonya stayed in her hospital room

despite the physician's specific prescription for her to walk around. Tonya also exhibited eccentric habits when alone or around people such as shuffling her feet, overwringing her hands, and constantly clearing her throat. Concerned these odd habits may repel other patients but determined to socialize Tonya, Nancy arranged for Tonya to sit in the lounge room next to another cardiovascular patient, also learning about nutrition. Nancy prompted Tonya to tell the new patient one or two of the details about meal planning taught to Nancy earlier. That brief sharing of information constituted a "practice" social exchange. The social exchange blended into the overall therapeutic milieu.

6. SUPERVISOR RELATIONS (AVERAGE). Tolerance of criticism is challenging for any person. A Cluster A personality type is particularly sensitive to any corrective feedback given no matter the saccharine or harsh tone of its delivery. Around supervisors, managers, foreman, or anybody in authority, the schizoid, schizotypal and paranoid consumers are rarely defiant. They are despondent, indifferent, affectively restrictive, or outwardly appear bland. They may respond politely or not at all, usually from confusion about the communication or from being distracted while spoken to. Preoccupied by disorganized thoughts or daydreaming, the Cluster A person is aloof, depersonalized, or temporarily in a nonreality. Supervisors may find this reaction not just strange, but offensive. Failure to respond, either positively or negatively, may be misinterpreted as rude, disrespectful, or outright insubordinate. Similarly, when providers give instructions and look for responsiveness to affirm or disconfirm understanding of the instructions, the consumer's catatonic-like and empty stare may be misdiagnosed as *disconnection.* From this peculiar silence or long gap (delay) before responses occur, poor or nonexistent relations may result with the supervisor or provider. This may jeopardize the individual's job or discontinue benefits of a service program.

Mending this schism between supervisor instructions and an individual's nonresponsiveness involves clearly definable criteria specified at the outset of the job or training and repeated intermittently over many verbal transactions. Providers or supervisors can give *instructional mands* in stating that whenever (a) any remarks are spoken to the employee/customer, responsiveness must occur within three to five seconds; and (b) when responsiveness is timely (within three to five seconds), the provider/supervisor will keep remarks brief and positive. A concomitant to this procedure is that, when the individual does respond but the context is tangential or irrelevant, the supervisor or provider can reprompt a cue for a relevant verbal response while *differentially* ignoring the tangential response (see Ayllon & Michael, 1959; Ruben, 1983).

Demara used this approach. She was a Certified Nurse Assistant in a nursing home that also housed postoperative orthopedic patients on a rehabilitation wing. She was assigned to Craig, who was diagnosed previously with Paranoid Personality Disorder. When Demara greeted Craig with an effusive "Hi Craig," Craig never answered. When Demara asked if he wanted more water or was ready for a bath, he also was stone-faced silent. On the few occasions he responded, Craig's answer elaborately pontificated about alien abductions and how alien implants removed during his recent orthopedic surgery will upset his galactic captives. Demara took a baseline measures of Craig's nonresponsiveness for later comparative data and also to refine her hypothesis on the functional relationship between her instructions and Craig's nonresponsiveness. Then, she told him that, when he responds to her within three to five seconds of hearing her questions or instruction, Demara would say very little afterward, and even allow Craig to return to whatever activity he was engaged in before she interrupted him with her instruction. In other words, he could resume talking about alien abductions and implants. This *additional incentive was to strengthen the establishing operation of her instructional mand within the limited hold period of three to five seconds.* Craig did respond more quickly, and Demara carefully and selectively responded only to his comments that corresponded relevantly to her prompts.

7. SUBSTANCE ABUSE (LOW). The rate of substance abuse among Cluster A personalities is so insignificant, it is almost a "nonissue." Occasionally, recreational drug use may surface as a byproduct of some permutation in the individual's life, but not as a habit. For example, on the rare occasion that Maxine, a schizoid personality type, visits her nephew and his wife, both of whom regularly smoke marijuana, Maxine may also smoke with them. Otherwise, Maxine never smokes marijuana. The greater risk with drug use is prescriptive medications. Maxine may take a cocktail of antipsychotics medicine (e.g., Zyprexa, Abilify, Risperdal, Seroquel, etc.), the side-effects of which may leave her in a zombie-like hypnotic trance or incapable of focusing on people or conversations. When consumers, instead, exhibit only *negative symptoms* of prodromal or active schizophrenia, medications may be

less sedating and more facilitative of normal or functional behaviors. Antidepressants are more likely to be the prescriptive choice to eliminate negative symptoms and rebuild energy and optimism. The problem, then, is not the addictiveness or side-effects of the antidepressants per se, but the erratic schedule by which the medicine is taken. Consequently, the major issue regarding substance abuse for Cluster A personality disorders is inaccuracy and inconsistency of self-administered medicine.

Medicines taken improperly fall into the six categories of overuse, underuse, erratic use, contraindicated use, abuse, and improper prescribing practices (see Ruben, 1990; Ryan, Popour, Arneson, & Ruben, 1983). Each of these are common and unintentional mistakes that may falsely convey symptoms resembling addiction or withdraw syndromes. *Overuse* is mistakenly taking several doses of the same medication or taking medication when it is not needed. *Underuse* includes both the failure to fill and forgetting to take medications. *Erratic use* refers to the failure to follow instructions. This includes missing doses, taking double doses, taking doses at the wrong time, and confusion over which drug to take at which interval. *Contraindicated use* occurs due to incorrect storage of medication, using outdated drugs or not monitoring side-effects. *Abuse* is drug misuse with intent to hurt self or with addictive purposes. Finally, *improper prescribing practices* is primarily a communication problem between physician and client. In elderly and disadvantaged (minority) populations, in particular, improper prescribing practice recur from *lack of explanations, complexity of explanations, and incongruence between explanations among different prescribing practitioners* (Ruben, 1984b; Ruben, 1987b).

8. VIOLENCE (LOW). The incident rate of violence among Cluster A personality disorders is very low. It reached this nadir by the fact that such consumers (a) avoid conflict, and are pacifists; (b) misinterpret cues of anger instigation and consequently would be slow or unaware to retaliate; (c) maintain a low or sedate body tempo of idleness, inaction, and indifference, incompatible with the autonomic arousal needed for previolent or violent anger; (d) are not impulsive or reactionary; and (e) lack the sophisticated social exchanges that foster contempt, annoyance, resentment, and feelings of powerlessness. In Cluster A, preponderant features of depersonalization, asociality, fragmented or irrational thoughts, and decrealization are all built-in safeguards against feeling aggression.

Not surprisingly, the sharp rise in reported domestic abuse cases nationwide has never correlated with personality disorders let alone Cluster A personality disorders. One exception has been when older adolescents labeled with Schizoid Personality also demonstrate fore-runner symptoms to antisocial conduct (Wolff & Cull, 1986). Pathological lying, hostilities to authorities, and general malice may emerge when the Cluster A personality is coerced into reciprocal aggression. Patterson, for example, pioneered research in parents and partners lured into mutual aggression as they quickly deplete their coping strategies (Capaldi, Kim, & Short, 2007; Patterson, Reid, & Dishion, 1992). For example, couple conflict escalates over unresolved discrepancies such as lack of sexual intercourse, misspending money, or cleaning rituals. When one partner is more dominant or assertive than the other partner, foisting opinions incessantly and ruthlessly, the passive partner may absorb this grief for a short period until reaching a threshold of anxiety. At that point, the passive partner retaliates. Retribution is not to even the score or counterbalance control; it occurs in desperation under an establishing operation to relieve anxiety and escape the confrontation. This is when a schizotypal partner, berated maliciously from his wife, may explode in childish rage to cause instant chaos. In that chaos, he interrupts and escapes from the barrage of insults. Once he burrows in some refuge, away from the cacophony of intraparnter conflict, the schizoid spouse instantly feels calm; the anxiety vanishes. In other words, onset of his anger or violence was *a byproduct of intimidation, his own inept social repertoire, heightened anxiety, and an overwhelming urgency to escape that anxiety.*

Mary, a health care homemaker, never saw this phenomenon coming. She routinely visited Chet's house on Tuesdays and Thursdays to help with Adult Daily Living (ADL) skills, based on Chet's psychiatrist's prescription for an assisted-living aide given the severity of Chet's Schizoid Personality Disorder. On each visit, Mary reviewed at the outset her goals of chores to be done either by herself or Chet and timeframes expected for each chore. Chet's poky resistance to initiate and complete chores meant the goals went unmet and this put Mary way behind in her chore completion list submitted monthly to her employers. To raise her monthly numbers on the chore completion list, she instituted a more persuasive instruction for Chet to get him motivated. She told Chet all of the reasons why he was lazy, incompetent, and lacking in social graces. Mary figured this paradoxical approach might build resentment in Chet, perhaps even guilt, mobilizing him to perform more quickly and efficiently. In the second week of Mary's intervention, she was astonished to see her words trigger Chet into a violent tirade; he yelled loudly, threw objects against the wall, stood closely to Mary's face and waved his fist furiously at her, and ran out of the house to a friend's house. She concluded that Chet's violence was a manifestation of his schizoid personality.

Chet was no more violent than a small mouse is against a large cat. However, Mary's inappropriate use of paradoxical statements backfired in causing provocation. It scared, antagonized, and aroused autonomic anxiety in Chet to a point where, in grasping for straws, he resorted to primordial aggression to avoid and escape from adversity. For many years, research has been extensive on the effects of escape behavior on anger-induced violence (Cherek, Sapiga, Steinberg, & Kelly, 1990; Dengerick & Covey, 1983). Violence becomes *a means to an end, impulsively occurring as anxiety spirals into a frenzy of terror.* With a limited social repertoire, worsened by a defective reactional biography for handling anxiety and stress, the Cluster A personality individual feels like a hostage imprisoned in the same suffocating circumstances that he experienced in childhood. This is when early symptoms of schizoid personality (i.e., ASD) were forming.

9. OFFICE CRIME (LOW). The tenacity needed to commit premeditative office crimes is beyond the social repertoire of individuals with Cluster A personality disorders. Crimes involve passions of jealousy, envy, resentment, anger, or revenge. Each of these emotions presumes a level of sensitivity, of caring about something to a point of being deceived, disappointed, distraught, or damaged. In the schizoid, schizotypal, and paranoid typologies, the overarching features include emotional coldness, apathy, disenfranchisement from people, and disregard for affection. In other words, *they don't care.* Detachment occurs from relationships, communication, and from any organizational system in which the schizoid consumer may feel slighted. They do not feel slighted. The person is unaware of the nuances of human interplay that foster *unfairness, inconsideration, and betrayal.* Failure to discern problems in very complex social behavior means the consumer operates in a bubble; his or her world is simpler, superficial, and lacks the impetus for selfishness that stimulates fierce competition in most people.

The up side of a crimeless personality type is that the consumer seems more trustworthy. The individual appears more moral, wholesome, and reliable. The phlebotomist Naomie felt, after 25 years in her profession, that patients lied about their diseases and even inflated diseases beyond their medical diagnosis. Naomie drew blood from patients on the psychiatric unit, and particularly she needed samples from Howard, diagnosed with Schizotypal Personality Disorder. Howard always greeted Naomie graciously compared to the malcontent patients on the other units. With other patients, complaints stacked up quickly when Naomie neglected to respond instantly to the patient's arbitrary requests. Patients blamed Naomie for slowness and carelessness, even filing petitions for her job suspension. This retaliation seemed unreasonable since Naomie worked at a rapid pace on each unit, outwardly had a smile on, and she always responded to STAT hospital requests, especially when the emergency order came from pharmacists and physicians. By contrast, when she took blood from Howard, he never made Naomie feel uncomfortable or under the ludicrous pressure to work faster. Howard never used leverage, that is, sneaky or deceiving threats, to plot revenge against Naomie. Howard *could not do these things, because he did not understand the setting events or conditions from which to abstract what people possibly did right or wrong to him.*

10. PROGRAM COMPLIANCE (LOW). A participatory consumer or client is one who gleans the value of reinforcement inherent in the training or other services received. In Cluster A personality disorders, motivation, in general, is sparse; the rewards targeted as "incentive-builders" have a short shelf-life. One reason for low motivation is the discompassion for anything. Schizoid and schizotypal personality types dissociate from daily priorities, world events, or even the transactions of people cohabiting with them. They seem impervious to any stimuli producing reinforcing or punishing effects, no matter the form. Absent of any impact effects, their continued role in some program is very precarious. They may quit or just decrease their frequency of attendance.

Matthew, a schizotypal individual went for an MRI of his skull. When Bethany, the radiologist tech, greeted him, she was unprepared for his dearth of social skills. She also felt uncomfortable when he elaborated on his imagery of game characters from his online game playing of Warcraft. She ushered Matthew onto the table and prepared him for the scan. When she finished the MRI, she tried to debrief him with soft comments and found her words just rolled off his shoulders like Teflon. She also gave him simple post-MRI instructions about unrestricted activity and time periods within he will receive medicine and the results. Matthew seemed adrift in a different world, consumed in his own thoughts, and totally unconcerned about the MRI and its results affecting his health. She learned that shortly after he left the MRI lab room, he did not follow any of the sequence of instructions so carefully outlined by her.

One simple way to tune-in the wirelessly unconnected schizoid, schizotypal, or paranoid individual is to build realistic (naturalistic) contingencies including establishing operations and a clearly seen coordination between some specific (desirable) behavior and a very concrete (reinforcing) outcome. Had Bethany told Mathew *what exactly he needed to do after the MRI, whom to call, and the importance of that call to let him return to playing online games,* Matthew's motivation suddenly might increase. Contingencies of relevance, that connect behavior with highly preferred rewards, can break through the barriers of emotional distance or insensitivity. Matthew may show a remarkable burst of energy and motivation, and may even cooperate fully with instructed tasks. But once the incentives lose visibility or magnitude, Matthew's ambition turns off.

PREDICTORS OF PERSONALITY FOR SPECIFIC VOCATIONAL OUTCOMES
CLUSTER A (PARANOID, SCHIZOID, SCHIZOTYPAL)

Program Attrition:	HIGH
Absenteeism:	HIGH
Motivation:	MODERATE to LOW
Hx of Transient Jobs:	HIGH
Coworker Relations:	POOR
Supervisor Relations:	AVERAGE
Substance Abuse:	LOW
Violence:	LOW
Office Crime:	LOW
Program Compliance:	LOW

Figure 5.1.

C'mon, remind me:
76. For Cluster A, program attrition is very _____.
77. Coworker relations, for Cluster A, is usually very _____.
78. Office crime is nearly always _____ since Cluster A types are asocial.

Cluster B Personality Disorders
(Antisocial, Borderline, Histrionic, Narcissistic)

1. PROGRAM ATTRITION (HIGH). Cluster B personality disorders uniformly involve five features: (1) impulsiveness, (2) risk-potential, (3) inflatability of circumstances ("drama"), (4) egocentricity (self-centeredness), and (5) severe mood swings (i.e., cyclothymic or bipolar). On program or job entry, the Cluster B personality consumer may be ecstatic with unrealistic expectations of their own past and future behavior repertoire. They idealize their potential with hyperbolic verbal statements about the ease with which they will master difficult goals and be victorious at the end. They overlook palpable flaws in character, judgment, or uncorrected mistakes that may undermine their effusion, investment of effort, and diminish production rates. When this whirlwind of effort faces its first obstacle, no matter how easy the obstacle is to resolve, excitement about the program instantly plummets. As the second, third, and finally a cascade of obstacles roll into the path of the consumer, the consumer's vitality and egocentricity not only stops, but causes resentment and depression. The consumer feels deflated, defeated, cheated, betrayed, is overcome with embarrassment or anger, and blames the provider and the program for failing to deliver its promises. Cessation of the program is *an absolute decision entirely attributed to external reasons.*

Betsy was a Unit Coordinator on B-wing North at a local hospital. This wing housed labor and delivery and generally had upbeat staff celebrating the births of children. The patient in room 213, Cara, a 24-year-old first-time mother, previously was diagnosed with histrionic personality disorder. Cara was recovering from her cesarean section of a healthy boy two days ago. She was grateful to be spared the long labor (painful) period, and elative about her prospects of motherhood. Her husband, Mark, also was there visiting regularly and excitedly boasting to Cara's family about Cara's amazing recovery and its auspices for a perfect family of three. In Betsy's observation, she always noticed Cara was hypertalkative, out of bed visiting, making plans on her I-pod, and being impertinent with nurses. The nurses always urged Cara to slow down and recuperate. Betsy even overheard Cara on her cellphone elaborately describe labor-intensive aerobic exercises she *believed she* could perform now and planned to do more of in the next two weeks. On consultation with the OBGYN, Betsy received a prescription for a social worker to talk to Cara about her runaway enthusiasm and to be more respectful of her stitches and timetable for body healing. After this discussion occurred with the social worker, Cara burst into a towering inferno of anger and protestations. She blamed the labor and delivery unit for botching her surgery, and for corroborating to sabotage her dream (i.e., fantasy image) of being a loving mother. She abruptly decided to self-discharge from the hospital two days before medically advised.

Cara was determined to live out her idealized fantasy of parenting despite the ostensible roadblocks clogging the pipeline to her dream. She did not want to hear, believe, or accept any words from the social worker about responsible rehabilitation, since it conflicted with her egocentric image of being invincible and a perfect parent. In the wake of Cara's locomotive-like determination, is there a way to educate her about her medical condition and respect her bloated impression of motherhood? Yes, with Cluster B personality disorders, and particularly with the histrionic personality disorder, the goal of program retention does not lie with planning the goals they will reach in the future. *Instead, the focus is on the measurable, concrete, and practical goals they can reach today.* Goal setting is a mutual activity immediately begun postoperatively when she is conscious and can focus. A provider (unit coordinator, nurse, social worker, etc.) meets with Cara and her husband to outline the exact behaviors taught, or expected (for her to try) per day, and how each response is measured. When Cara hears the definite parameters and criteria of behavior, and how it is monitored, she is more likely to comply and take faster egocentric pride from the attention (i.e., reinforcers) given to her by hospital staff for this compliance. In other words, eliminating the ambiguity of goals during recovery can prevent Cara's inflation of unobtainable goals; it can also prevent possibly unhealthy goals contraindicated by her medical condition.

2. ABSENTEEISM (HIGH). Tardiness and absenteeism are frequent occurrences for Cluster B personality disorders. Features of the personality responsible for the probability of this absenteeism lie with (a) impulsiveness, (b) distractibility, (c) retaliatory defiance, and (d) overconfidence (cavilarity). Consumers may change their schedule spontaneously and frivolously, disregarding promises made to providers. They renege on promises with alacrity and seem undisturbed by the inconvenience caused to other people. Distractibility, while similar to impulsiveness, may not involve a sporadic change in schedule or routines. The consumer, engaged in some activity, suddenly gets preoccupied or fixated on some diversion. This diversion absorbs their attention and competes with the target or relevant behaviors they are supposed to perform. Texting while driving an automobile is an example. The consumer overlooks the danger of texting while driving or even city ordinances prohibiting texting and driving. As the texting exchange heats up, the consumer may pull off the road, delaying the arrival time at some destination. This delay, *again,* inconveniences some other person. Retaliatory defiance is more pronounced in antisocial, borderline, and narcissistic personalities. It is a passive-aggressive or indirect expression of disobedience. The consumer may be angry over some perceived infraction by the provider, and retaliates for this imposition. One way to indirectly retaliate is tardiness or recurrent absenteeism.

Overconfidence and cavalierity follow a different path but are also indirect. Here, a morsel of approval at work or in rehabilitation spirals the consumer into an inflated self-perception as invaluable at the job and *advanced in* rehabilitation. They feel superior, privileged, and grandiose in their skills and trajectory of high success. Intense energy and high production of effort seen within the first week of a job or training suddenly shifts to a plateau. They engage in less effort and ride on the coattails of their past accomplishments. On this magic carpet of self-grandiosity, loyalty of routines fade and tardiness or absenteeism increase.

Daniel fell into this cavilierty trap at the chiropractor's office. He was referred there for cervical (vertebrae) pain unrelated to arthritis or disc degeneration. Daniel premorbidly was diagnosed with narcissistic personality disorder. He originally sustained cervical pain from whiplash in a vehicular accident. After one or two sessions of neck manipulations, Daniel instantly felt pain relief, and boasted about his healthy progress to the chiropractor. The chiropractor, impressed by this rapid recovery, praised Daniel for his dedication to rehabilitation and outlined a series of sessions over one month in which to stabilize his current progress. That evening, Daniel posted on Facebook to many of his friends about his *incredible recuperative powers to overcome cervical pain*, discovered after two chiropractic sessions. In return, Daniel received a plethora of laudatory responses from friends amazed by his self-discovery and wanting more insight on what Daniel did. In the meantime, Daniel deliberately did not go to the next two scheduled sessions with the chiropractor.

The problem here does not lie *exclusively* with Daniel. Self-grandiosity occurs as a function of (a) incorrect or absent feedback, (b) misallocation of reinforcers, and (c) establishing operations to generate self-worth absent of other productive ways to build confidence. Daniel never received realistic feedback from the chiropractor (provider) that, while initial progress is likely, any pain relief feels euphoric and is not a gauge of a permanent solution. In chronic headache sufferers, for example, nonsteroidal antiinflammatory drugs (e.g., Naprosyn) are for temporary relief of major symptoms (nausea, photophobia, distractibility). Health benefits of the drug can falsely imply the medicine alone is the panacea (Penzien, Rains, Lipchik, & Creer, 2004). On the other hand, when early feedback includes proper information about limited medicine effects *and also discusses the role of relaxation, biofeedback, and cognitive behavior therapy*, for example, the consumer is less idealistic and more pragmatic about the course of migraine treatment. Daniel launched a self-promotional campaign on Facebook operating on misinformation, and was more attune to his inflated image than to the truth or falsehood of his Facebook message. He received misallocated attention for his false claims, and lacked a better resource to boost confidence.

With Cluster B personalities, the precariousness of self-worth is the reason why consumers build pyramids of falsehood to bolster their image and overcome profound insecurity. One solution to absenteeism, tardiness, or the plateau effect is (a) realistic feedback given at the outset of training, (b) small doses of compliments per unit of measured progress only when the consumer attends the training (or rehab), and (c) in-house system of the consumer promoting his or her progress among peers. The chiropractor, for example, could tell Daniel in the first session the pros and cons of manipulations and outline a goal-based schedule for one month. He can even explain how attendance at each training would advance Daniel's progress faster. Moreover, the chiropractor might suggest an in-house or related whiplash support group in which Daniel can share his tidbits of self-admiration and receive *both praise and realistic criticism for his boastfulness.*

3. MOTIVATION (HIGH TO LOW). The impetus for any behavior is always a stimulus in some capacity. Either the stimulus is paired, presented, removed, or intermingles between the operant and respondent events, setting events, and behavioral segments. Properties of the stimuli evoke, elicit, or produce circumstances probable for some behavior. When properties of stimuli *evoke* behavior, that behavior is frequent or infrequent, strong or weak, or long or short, and depends on the rest of the three-term contingency – a contingency consisting of antecedents, behaviors, and consequences. A contingency that cues pleasant or reinforcing consequences always weighs more favorably than contingencies cueing the arrival of punishment. This conclusion comports with research culled from social exchange theory (Ruben, 1998, 1992b). In Cluster B personality disorders, attainment of reinforcers is paramount. Optimal reinforcement is achievable depending on *both* schedule and density of delivery. The consistency of these two variables – schedule and density – determines whether the consumer is motivated or unmotivated.

Motivation is a function of high density, a continuous reinforcement schedule (CRF), or a very low fixed rate (FR) schedule. For egodystonic individuals, their behaviors do not create a mood or emotional balance consistent with some social norm. Instead, they defy social norms by impatiently and insatiably seeking immediate gratification through legal or illegal means. When rewards are instantly available, in large quantities or potency, and the effort exerted for the reward is facile, the motivation (establishing operation) for that reward is very strong and unwavering. For instance, a consumer diagnosed with narcissistic personality learned that punctual attendance for two consecutive days in vocational training earned money. The money also accompanied a chance to earn a job promotion. On this low fixed rate schedule (two-days for the reward), with many (high density of) rewards promised (money, job promotion), motivation is very strong to act immediately.

However, when this schedule thins out, and seems less generous for more effort, motivation disappears rapidly. In other words, as the reinforcement schedule increases (on fixed ratio, variable ratio, fixed interval, or variable interval), plus the amount and rate of behavior increase, as the variety or density of reinforcers decrease, three results can be expected: (1) the establishing operation or motivator is delayed, (b) responses are less robust, and may extinguish (i.e., ratio strain), and (c) extinction may result in nonrecovery of the response (Ferster & Skinner, 1967; Schneider, Sealy, & Montgomery, 2005; Zeiler, 1968). This phenomena explains the predictable cycle of consumers with Cluster B personalities, who shift *arbitrarily* from high production to low production on some task, from eagerness to apathy at work, and from admiration to antipathy toward coworkers or supervisors. Properties of reinforcement are that influential and can be reified into strange or irrational beliefs about people. For example, narcissistic individuals will mistakenly perceive the transition from continuous to partial to intermittent reinforcement schedules as sinister and malicious. They will feel painful deprivations, and blame somebody for acts of irredeemable betrayal.

Robbie, a rehabilitation assistant for brain-injured consumers, met daily with Leroy. Leroy suffered a left-sided, frontal-lobe brain injury three years ago and now lived independently in an apartment contracting with an agency that dispatched Robbie. Before the accident, Leroy was a prominent drug dealer in a local area and accustomed to living an impulsively selfish life of expecting and receiving fast service and pleasure. He also was diagnosed with antisocial and narcissistic personality disorders. He was impatient, angry, and even explosive when his needs went unmet. Three years later, struggling with memory and speech problems (particularly from effects of Broca's aphasia), Leroy appeared *more* humble and tolerant, but was still impulsive. Robbie's goal was to help Leroy with Adult Daily Living Skills (ADLs) and chauffer him around to planned recreational activities. He found Leroy demanding and recalcitrant; but Leroy's anger was most abusive when obstacles arose that forced changes in plans or delayed fulfillment of Leroy's idiosyncratic needs. Robbie felt helpless, clueless, and servitude around Leroy. He knew his capitulation was not benefiting Leroy's overall rehabilitation.

Robbie was grasping for the elusive solution to manage excessive selfish behaviors. This is very difficult since antisocial and narcissistic personalities lack an alternative repertoire of sensitivity or altruism, from which to borrow or even expand upon. One way to manage impulsiveness (establishing operations) for immediate gratification is to employ *concurrent schedules of reinforcement.* Concurrent schedules are when the consumer can choose between any one of two simultaneous simple reinforcement schedules available at any time. One schedule is on a fixed ratio (FR) and variable ratio (VR) schedule. On fixed ratio schedules, some behavior or tasks slow down right after the reinforcer is given, and then picks up again. On variable ratio schedules, there is a high rate of responding, more continuously and resistant to response decay (i.e., a better ratio run). For example, suppose we want to teach Leroy to stay on task talking about relevant tasks for the day. On the FR-schedule, Leroy can listen to whatever radio station he wants (i.e., turn channels continuously) while talking on-task about the day events; or, he can forgo listening to the radio channels, and talk on-task about the schedule for the day (for varying lengths of discussion), followed by the reinforcer of (a) talking about his past drug-dealing days, and (b) engaging in an recreational activity (VR schedule). On the surface, this compound schedule of reinforcement may sound complex or even difficult to implement. However, blended into the natural field segments of Leroy's life, while he is in the car driven to his recreational activity, the procedure flows much easier and is faster for Robbie to control.

4. HISTORY OF TRANSIENT JOBS (HIGH). Job turnover rates are very high among Cluster B personality disorders. The same is true for transience across programs or across different providers. Cluster B-type personality types are impulsive, snap-deciders, and unrealistically expect instant benefits (results) with little investment of effort. On the obverse, when efforts are exerted, proportionally high expectations exist to receive benefits that match the time and effort invested. When this match does not occur, disillusionment results toward the job or program, and it triggers shopping around for new programs or providers. For Cluster B personality disorders, then, self-termination from jobs or programs may occur for five reasons. *First,* the short-term expectations fail to be met. *Second,* approval of the consumer is slow, unlikely, or replaced by disapproval. *Third,* mounting negative feedback or formal reprimands threaten the potential of dismissal. *Fourth,* the consumer cannot perform a task and masks this job deficiency with anger or deflects it onto other problems. *Fifth,* despite how enjoyable or successful the job really is, the consumer obsesses on the prospect that other jobs may pay better, be more challenging, and advance their personal or professional career. The latter belief belongs to the fallacy that the "grass is always greener" somewhere else.

Short-term expectations fail to be met. Entry into any job comes with a natural expectation of hopes, goals, and earning potential. At first sign of these goals falling short, many people may *assertively confront the situation and troubleshoot the problems to either restore goals on track or amicably part from the job if goal recovery is not possible.* Individuals with borderline, narcissistic, and antisocial personalities, in particular, take a different approach. They are impatient when perceived or promised goals remain unmet within a very short latency from the point of being hired. Failure of goals is blamed on the agency, providers, types of services, and underlying prejudice presumably conspiring against the consumer. Rather than diplomatically discuss the unfulfilled goals and amiably compromise on solutions, the consumer adopts a "black and white" or rigidly dogmatic conclusion that unmet goals were intentional and the agency or provider is unworthy of a second chance.

Deshawn, a health coach, witnessed this type of decline in motivation overnight. He was assigned to meet once weekly with Lori, a 45-year-old, recently diagnosed diabetic (type II). His job was to teach her proper dietary food choices, self-administration of insulin, and self-awareness of blood sugar fluctuations to prevent low blood sugar fainting and unconsciousness. Lori, comorbidly diagnosed with narcissistic personality disorder, entered training with a burst of excitement and was overtalkative about the ways she already eats properly and controls her blood sugar. Training involved one-on-one reviews of good practices and some homework given to Lori to log her food-menu and insulin injection schedule. By the third meeting, Lori, of the Jewish faith, saw her glucose levels remain unchanged and noticed her ravenous appetite double. She felt Deshawn was deliberately sabotaging her progress and was anti-Semitic. At the third meeting, her disposition shifted to indifference, cynicism, sarcasm, and she was slightly debative about suggestions given to correct her overeating and unmanaged glucose levels. She quit the program the next day.

The irony is that Lori had a genuinely medical establishing operation to complete the program; she needed to control her diabetes. Deshawn's technical knowledge also was consistent with the curriculum appropriate for Lori's level of learning. The difficulty here was not the pedagogy; it was the absence of any immediate gratification from goals with measurable progress. Detection of measurable progress is very easy using self-monitoring. The use of self-monitoring in behavior change procedures has been highly effective for many challenging, medical symptoms (e.g., Burke, Wang, & Sevick, 2011; Collinge, Yarnold, & Soltysik, 2013; Miltenberger, Fuqua, & Woods, 1998). In Lori's case, and with Cluster B personality disorders, self-monitoring provides instant proof that a procedure is beneficial and worthy of continued practice. Deshawn can supply very simple recording sheets to log daily glucose readings and foods consumed; or he can request the same information be transmitted daily by email to DeShawn. Second, DeShawn can predefine the criteria per day that allows Lori, on her own, to repeat a step or advance to the next step of the procedure. For example, after eating and recording three fruits consumed by mid-day, and three glucose readings of 90-100 mg/dl, Lori can begin Step two of eating only two fruits per day and taking two glucose measures. Self-paced progression through any programmatic steps can provide immediate reinforcement; consumers will *feel motivated and feel they are the ones in charge of their health improvement.*

Disapproval. Self-termination also occurs when the consumer misperceives the provider as an antagonist. More than a conspirator or prejudicial toward the consumer, aspects of the provider's behavior may seem outright mean, negative, or disapproving. The fragile balance between approval and disapproval is very tenuous and may shift unpredictably based on events at the job or training misinterpreted as criticism or rejection. Cluster B personality typologies may react to perceived disapprovers with either hostility, distractibility, or detachment. Hostility, the more common reaction, is defensiveness or verbal combativeness toward the provider's feedback. Distractibility is when the provider deliberately diverts the feedback or discussion to another issue. Detachment is the consumer disconnecting from the perceived aversive situation to escape anxiety, anger, or anguish.

Jerald was a bowling pro (instructor) at a local bowling alley where Shayna went for recreational therapy. Shayna bowled there twice weekly, recovering from a mild temporal closed-head injury. She bowled on two leagues per week at the same bowling alley before her accident, and the recreational therapist recognized the value of this activity to overcome retrograde amnesia and rebuild her confidence. Shayna also was diagnosed with histrionic personality disorder. When she bowled in leagues, she always consulted the pro, who helped to boost her scores beyond a score of 200 points. Currently, however, she found the pro Jerald unsettling. She complained he was uncaring, aloof, rude, and impatient with her. She became frantic, self-deprecatory, and immediately concluded she was unattractive, a bad bowler, and that the pro disapproved of her playing quality. Without consulting the recreational therapist, she unilaterally quit bowling.

Shayna's impulsive decision to end bowling defied her premorbid repertoire of bowling enjoyment and a high bowling average. She clearly mastered the skill of advanced bowling and was comfortable in that exact setting mingling with the pro, Jerald. The error here lied in presuming the environment *qua environment (i.e., the environment itself)* would motivate her bowling and restore her game-playing to baseline levels. Although Shayna threw the ball identically on the soft synthetic lanes, even on her favorite Lanes 24 and 25, she interacted with Jerald differently than before her accident, producing uneasy reactions between both of them. To alleviate her misperception and foster the stimulus generalization hoped for by her bowling at a familiar bowling alley, the recreational therapist can introduce three changes. First, before throwing a bowling ball for practice or the first frame, Shayna can estimate her points overaverage she wants to earn and even identify personal incentives for approximations to her goal. Second, introduce another bowler to bowl in the adjacent lane against which Shayna has to "compete" as she does during her leagues. This change arouses a metaphorical establishing operation; it generates motivation for self-monitoring and incrementally enhances her bowling accuracy per frame. Third, coach Jerald to give feedback on Shayana's bowling in similar words and delivery as done prior to her accident. The histrionic personality feeds off of a high-density reinforcement schedule that can be integrated more naturally through these three interventions.

Negative feedback threatens dismissal. At jobs or in training programs, performance compliance and accuracy depend on the regularity of corrective feedback to guide the learner-consumer on error-free tasks. When feedback is objectively descriptive, points out the functional reasons for errors and ways to ameliorate these errors, and provides opportunities to practice these corrections, most consumers likely view the feedback as constructive and even reinforcing. Individuals with Cluster B personality disorders may view the feedback, no matter how friendly it seems, as a forecast of *worse things to come.* The foreboding fear is that *any feedback* constitutes a threat of job or training dismissal. This traces to a history of conditioning in the reactional biography from severe verbal or physical punishment delivered arbitrary and capriciously for *appropriate or inappropriate behaviors.* The randomness of verbal punishment – its schedules and varying intensities of impact – conditioned the individual to anticipate that *any verbal statements made are automatically condemnatory, humiliating, and induce helplessness.* Such victims of random punishment are notorious for responding in three ways. First, they engage in superstitious-like routines that accidentally and coincidentally in the past delayed or mitigated the punishment (cf. Azrin & Holz, 1966; cf. Skinner, 1948). Second, they engage in preemptive or overreactive aggression to thwart, avert, or escape from the onset of punishment (Ruben, 2014). Third, they resign unrelentingly to the inevitable; they can neither avoid nor escape from punishment other than by immobilization; they become idle, apathetic, labile, and just pout in sorrow (cf. Davis & McIntire, 1969; Jones, 2007; Ratner, 1977; Seligman, Maier, & Greer, 1968). These patterns may occur independently, concurrently, or sequentially.

Janine was a cosmetologist contracted with the psychiatric hospital to cut or trim hair weekly for adult patients on Unit 6, a transitional unit preparing nonsuicidal patients for discharge and aftercare adjustment. She regularly trimmed Maxine's hair, a young 25-year-old female diagnosed with borderline personality who, three months ago, was self-cutting and suicidal. With her moods stabilized on Risperdal and Seroquel, Maxine interacted calmly with unit staff and complied with routines. On the third weekly contact with Maxine, Janine greeted Maxine with praise for combing her hair and freshening up her hygiene. Maxine blinked several times, and then started to roll up her sleeves, roll down her sleeves, and roll up her sleeves again, all synchronized with her blinking. Janine ignored this odd behavior and asked Maxine more about her hair-care for the week. In response, Maxine exploded with a startling utterance of profanity, followed by a series of snipes and cynical comments sprayed at Janine. Again, Janine ignored her; Janine recalled her orientation training of how to selectively ignore strange behavior and instead attend to on-task behaviors. Janine slightly changed the topic to hair styles and what Maxine wanted her hair to look like today. Within minutes, Maxine just sat in the chair mute; she appeared numb, indifferent, placid, and stared in space.

Janine's training in Differential Reinforcement of Alternative Behaviors (DRA) was a lifesaver, in some respects, because it prevented her from overresponding to Maxine's shifting moods or verbal insults. However, what Janine did not realize is that she perseverated on hair-and-hygiene topics provoking Janine into a frenzy of over-reactions. Janine had no idea her questions about hair-and hygiene care during the week *triggered toxic memories of her mother demanding rigid and compulsive rituals of daily hair-washing or else be spanked and yelled at.* To make matters worse, the antecedent of her mother's tirades always began with praise to Janine for hair care and hygiene. In response, Maxine commenced a pattern of field-integrated responses. That is, she connected responses from different "fields of her history" successively merging with the current field of being in the psychiatric hospital with Janine asking her a question.

Despite a strongly intact history of punishment and generality of responses, Maxine can interrupt this predictable cycle of her behaviors. First, when Janine observed the first response class, that of superstitious or ritualistic sleeve-rolling and unrolling, Maxine needed to, not just change the subject-matter, but also change the setting events. She could walk Janine outside of the building or in another room. This escape behavior would relieve anxiety and restore her normal disposition. She can return in the hair salon room after initiation of a different conversation or one started by Maxine. Second, at any time during the cycle of behavior, Janine can provide opportunities for Maxine to regain ("feel in") control. This strategy involves, for example, (a) asking her questions about anything she does well and enjoys talking about, (b) allowing her to move around (stand, sit-down, flounder), and (c) possibly be the planner of the hair-cut from topics to discuss to how she wants her hair done. The essence of this (stimulus) control is to allow escape from aversive setting events, symbolic or otherwise, that reminded her of unpleasant past behaviors.

Failure to perform a task and hiding it. Job or training transience is not always impulsive. Individuals with Cluster B personality disorder may be methodical in their systematic disguise of performance errors to delay being fired or terminated from a program. Anxiety spikes immediately at the mere risk of their mistakes exposed; this arouses humility, vulnerability, and a disturbing feeling of contempt for any person causing them to make this mistake. Anger follows in escalating or explosive rages against the scapegoated instigator; this deflects attention away from the actual person making the error, a subterfuge that allows the individual to appear the perfect employee. Traits of inculpability, nonremorsefulness, and externalization of blame onto other people are prototypical of the antisocial personality disorder. Such individuals may go through extraordinary efforts to justify their innocence, even in the face of obvious facts indicting their performance errors.

Cody worked as a dishwasher at a chain restaurant in a college town. His afternoon shift started at 3 PM and finished by midnight or thereafter. However, by 10:00 PM, Cody became extremely tired. He was never a night owl and loathed his body trying to stay energetic when he wanted to sleep. By the last two hours of his shift, from 10:00 PM to midnight, Cody received his highest volume of dishes to clean since crowds slammed the restaurant in these hours. Cody needed to push his body into overdrive, but he was too exhausted. Instead, he coasted mechanically through the dish-cleaning process and was careless, leaving several dishes marred with food residue before placing them into the dishwasher. When the quality-control supervisor inspected Cody's job, the supervisor politely described the errors of residue and corrective action needed. Cody became livid and erupted with profanity and allegations of harassment. He also accused the bus boys of improperly stacking up foods onto the plates, causing more resistance to feedback. He was so boisterously angry, that he threatened to leave the job unless the bus boys or supervisor apologized for falsely accusing him of wrongdoing.

Cody's exhortations of blame and self-vindication are part of the predictable cycle in Cluster B personality disorders. The rapid onset of an establishing operation to avoid and escape criticism triggers a torrent of fault-finding, while masking the real or underlying deficits (errors) of the accuser. For on-site job coaches recognizing Cody's proclivity for anger, one intervention is to design in advance a highly reinforcement contingency for honest disclosure. Cluster B personalities share traits of selfishness, optimization of personal needs, immediate gratification, and eschewing any obstacles in their paths. When Cody knows, for example, the exact benefit he receives for "admitting a fault," and feels that benefit or reward deeply satisfies him, it will compete with the concurrent avoidance/escape (anger-producing) conditioning paradigm. For example, suppose the supervisor tells Cody that admission of fault, when validated, earns an additional $3.00 bonus. That means, when Cody voluntarily confesses he made a mistake, without rudeness or deception, either before or after the supervisor points it out, he earns this bonus money. The contingency will tempt Cody to engage in honest-expressive behaviors *incompatible* to anger-expressive behaviors.

Other jobs hold better prospects. High job turnover rates can be motivated by an illusion. The illusion is grandiose and evolves from the faulty premise that other higher-paying or more enjoyable jobs are available immediately. In a jobless economy, where the rate of unemployment is 5.5 percent and long-term unemployed is 2.6 million, competition for minimum wage, trade, and many professional jobs is fierce. Job prospects are fewer and require more ingenious craftsmanship on how to carve a path around the flood of job applicants. The disgruntled worker, who has a job paying a livable or even impressive wage, is neither aware of nor cares about this reality of a jobless marketplace. They idealize that *they deserve a better job and anything is better than the monotony of their current job situation.* While it is not unusual for employees to dislike their jobs and imagine a nirvana-job, the plight of Cluster B personality disorders is quite different. Underlying this illusion is a selfishly impulsive reaction to (a) feel victimized, (b) feel deliberately targeted for persecution, and (c) have the magical belief of entitlement to other tempting prospects.

Victimization is when the Cluster B individual mistakenly sees self as the center of the universe. They feel besieged, overwhelmed, and tortured by a merciless supervisor or system operating illogically. The consumer is poorly objective, and cannot see the bigger picture of other employees possibly sharing similar agony *and effectively coping with it.* Instead, their agony seems personal, deliberate and condemnatory. The consumer feels there is an abnormal conspiracy, or collective effort by other coworkers or supervisors to scapegoat the consumer for faulty job performance. As standards change at the job mandating higher volume of or more accurate work, that standard is misinterpreted as singling out the one consumer as the target to "be made an example of." This self-absorbing paranoia launches into a *magical mand* (Lamarre & Holland, 1985; Skinner, 1957) of the employee announcing he or she is really invaluable, overlooked for their greatness, and would be unconditionally courted at any other job.

This same magical mand regarding inflated value at jobs also applies to any service or training the consumer receives; the belief is that there is always a better service than the current one received. In physical therapy for five weeks, individuals with Cluster B personality may entertain the luring notion of switching to another physical therapist. While the therapy received at the current physical therapist is appropriate and positive, the *illusion that a better physical therapist exists and is superior to the current inferior one* is the visceral spark that motivates therapist shopping.

Mckenna was a vocational counselor trying to stabile the precarious job performance of 62-year-old Sheila, employed as an examiner analyst in a state position. With only a Bachelor's degree education, Sheila was earning an exceptionally high income combining her regular and overtime pay. She fully admitted this income would be hard to duplicate in the private sector for her limited education and background. Still, she constantly complained of job tedium, supervisor harassment, unfair management practices, and feeling powerless. She overlooked the perks of the job, her financial autonomy and materialistic purchasing power, her convenience of working close to her house, and the fact that she could stay at this job undisturbed for three years until she retired. For Sheila, diagnosed with borderline personality disorder, her universe was always incomplete. She felt empty, useless, cheated, betrayed, deprived, and prohibited from pursing self-enriched jobs she insisted were available outside of the state system that fit her needs perfectly. McKenna focused purely on the advantages of Sheila's current job, and ignored speculations about Sheila leaving this job to be happy in nonstate jobs.

Sheila's perception of job paradise predicated on the illusion that greatness lied at her fingertips for another job. She persuaded herself to believe her credentials were impeccable and likely respected and admired by imaginary employers. This inflated perception is like making a request for a consequence that never occurred for that mand (i.e., her belief she can get hired), but seems probable *of occurring* given the distortion that *it should occur under similar circumstances.* Prayer is a good example. People pray on the *faith* that they may go to Heaven. Since this mand never directly produced this outcome for them, they rely on similar mands that generate proximal goals. Examples might be prayer during confession or fasting on holy days to receive exoneration of misdeeds during the year. Cluster B personality traits typically include many magical mands often compelling irrational decisions, later regretted. Several strategies to reduce magical mands begin with common workplace interventions for job satisfaction and autonomy. These include (a) increasing independent decision making, (b) setting one's work hours with flex time. (c) more control over job performance criteria, and (d) balanced distribution of negative and positive feedback (Ivancevich & Konopaske, 2013; Ruben, 1989). After engineering a more self-reinforcing (self-managed) workplace, the next step is training of realistic mands. This involves a series of achievable goals agreed upon in advance with the consumer that the consumer "promises to reach," in small gradients. For example, McKenna and Sheila together might agree that her accrued hours allow her to take off every other Friday. During the week, McKenna encouraged Sheila to state *what she plans to do on that day off, and how the task needs to be achievable that day.*

5. COWORKER RELATIONS (POOR/BAD). Coworker relations is a subset of the cultural peer matrix embodied in the consumer's job or training environment. It describes the capacity to interact interpersonally, both on verbal and nonverbal levels, reciprocally, and without hostility or passive-aggressive (indirect) sabotage of the social exchange. In many work settings, ample time exists for formation of casual coworker relations, whether at break, lunch, before or after work, or while in collaborative-team meetings and projects. Coworker communication varies from brief sharing of conversational topics (e.g., "Gee, it's really hot out today, isn't it?") to formal discussions. When coworker exchanges run smoothly, interoffice friction is minimal, communication is bilateral, and production rates remain steady or increase. Contrariwise, when coworker communication is poor or hostile, interoffice friction intensifies and sabotages morale, let alone decreases overall production rates. Individuals with Cluster B personality commonly contribute to the latter work environment. They are selfishly ostentatious, rebellious, aggressive, controlling, noncooperative, and randomly moody. Their unpredictable behaviors not only upset the workforce equilibrium, but, on a personal basis, it repels coworkers from closeness. For this reason, Cluster B personality types may outwardly seem fond of the spotlight and courageously outgoing. But their clownish, sarcastic, or excessive demands are too intense, impersonal, or offensive to tolerate on a daily basis.

Keanna was a psych tech in an outpatient community center in the suburb of a metropolitan city. She frequently saw patients (consumers) once or twice weekly who attended the center for group or individual therapy and joined in with other healing groups involved with handcraft projects. Clarence was one of the patients, diagnosed with antisocial personality disorder from a chronic history of juvenile and adult felonies, nonremorsefulness, gross disregard for other people's feelings, and a volatile temper. In the community center, Clarence both attended therapy and worked for pay as the janitor. After one week of his new job, Clarence was outspoken about the need for (a) updated supplies for cleaning, (b) the mediocrity of coworkers, and (c) the moronic nature of his job. He also teased the shorter men of having a Napoléon complex and teased the women for never wearing make-up. While none of his comments were offensive per se, they bordered on harassment and insults. Other workers and consumers at the outpatient center politely laughed at Clarence's jokes and humored him about his job-related complaints. But none of the coworkers invited him to after-work functions or confided personally in him. When given their druthers, they preferred to stay away from Clarence.

Clarence never felt abject regret for his mistreatment of coworkers and other consumers at the community center. He dismissed their feelings and felt arrogantly righteous about voicing his opinions until somebody listened to him. Keanna, a witness to Clarence's improprieties, recognized two problems. One was that his negative comments repelled people. A second problem was Clarence's insensitivity to the physical or other traits of other people. Keanna consulted with personnel at the community center to rewrite the job contract with Clarence entailing two new duties. First, included was that he must pay three to four compliments per daily either to different coworkers or consumers. Compliments were general about the activities or work efforts he observed. Second, he was introduced to two subcomponents of the sensitivity and benevolence training package used for shaping uncaring adolescent and adults with empathy skills (Ruben, 2000). The two components consisted of (a) asking how the consumer or coworker felt about something, and (b) an unprompted gesture of assistance with some task or project for the coworker or consumer. Coached rehearsal of these duties on the job, including reminder prompts, helped Clarence spot the right opportunities to apply the skills, and to proportionally decrease his cynical and sarcastic remarks.

6. SUPERVISOR RELATIONS (POOR/BAD). Job relationships presume a degree of trust among coworkers. But a more difficult relationship for Cluster B personality types to trust is with supervisors. Supervisors signify "authority" roles in the hiring, firing, and administration of job duties including feedback on those duties. In nonjob capacities, "authorities" may be the provider as monitor, coach, advisor, or liaison between different paraprofessionals overseeing the larger picture of training implementation. For example, the authority may be a site manager or clinical director of a program observing a physical therapist administer a protocol of techniques. Dislike of that authority (supervisor) partly may stem from past aversive contact with that same or dif-

ferent authorities, for which the consumer or client is now suspicious and anticipates an unfriendly encounter. Dislike may also stem from metaphorical factors, or those relevant features closely or remotely resembling authority-like figures in the past, with whom the consumer had altercations. Such past incidents of aversive contact possibly included with a parent, school principal, police officer, football coach, probation officer, or even camp counselor. Dislike of the authority may also stem from no-relevant or *irrelevant* properties of the current or any past contact with authorities. For example, it's not *what the football coach said or did to the consumer years ago, it was his beard that muffled his words. Now, every time the consumer hears criticism from an authority-male wearing a beard that muffles his words, instant animosity arises.*

Stimulus (verbal) control from irrelevant features is called *metonymical extension* (Skinner, 1957). This extension may be hard to trace to subtle or remote irrelevant properties, most of which elude the consumer. When subtle irrelevant properties cannot be readily found, generalized beliefs emerge to replace detection of subtle stimulus properties. These beliefs or *rules begin to govern how the consumer perceives and reacts to the authority figure (with irrelevant properties).* The rule likely states that any person *who challenges, delays, or prevents fulfillment of my immediate needs is the enemy.* Antisocial, borderline, and narcissistic personalities, in particular, are inventors of these common rules regarding authorities or supervisors; they conclude the authority figures are deliberately malicious, surreptitious, and controlling. Fears abound that the controller will somehow infiltrate and expose the consumer's weaknesses, rendering the consumer indefensible. Consumers then feel inferior, helpless, paranoid, and highly susceptible to *what feels like an* avalanche of manipulation by everybody they know.

Operationally, *paranoia is an adventitious effect of random punishment occurring over many behavioral segments, each involving similar conditions of inescapable and unavoidable exposure to unpredictable aversive events.* In the most classic example, children spanked for arbitrary reasons at home, and later in schools are harassed in school by teachers or peers for arbitrary reasons, come to expect that everybody *is arbitrary and cannot be trusted (i.e., paranoia).* One way that children, or in adulthood, consumers counter this powerlessness is with anger. Cluster B personality types frequently explode into verbal rages at any time they sense arbitrariness of punishment, even when the punishment is not arbitrary and instead is very logical. A police officer pulling over a motorist for speeding may present the obvious facts of how fast the motorist drove over the speed limit. However, despite this palpable evidence, the motorist erupts instantly with defensiveness and vulgarity, charging the officer with scapegoating and ethnic profiling. The motorist *anticipated punishment and immediately engaged in aggressive behaviors to delay, mitigate, or terminate the punishment entirely.*

Damian was a new employee in a welding shop. He received impressive recommendations from his job references. On the job itself, Damien performed impeccably, was safety-sensitive to OSEAH policies in the shop, and respectful of his coworkers. He also was previously diagnosed with borderline and narcissistic personality disorders. After two months of uneventful production in the shop, new materials for welding arrived in the shop that required extra cleaning and prepping of materials to prevent foreign matter from getting into the bead. Damian's supervisor Garrett kindly sent paper notices around to each welder of this safety precaution. Garrett also took the time to visit each welder personally and explain this enhanced policy in case questions arose and to assure compliance. When Garrett approached Damian, Damian was immediately livid, curt, insulting, and accused Garrett of belittling him with the indignity of thinking Damien might "screw up" and not form a proper bond to weaken the weld. Damian's temper also seemed "to be on auto-pilot." His face got red, arms and hands tensed up, and his speech quickly got louder and faster. As he shouted, his rapid words became more vulgar and intense, as if his words triggered more of his anger.

The two common observed behaviors in Damien's outburst included *anticipatory aggression* and *self-stimulatory (autoclitic mand) behaviors.* As discussed earlier, anticipatory aggression is a common behavior found in children and adults. In Damien's case, he pre-emptively responded with anger to avoid or escape from any risk of confrontation with Garrett, although, in reality, there was no confrontation with Garrett. Damien falsely anticipated there would be conflict, improperly generalizing his behavior from other behavioral field segments in Damien's life. The second behavior is self-stimulatory behaviors ("stimming"). Here, also discussed earlier, is when the autonomic arousal (e.g., proprioceptive stimuli) by itself generated more excitability in Damien's body and speech, regardless of the events around him. This means his vestibular, auditory, tactile, and other senses propelled more of his behavior independently. The calmness of Garrett, although visibly obvious, had no effect on the self-generative or self-reinforcing pattern of Damien's escalation. In addition, each verbalization Damien made (e.g., profanity, name-calling) occasioned a cue to spiral Damien's anger further. Since anger is self-stimulatory, it would seem resistant to external intervention.

Reactionary and self-stimulatory angry behaviors risk high resistance to external contingencies (particularly to "extinction" or ignoring it), unless the contingencies have properties more influential than the rewarding properties of self-stimulation. Research over the last four decades have amassed a litany of effective interventions designed to displace the powerful reinforcing properties of self-stimulatory behaviors (Lovaas, Newsom, & Hickman, 1987; Rincover, Cook, Peoples, & Packard, 1979). One particular intervention, originally used for autistic children and adult self-aggressors, is called *evoked response arousal plus sensitization* (Ruben, 2009). It is designed to reproduce the same, *if not more*, visceral (autonomic) arousal experienced during self-stimulation. However, the new competing sensation is paired with unpleasant properties. The goal of this procedure is for any angry child or adult to increase anxiety and awareness of other people observing him or her during the angry episode; this decreases the child's and adult's spontaneous and automatic angry outbursts. Let's consider this procedure more closely.

Two preconditions for using this procedure for adults include:

1. *The aggressive adult must possess basic social skills.* This means simple communication skills are intact. Social skill facility does not mean a popular, likeable, or attractive adult.
2. *Select a minimum of three adults who are reinforcing to the aggressive adult.* "Reinforcing" means the preselected adults all share the following properties of interest to the aggressive "target" adult.
   a. The aggressive adult looks for and is aware of the presence or absence of the reinforcing adults. The aggressive adult may "prospect" by looking to see where the reinforcing adults are.
   b. The aggressive adult imitates the gestures, postures, speech, or other behaviors of the preselected adults.
   c. The aggressive adult never exhibits the aggressive (violent, self-stimulatory) behavior around these reinforcing adults.

The steps of evoked response arousal plus sensitization follow this sequence:

1. During the adult's outburst, ask one selected adult to stand far away from the aggressive adult and watch the aggressive adult. Distance guarantees the aggressive adult will not dart after and hurt the spectator. Nobody around the self-stimulator says or does anything directly to the stimulator.

2. After the adult engages in verbal or other self-stimulatory anger, wait for the outburst to expire or subside. Remove objects around the aggressive adult during the burst, as if the adult had a grand mal seizure. Pay no attention to self-stimulator while the burst progresses.

3. Once the aggression stops, verbally (or otherwise) prompt the angry adult to walk in front of, first, one adult peer he or she knows. These peers hold a special relationship with the angry adult. Around these special adults, the angry adult rarely blows up, and may even show respect. In fact, the angry adult may show exceptional maturity around these selected people. Recruit only one of these people the first time around. Tell the angry adult to apologize for the outburst. No matter what the adult says or does not say, note the discomfort or mild anxiety manifested when facing the adult peer. *It is not necessary for the angry adult to actually apologize or say anything verbally to the adult you selected.*

4. After each successive angry outbursts, after it subsides, repeat the same steps. Now increase the number of "special people" selected to watch and be in front of the angry adult as the outburst occurs. Prompt the angry adult to apologize to each of these "spectators" at the end of each burst. Even if no apology is made, keep the angry adult in visual contact with the adult peers for two to five minutes after the anger expires.

5. When visual contact with special people is impossible, since there are no other people physically around, use the telephone for an *auditory contact or camcorder* for visual contact (e.g., with I-pad, I-phone, Skype). Repeat the same directions with the angry adult on the phone or other social media with the special, selected person.

Why does this procedure work? Here's the first clue. Let's begin with a well-established phenomenon that anxiety sharply increases an individual's acuity or awareness of objects and people surrounding that individual at the moment (e.g., Kimble, Boxwala, Bean, Maletsky, Halper, Spollen, & Fleming, 2014). This enhanced state of sensory sensitivity or *hypervigilance* usually involves an exaggerated or *hyper-aware-ness* to relevant and irrelevant details affecting the individual. More practically, as anxiety rises and triggers hypervigilant states, the angry consumer is now more acutely aware of his or her surrounds; they are clued into other people's verbal and nonverbal (body) language. Abnormally high responsiveness is to *external* stimuli, and not to the adult's *internal self-stimulation*. This redirected attention (to external stimuli) interferes with the pattern of self-stimulatory behaviors. That is, the angry adult experiences nervousness or anxiety (unpleasant effect). This anxiety competes with and replaces the self-stimulation (pleasant effect) as the new controlling stimulus for the anger. Anxiety sensations (unpleasant effect) interfere with and disrupt the seamless sequence of ritualistic self-stimulatory (angry) patterns. When this seamless sequence unwinds, breaks apart, and loses its chain-link effect, the self-stimulatory (angry) behavior rapidly deteriorates. The result is a major reduction in subsequent self-stimulatory angry outbursts. In future episodes, the angry adult may look around, first, before launching into anger. Or, during angry outbursts, the angry adult may suddenly stop, look around for the adult spectators, and then resume the outburst. In both cases, the frequency and magnitude of self-stimulatory anger reduce significantly.

In Damien's case, Garrett would, first, ignore Damien's self-escala-tive angry answers. Second, during Damien's outbursts, Garrett might arrange one of Damien's close coworkers to watch Damien's outburst from a remote spot. As soon as Damien stops yelling and is calm, Garrett asks him to apologize for his behavior to his observer-friend. Damien will likely refuse, protest, or even rebelliously challenge Garrett, who again ignores Damien. An hour later, Garrett approaches Damien a second time about a job issue; Garrett now arranges two of Damien's close friends to watch him. Damien, again, is vehement about not apologizing. By the third time Garrett approaches Damien in the day, *Damien does not immediately explode with rage*; he first scans the room to see if any of his buddies are on patrol, watching him. When nobody is found, Damien slightly escalates verbally and, then, sudden-ly stops his verbal ranting. He looks around the room again to make sure none of friends are present. He then resumes his anger but with less intensity. The anxiety of knowing if his friends were present super-seded the adrenaline or other sensory excitement of verbally yelling. Within two to three days, Damien ceased the anger response to Garrett and just thanked him for sharing OSEAH's new regulations.

7. SUBSTANCE ABUSE (HIGH). Substance abuse in the workplace is a universal problem (e.g., Bush & Autry, 2002). Reduced work production, unsafe work performance, low morale, peer rivalry, and violence all rank as the top reasons for antidrug polices enforcing strict penalties for violations. One of these policies for positive drug screens, when unexcused by preauthorized medical statements, is a substance abuse evaluation. Likewise, a positive score on a random breathalyzer test may invoke immediate job suspension while the evaluation is scheduled. Under Federal regulations (49 CFR, part 40, subpart O) for the Department of Transportation, all state, federal, or private sector agencies engaged in safety-sensitive duties (e.g., driving a UPS or FEDEX truck) mandate the use of evaluations as the first step of triage to determine the corrective rehabilitation steps needed before the employee can return to work (US Department of Transportation, 2015). This means the employee's job is retained for a period of suspension while he or she undergoes the recommended course of residential or outpatient treatment. Once evidence appears the employee met the recommendations and is now drug-free or otherwise capable of return to a safety-sensitive job duty, medical release is given to the employee, providing he or she still submits to another drug or alcohol screening on the day of work re-entry; the employee also agrees to up to six more drug or alcohol screenings over the next year.

Despite these office safeguards, the highest risk employees or consumers abusing substances on or around the job are Cluster B personality disorders. Their traits of impulsiveness, mood and anger volatility, disregard for social norms and rules, selfishness, and propensity for self-stimulation correlate positively with careless drug habits that are dangerous in work settings (cf. Haase, 2009). Frequently, "the drug or alcohol problem" results from self-medication of unwanted symptoms of hyperactivity, cyclical anger, mood dysregulation, or in coping with anticipated conflict situations. In treating alcoholic individuals with borderline personality disorder, for example, recidivism rates were very high since the abuser feared a deluge of unhappiness, vulnerability, and anxiety in sober states (Gianoli, Jane, O'Brien, & Ralevski, 2012). Similar fears of returning baseline symptoms occurred in post-traumatic stress disordered consumers with comorbid Cluster B personality disorders (cf. Leeies, Paguar, Sareen, & Bolton, 2010). In both cases, overuse of substance was to mask the anxiety precipitating unwanted symptoms. Consequently, the central variable among Cluster B personalities involving substance abuse is *panic*.

Histrionic personality types *panic* when they feel overwhelmed by routine stressors and immediately dramatize the expected catastrophes that lie ahead. Borderline personality types *panic* when entrusted people abandon them and they feel anxiously lonely and desperate to reconnect to another lifeline for support. Narcissistic personality types *panic* when the spotlight on them fades or is abruptly removed and replaced by a torrent of inescapable and unavoidable criticism that restricts their hedonistic lifestyle. For example, take the partier and charismatic drinker who enjoys the "fame" from his karaoke talents. He gets a DUI on the way home from the bar. Now he must avoid bars, and remain sober tethered to a leg bracelet that randomly samples blood alcohol content, also called Secure Continuous Remote Alcohol Monitor (SCRAM). In his perspective, his world "just ended." Anti-social personality typologies panic when their rebellious or over-the-top aggressive behaviors backfire with social or legal consequences, forcing them to be humble, benevolent, and martyrdom-like. For example, after overdrinking at two parties and cavalierly engaging in sexual relations with two no-strings-attached partners, the consumer learns nine months later he fathered a child in both of them; this news suddenly means a drain on his finances, and doubles his social and legal responsibilities. He must change his sociopathic behaviors to accommodate his new paternity-benevolent role. These "systems-like" factors impinge on his life from multiple directions, ruining his optimal stimulus control over *simple contingencies* and exposing him to *complex contingences* under the new control of the children's mothers and Friend of the Court (or equivalent legal system) (cf. Ruben, 1999).

Panic reactions require panic reduction methods. Such methods coexist with substance abuse prevention in the workplace and in training programs. Whether on a high-demanding job or in rehabilitation program, the solution lies with *reinstatement of control*. Panic escalates when reinforcement abruptly stops or aversive conditions abruptly start, in either case challenging an unprepared individual to respond in ways atypical or incapable with their existing repertoire or from a deficient reactional biography. When clearly definable steps provide the "bread crumbs" that *guide or promise* a pathway to restored contingency control, panic levels diminish quickly. Trust is regained in the provider, agency, or employer who supplies that contingency control. Since panic reduction methods eliminate the anxiety triggering panic, less substance abuse may be needed to mask anxiety and panic symptoms. However, *just how much* substance abuse is reduced depends on the pre-existing (premorbid) rate of substance use before panic symptoms became a problem in the consumer's life.

Matilda was a regular client (consumer) of John, her Health Professional Coach hired by Matilda's employer; John oversaw Matilda's drug recovery aftercare program. He monitored her attendance at Narcotics Anonymous (NA) meetings, weekly therapy sessions, and twice weekly random urine drops, a part of relapse prevention for her prescription opioid addiction (Vicodin, Darvocet, Oxycodone). Her job depended on Matilda's adherence to this drug-rehabilitation regimen and compliance with John's advice and feedback. Matilda also was diagnosed with borderline personality disorder. Within two weeks of abstinence, Matilda felt anxious, worried, obsessive, and realized these symptoms resembled the frenzy of feelings suffered before she got hooked on opiate synthetics. Matilda panicked and called John nightly complaining that her world had turned upside-down; she felt suicidal, hated, abandoned by her support system, and passionately pled for John to "rescue" her. John recognized Matilda's panic reaction was tempting her to relapse with self-medication. He outlined a very concrete series of simple steps for her to interrupt the anxiety symptoms, including which providers to see, how to follow their homework assignments, and how much to expect her symptoms to subside each day over the duration of one to two weeks. He also provided her access to check in with him via email every day. John's structure of new (reinforcing) contingences prevented Matilda's "meltdown." More importantly, his intervention restored her control over *some contingencies* to relieve helplessness and prevent self-medication with opioids.

8. VIOLENCE (HIGH). Angry or violent reactions in a work or therapy setting are always variable. Variability depends on (a) poor control over establishing operations (i.e., impulsivity), (b) history of aggression reactivating delayed establishing operations, (c) absence of any systems effects of punishment for volatile or lethal behaviors, and (d) other concurrent reinforcing properties produced from the aggression proportionally stronger than the punishment effects. All four of these criteria for variability of violence exist in Cluster B personality disorders. This makes the Cluster B personality disorder at high risk for workplace or agency violence. The most interesting criterion for violence is (d) that

of reinforcement generated from violence that supersedes the punishing effects of violence. This is due, in part, to a phenomenon called *behavioral contrast effects.* Behavioral contrast effect means that the rate of responding to a stimulus in one setting changes when the condition of the reinforcement changes in another setting. There are two types of contrasts: positive and negative. Positive contrast is when the response *increases* to a more favorable reward after being exposed to a reinforcer (stimulus condition) that has become less-favorable. In negative contrast, the response *decreases* for a less-favorable reward after being exposed to a reinforcer which is clearly more favorable; in this case, research on behavioral contrast effects largely if not exclusively pertained to properties of reinforcement (Catania, 1992; Gross, 1981). The essence underlying behavioral contrast effects it this: *exposure rates to different stimuli within and across multiple, integrated fields in one's life can directly influence how the individual responds in any one of those fields.*

In everyday life, we see the phenomenon of behavioral contrasts at work for "normal reasons." Billy dated Susan on Tuesday night and saw a movie together after they ate at a steak restaurant. While this was reinforcing, the next night Billy dated Beth and not only enjoyed a steak meal and a movie but had sexual intercourse with her that night. Billy, we would say, experienced a *positive contrast effect in that he increased his future responses to Beth (the more favorable reward) after exposed to a reward (Susan) who became less-favorable.* But with respect to violence, there is a different spin on this contrast effect theory more aligned with the study by Harrison and Pepitone (1972). Here, in a study using rats, two conditions existed. In the experimental condition, a prohibited degree of punishment (extremely painful lever) is present but not accessible, while a lesser degree of punishment (moderately painful lever) is permissible. The rats, like human beings, chose the absolute frequency and relative intensity of a weaker permissible level of punishment providing the stronger level of punishment was unavailable or inaccessible. If the stronger level of punishment were not prohibited, the rats, like human beings, would choose it instead. Results comported with the classic Milgram study showing how a person's propensity for inflicting violence varied with accessibility to (authority who permitted) higher levels of punishment (Milgram, 1963, 1974)

Similarly, in the workplace or in rehabilitation settings, when opportunities *provide a contrast of permissible and nonpermissible levels of punishment options, higher-risk violent consumers may choose the least punishing option if the most punishing option is prohibited.* Cluster B personality types may listen to a calm, soft-spoken supervisor give criticism (i.e., permissible, moderately painful stimulus), while informed of a zero-tolerance policy for any jobsite violence (prohibited extremely painful stimulus). Here, the consumer selects to listen to the supervisor's criticism versus face the risk of violating policy and being terminated. The clarity of these contrasting contingencies occasions more accurate discrimination and thereby controls the Cluster B individual's proclivity for aggression and violence. However, the problem in most job or rehabilitation sites is *the ambiguity of permissible and nonpermissible contingencies, about which the consumer has received inconsistent consequences.* When the conditions are unclear and options for extremely painful infliction remain permissible (available, accessible), aggression readily turns to violence.

DeMar sewed military uniforms at a local factory contracting with the federal government. His job entailed following a template for sewing zippers onto clothing and passing on his unit to a quality inspector. Renee was DeMar's onsite therapist and job coach, making sure he followed instructions and generally met the quota of certain clothing units per hour. DeMar began the job six months ago after serving 15 years in prison for drug delivery and possession, a trade he capitalized on since he was 12 years old. As a child, he went in and out of juvenile detention, was diagnosed with conduct disorder, and in adulthood received the diagnosis of antisocial personality disorder. DeMar, having a bad temper himself, once witnessed a supervisor down the corridor yelling at a worker. When the worker yelled back, the supservisor grabbed the worker and police were called to tackle the worker, numb him with a taser (an electric-shock, nonlethal weapon), and escort the worker out of the building. He witnessed a second occasion of a supervisor-employer argument; in this case, the supervisor got angry, triggering a violent threat by the worker to hit the supervisor. The supervisor backed down immediately and surrendered to the worker's terms. DeMar figured the second example gave him the courage to repeat a similar protest against the quality inspector when the inspector told DeMar he was lazy and a bad worker.

The problem with one field of events availing permissible lethal punishment while another field of events prohibits lethal punishment is that individuals prone to inflict harm will nearly always select the route of lethal punishment. When harmful words or objects (weapons) are visible, it provokes a propensity for infliction of aggression, such as when the National Guard dress in riot gear and weaponry to control unruly crowds and the crowds intensify violence in response. One option, in the police field, was to use less lethal weapons such as rubber pellet guns, tasers, or tear gas. However, aversive effects of even these alternative, less violent devices can equally instigate crowd aggression.

On the job or in an agency, and relative to the behavioral contrast phenomenon, the task is to (a) conspicuously and consistently present clear delineation between prohibited (extremely painful) and permissible (moderately or low painful) punishment, (b) provide opportunities for the at-risk angry consumers to not only apply but then to teach to others this delineation, and (c) a concurrent contingency of more-favorable reinforcers for abiding by the proper discrimination of punishment. That is, reinforcement is for *not getting angry or volatile on the job and teaching this rule (based on the contrast effects) to other coworkers.*

9. OFFICE CRIME (HIGH). Impulsivity and retribution are the primary pathologies in Cluster B personalities contributing to a high degree of office crime. Violent or nonviolent office crimes are rarely the product of methodical, collaborative, or time-patience planning. Reactions are robustly spontaneous when office politics, supervisor insults, or other roadblocks disrupt the consumer's establishing operation (EO) for wanting *anything*; these disruptions to the EO exponentially increase instant revenge, even if the revenge (and crime) threaten imminent job termination. More closely understood, the impulsiveness of anger, as suggested earlier, is a function of *anticipatory aggression.* The consumer reacts pre-emptively to avoid or escape the anticipated confrontation. Rarely does impulsive anger occur *purely* for the reinforcing valence of a hostile interchange. Hostility for *the sake of hostility (i.e., automaticity of reinforcement)* is uncommon and may occur when: (a) there is self-stimulation or visceral arousal paired with anger responses, or (b) there is normalcy and sense of comfort from a childhood history of exposure to extreme punishment. Otherwise, anticipatory aggression is a deflector, a decoy, and never really intended to inflict damage on a person. As for retribution, this behavior functions to relieve current anxiety and *anticipatory anxiety* of some impending and recurrent punishment. That is, to "get one back for what he did to me" translates (operationally) into "I must stop the ongoing punishment and try to stall or prevent more punishment in the future." Acts of retaliation for many people can be indirect or subtle such as stealing clerical supplies.

But for Cluster B personality disorders, retaliation is more immediate, grandiose, violent, or threatens violence of a more audacious and conspicuous nature.

Marlene was a nurse practitioner in an OBGYN's office and saw her patient Madelyn once weekly during her pregnancy due to high-risk factors such as Madelyn having three prior miscarriages, and her prepartum diagnosis of Hepatitis C. Madelyn was also diagnosed by her psychiatrist with borderline personality disorder. By her first trimester, Marlene noticed signs of increased hypertension and inquired about any lifestyle problems possibly accounting for the elevation. Madelyn exploded into anger and rebuked Marlene for insinuating she was "mental" and not in control over her life. Madelyn also threatened to contact the local state Board of Nursing to report Marlene for her unethical misconduct of making these accusations. Dumbfounded, Marlene initially defended herself and then apologized for the misunderstanding. But Madelyn did not accept her apology; she continued to complain about her emotional injury from Marlene's comment, and then stormed out of the examination room. On her way out, she took five of the pens with the office practice logo on them. She also took the latest *People Magazine* out of the lobby.

Madelyn's anger is *not because she is an angry person*. Madelyn felt vulnerable, became frightened (anxious), and immediately raised her shield of defensiveness with anticipatory aggression. She also filched items from the doctor's office to relieve her anxiety and to hopefully *send a message to them that they (i.e., Marlene) better not do this again to her.* The "message" is a magical mand, in that this crime never *really produced the consequence idealized by the mand.* Marlene reified her theft to believe it might generate this outcome, when actually all the theft did was to temporarily relieve Madelyn's anxiety about the future, that is, relieve her *anticipatory anxiety.*

One possible solution is for Marlene to inform Madelyn that, at the outset of the brief physical exam, Marlene will be looking at Madelyn's maternity health and offering comments. Marlene can also describe *exactly how Madelyn can respond to the questions asked of her and how both can handle the criticism.* This preparatory behavior sets an occasion for the consumer to prepare for and not be surprised by the imposition of fear-induced behaviors; the consumer (i.e., Madelyn) also knows the outcome is favorable. This preparatory instruction is a type of mand requesting behavior and creating an establishing operation for some likely reinforcer. Such mands also reduce potential for aggression since it allows the volatile consumer to *know what is going on, and to control the circumstances.* For example, Marlene might invite Madelyn to answer "yes or no" or permit her to elaborate on one or two replies, in response to which Marlene kindly thanks her for calm answers. More than a deterrent to anger, engineering this stimulus control for Madelyn also lowers lingering anxiety and the need to eliminate the anxiety with stealing.

10. PROGRAM COMPLIANCES (LOW). Job and program compliance presumes a prerequisite of conformity. Cluster B personality disorders characterize individuals who are nonconformists; they defy rules, norms, mores, boundaries, policies, and any structure governing therapy or rehabilitation. They operate on egocentric motives for immediate gratification at the unremorseful expense of the surrounding social community. They may disagree, challenge, or outright rebel against traditions and institutional practices, not on philosophical or political principle, but because the standards delay, reduce, or prevent fulfillment of their personal goals. Their perception of self-fulfillment goals also differ widely from the "normal" or commonly prescribed goals in some job or agency setting. For example, in an outpatient treatment using Suboxone as the antagonist to control opioid addiction, the consumer may voluntarily quit therapy after one month of "feeling" his or her addiction is permanently in remission. Or, in alcohol outpatient programs using SCRAMs or weekly random drug screenings, the consumer may demand the removal of SCRAM or to thin out the random schedule of drops in view of his or her *amazing* display of sobriety. This self-imposed goal pleases the consumer but is discrepant with or even contradictory to the medical goals of using Suboxone or SCRAM.

Overconfidence leading to violations of rules or standards in agencies is not any different than rewriting the criteria for success in jobs. Cluster B personality consumers employed at entry levels in apprenticeship (electrical, plumbing, heating-cooling) programs are neophyte tradesmen; they may inflate their projected skills and expect honorable recognition in a short time. They are unwilling to pay the "sweat equity" dues expected in most training or apprenticeship programs, in developing a skill through exhaustive trials and error under the guidance of an experienced mentor. In degreed-occupations such as a school teacher or engineer, the nascent learner who is Cluster B personality is the same way. The consumer believes his or her knowledge after two or three months of employment matches, if not exceeds, the senior or more experienced peers in the same field. On this misassumption, they are bewildered when overlooked for job promotions. Egocentricity interferes with acknowledgement of their inexperience and the consumer becomes livid and blames the employer with ignorance and discriminating against youthful workers.

One nationwide trend that, ironically, sympathizes with sentiments of the Cluster B personality type in young workers, views the plight of millennials or *generation Y* as misunderstood. Generation Y is the demographic cohort that follows generation X, and typically covers birthdates ranging from the 1980s to the early 2000s (Strauss & Howe, 2000). This same generational group also received the undistinguished label of *boomerang generation or Peter-Pan generation*, since the members' perceived the need to go through rites of passage into experience as useless. They believed emergence to adulthood began in their younger adult years and entitled them to fame and fortune enjoyed by their senior competitors. These senior competitors, as often overlooked, took a lifetime to achieve these accolades (cf. Alsop, 2008). One organization even dispatches what are called *generational experts*. These are millennials (20-, 30-year-olds) and baby boomers (40-, 50-year-olds) who lecture and consult on the art of closing the generation gaps between younger and older workers (millennials vs. baby boomers). The multigenerational solutions provided for a harmonious workplace include, among other things, (a) respecting the millennial's knowledge of social media and seeing its business value, (b) reducing ageistic stereotyping (particularly of the millennials), and (c) understanding differences in the personality of each generation (cf. Lancaster & Stillman, 2003). On the latter, Lancaster and Stillman (2003) described generational personalities of Americans born between 1900 and 1945 as "God-fearing," hardworking, and patriotic. The Baby-boomers, also hard-working, were more idealistic, born in late 1950 through 1970s. The millennials, albeit stereotyped as slackers with a poor work ethic, are viewed as visionaries, motivated, and question indentured traditions.

The upside of this personality-driven theory of a multigeneration workplace is the respect for younger workers and the advocacy for them to compete fairly for top positions, largely occupied by highly experienced workers. The downside of this personality theory is its lack of empirical and *social* validity. Earlier sociological research apparently disputed this multigenerational, personality theory; put simply, results showed, as it always has with workers, that focus belongs on *individual behavior and work differences* rather than on generalized stereotypes about generation demography (see Wong, Gardiner, Lang, & Coulon, 2008). More to the point, the opinions proselytized by generational experts unmistakably echo the same rhetoric expressed by Cluster B personalities. This conviction is that *young consumers have the same selfish right to privileges despite their limited world experience or knowledge base, or even actual skills needed for a job.*

Karen was a 24-year-old computer programmer fresh out of Brown University and excited about her first job in advanced database and software engineering. She took several classes outside of her major in computers, particularly in business, to strengthen the attractiveness of her resume. Her resume strategy worked. The firm hiring her had been a premier social media mogul for 20 years, and placed Karen at the entry-level programming position. Karen, also diagnosed with histrionic personality disorder, took issue with their relegation of her into a puny robotic job, when she felt her talents exceeded her older peers. She believed her talents and skills deserved the same premium salary package as her boss, or even two administrative layers higher than her boss. When she asserted this conviction, her immediate supervisor asked if she had been working for 30 years, and knew the technical as well as political nuances inherent in consultation with their Fortune 500 company clients. Karen looked at her supervisor a bit miffed, and asked what political nuances she was talking about. The supervisor quipped, "You'll understand them in 30 years."

Admittedly, the supervisor's remark was a bit sarcastic. But Karen was unrelenting, with her penchant for drama. She appealed twice to her supervisor for a promotion, arguing equity in pay for her job talents, before she finally abandoned the cause. She quit her job four weeks later blaming her decision on the antediluvian thinking of its owners and for Karen's failure to advance up the executive ladder.

Karen's plight is a common theme in Cluster B personality typologies, who are narcissistically convinced they are superior with unimpeachable credentials. Karen may migrate among many jobs, each at first challenging her fierce winner's instinct to outperform her peers; within weeks to a month, she will feel unbeatable and euphorically desire to skip beyond her assigned job station into more advanced jobs. She will believe this rapid progression is not only possible but deserving, unlike her predecessors, who followed the pecking order of experience to win their trophies of lifetime achievement. Not Karen, and not Cluster B personality types; they want their trophies *now, and for exactly the reason they received the trophies growing up in childhood – for whatever they did good, mediocre, or just for showing up.*

One real solution to job noncompliance among Cluster B personalities (or, by analogy, among millennials) is to construct a clear hierarchy of stepwise skills permitting forward or backward movement along the company executive branches. Job coach Sally, who regularly visits Karen at her new position, can prepare a functional job description that lists five or six criteria to reach for Karen to qualify for promotions. Karen can seize unilateral control over these criteria and progress at whatever slow or fast pace she wishes, knowing, noncompetitively, that her attainment of goals is entirely up to her, and not due to some personified ageistic bigotry of her generation colliding with an older generation.

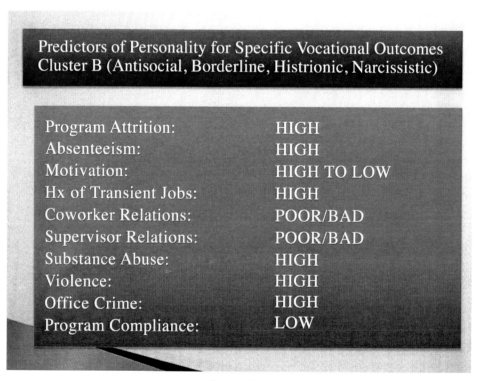

Predictors of Personality for Specific Vocational Outcomes Cluster B (Antisocial, Borderline, Histrionic, Narcissistic)	
Program Attrition:	HIGH
Absenteeism:	HIGH
Motivation:	HIGH TO LOW
Hx of Transient Jobs:	HIGH
Coworker Relations:	POOR/BAD
Supervisor Relations:	POOR/BAD
Substance Abuse:	HIGH
Violence:	HIGH
Office Crime:	HIGH
Program Compliance:	LOW

Figure 5.2.

C'mon, remind me:
79. For Cluster B, program attrition is very _____.
80. Coworker relations, for Cluster B, is usually very _____.
81. Violence is nearly always _____ since Cluster B types are antisocial.

Cluster C Personality Disorders
(Avoidant, Dependent, Obsessive-Compulsive)

1. PROGRAM ATTRITION (LOW). Cluster C personality disorders centrally converge into the vortex of four common traits: (1) poor interpersonal (social) skills; (2) strong tendencies for avoidance and escape of many anxiety-driven situations; (3) overreliance on people, places, or belief systems to navigate through their social anxiety: and (4) appeasement of people including profound self-sacrifices to maintain stasis. In jobs, therapy, or other rehabilitation programs, the Cluster C personality type is an unwaveringly loyal and enduring worker. They are conformers, chameleons, and silently inconspicuous drones in the cubicle or backroom, arduously working on layers of tasks neglected by coworkers and supervisors. They rarely complain, abide unconditionally by policy, and accept traditional company standards as the gospel. Since they are noncomplainers, they effectively hide their skill deficits or task inadequacies behind a superficial veil of constant activity, none of which appear suspicious to the supervisor.

One recent problem frequently arising in job situations involving Cluster C personalities concerns racial or other ethnocentric insults subtly conveyed and overlooked to avoid conflict. The subtle messages that verbally or nonverbally, intentionally or unintentionally, mistreat an individual are called *microaggressions* (Delapp & Williams, 2015; Sue, Capodilupi, Torino, Bucceri, Holder, Nadal, & Esquilin, 2007). Three subtypes of microaggressions inclue (a) microassaults, (b) microinsults, and (c) microinvalidations. Microassaults are explicit racial derogations, such as a slang or ethnocentric expressions used to deliberately discriminate against another person. Saying "You Jews control the financial marketplace," not only is antisematic, but the antisematicism is a purposeful assault. A less conspicuous insult, relying on innuendo or inference, is a microinsult. Here, the message conveys rudeness and insensitivity in demeaning a person's racial or ethnical heritage and identity. Saying instead that "I jewd the price down in bargaining with the car salesman," implies that Jewish people are cheap or always negotiate a better price. While the speaker did not explicitly deprecate Jewish people or impeach their negotiation skills, the message exploits an ethnic fallacy about Jewish people. More peculiarly, the speaker probably was unaware while saying the microinsult that it was actually offensive. Another good example of microinsults recently integrated into the social lexicon of vocabulary is a *wife-beater's shirt*. This sleeveless white T-shirt, the kind famously worn by Sylvester Stallone in *Rocky*, gained infamous popularity as the shirt frequently worn while engaging in domestic violence. Today, many manufacturers boast sales of this t-shirt and young buyers proudly display this shirt, calling it by name, not ever realizing its pejorative insult to women.

A third type of microaggression are microinvalidations. This is a type of communication that intentionally or unintentionally excludes, negates, or *invalidates* the thoughts, feelings, and realities of some person belonging to a racial or ethnic heritage. In a job-hiring situation, among a panel deliberating prospective applicants, a remark from one panel member is that "John, who is from Michigan's Upper Peninsula, is more Hillbilly-like, and will probably not have the sophistication we need at this job." The assumption of John's lack of skills, entirely based on his geographic locality and the people negatively and stereotypically associated with that region, disqualifies, dismisses, or mitigates the integrity of the applicant. Microinvalidations are very common mistakes attributed to Cluster C personalities, since the consumer is docile, placid, and rarely objects to any obvious or subtle criticism attacking him or her.

When Cluster C individuals politely "hold their tongue" and suppress resentments about microaggressions, the resentments slowly ferment until an incident triggers an explosion of infuriation over the long-withheld anger. In recent months, for example, in racially charged cities such as Baltimore, Cleveland, Detroit, North Charleston, South Carolina, and Ferguson, Missouri, residents outraged by police shootings of unarmed black victims provoked riots, involving looting and retribution against the police. The "final straw" that tipped the silent minority into a rage of revolt was the microinsults and miroinvalidations by the police and local governments, demeaning the urban neighborhoods as high-crime ghettos. In less dramatic form, a consumer employed at Macy's, with Avoidant Personality, told that his shyness means he lacks the intelligence to handle more demanding customers, may erupt volatilely or even file a lawsuit for wrongful discrimination.

One possible solution for Cluster C personalities prone to microaggressions is to give them a variety of less-threatening modalities through which to communicate continuously to supervisors. For example, Lisa, a Geek-Squad customer-service representative, struggled to interact on the phone with customers. She was incomparably superior to her peers in troubleshooting computer problems and thrived on the challenge of difficult cases. But she loathed and did not perform well during phone conversations. She was diagnosed with Avoidant Personality Disorder. Peers chastised her for being a nerd, asocial, and being anhedonic (dislike of people). Demill, the vocational coach, observed her skill deficits with on-phone direct contact with people, and suggested an alternative way she could communicate with customers and her peers. Since she was a fast typist, grammatically accurate, and a multitask, high-rate performer, Demill suggested she restrict her communication only to remote online dialogues and refer cases involving telephonic dialogue to other Geek agents. Likewise, if Lisa objected to in-house criticism or microaggressions of her, she could use the same system to contact the human resource office. In this way, Lisa had an accessible communication outlet enabling her to assert herself immediately and it could prevent her habit of avoiding live-contact situations that invoked anxiety.

2. ABSENTEEISM (MILD TO LOW). Frequency of absenteeism is often a byproduct of passive-aggressive behaviors. A person indirectly sends a message of resentment, or s*o he or she thinks*, to the employer by refusing to show up or denying the employer income generated by the employee's work performance. The presumption is that the employer *will somehow connect that the absent employee and lost income meant the employee was mistreated.* Cluster C personality types rely on such inferences in the miscalculation of their actions. They are conflict-avoidant, unassertive, docile, secretive, and take circuitous detours around any natural course of solving problems. Despite their clandestine approach, it is still easier for such consumers to attend work and suppressively tolerate the injustices perceived at work. For this reason, absenteeism rates are generally low for Cluster C personality types. On the downside, suppression of feelings directly correlates with lower work performance rates (e.g., Van Gelderen & Bakker, 2011). Interference of low motiva-

tion, and perceived futility of worth, combine with confusion about how to generate reinforcing or positive employer feedback. Consequently, there are spiked increases in the error rate, production speed, production consistency, and communication about job performance problems. Similarly in rehabilitation and therapy programs, timidly suppressive consumers may mechanically and indifferently go through the motions of treatment steps instructed of them, and appear reliable attendees and leaners. However, after two to three weeks of repeating similar units of unmastered skills, they make very little progress over baseline or pretreatment levels.

Darla, an art therapists specializing in Adult Children of Alcoholics (ACOAs), ran an art therapy group for family victims. Corrissa was her patient/consumer enrolled in the five-week program. Corrissa also received the premorbid diagnosis of Avoidant Personality and Dependent Personality Disorders. Corrissa always fancied herself a sketch artist and eagerly looked forward to using skills gained in Darla's program to possibly pursue forensic police artwork. At first, Corrissa enjoyed her creativity in the art assignments, receiving rave remarks from peers and Darla. On a more complex assignment, asking her to sketch a caricature of barns from neighboring rural areas, Corrissa struggled to conjure an image and had "artist's block." Darla explained a naturally talented artist never gets *artist's block* and can configure a mental montage of images from a wealth of life experiences. The next day group met, Corrissa was absent. She also missed the second and third consecutive meetings. When she did return, she provided an unexcused reason for her absence, blaming it on her pets' medical condition. Thereafter, she hardly penciled any marks on her sketchpad, and the few drawings she made were hidden from her peers. Asked why she drew less sketches in class, Corrissa nonchalantly explained her "heart was not into the assignment."

Corrissa's diminished production of art drawings, including her precurrent behavior of absenteeism, demonstrates passive-aggressive symptoms. She deliberately did not attend class to convey a "subliminal" (indirect) message to the teacher she was angry at her. When Corrissa did return, morale declined rapidly and she further diminished her energy and output of assignments. While one solution, the obvious one, lies in altering the future negative remarks Darla makes to Corrissa or other consumers, the negative feedback alone was not responsible for Corrissa's apathy. It was the tip of the iceberg. In Adult

Children of Alcoholics (ACOAs), preponderant behaviors are vulnerability (helplessness), overtrust, overhelping, and hypersensitivity. Corrissa was severely hyperalert to criticism, rejection, and any risk of abandonment. Darla's remark about artist's block *threatened* that Corrissa would be rejected, abandoned, and invalidated. Corrissa also immediately assumed she lacked talent, competence, and this disillusionment launched rule-governed behaviors about how *she never will be a good artist since only good artists can draw without an artist's block.*

A more productive way to help Corrissa with approximations of drawing accuracy, without evoking her reactional biography of ACOA-related (Avoidant and Dependent personality disorders), is to *ask her or mand what she observes is the beauty and shortcoming of the drawing.* Inquiries or mands for verbal behavior enjoin the listener to tap some establishing operation or motivator existing at the moment to help form the verbal answer. The establishing operation (EO) might pertain to Corrissa's drawing and her desire for approval for it; or she may fear criticism of the drawing and give any superficial answer to escape from Darla's scrutiny; her perfunctory answer may function to move Darla on to another student. *In both cases, Corrissa has a choice, remains in control, and does not blame or feel punishment from Darla. Either choice of verbal behavior, to gain praise or escape from perceived scrutiny, keeps Corrissa on task and eliminates her fear of rejection and abandonment.*

3. MOTIVATION (HIGH TO MODERATE). The cornerstone of Cluster C personality typology is compliance. Motivation entirely predicates on the operational premise that social approval and disapproval are predictable outcomes. Calculated efforts exerted to gain approval and acceptance equal the response calibration that go into avoidance of disapproval. For example, in a recent investigation by the New York City Attorney General's Office into the underpayment of undocumented foreigner manicurists (Noe, 2015), results showed wage theft and unfair labor practices; salons, for example, often charged each new employee $100 for her job, in addition to supplying her own nail tools. Although enforcement of new labors laws protecting these foreigners may stop this illegal wage practice, the point remains that employer mistreatment was easier around passively non-English-speaking immigrants in financial despair. The workers *calculatedly conformed to the illegal practices for approval, acceptance, and wages. Moreover, they did not arrogantly or aggressively uphold their civil rights to protest unfair practices.* Cluster C individuals are rarely so politically inclined. They are not boldly Randian in

campaigning for individualism and capitalistic entitlements (see Burns, 2009; Den Uly & Rasmussen, 1984). By contrast to the liberal rights-advocacy of objectivism, the foreigner manicurists, and Cluster C personalities in general, are sheep. They are submissive and self-sacrificial. They self-sacrifice for the greater good of other people, dismissing or marginalizing personal indignities if it means the outcome of their martyrdom benefits some lesser-abled party. Their altruistic role of benefactor is not like a philanthropist, a donor of large sums of money to, say, an art museum or venue for performing arts. In Cluster C personalities, altruism is synonymous with *avoidance behavior. The giver generously forfeits self-value for the value of others to avert, delay, diminish, or eliminate adversity.*

Darnell, a retail-clothing advisor and purchaser, marketed her services to busy working women, who needed stylish and affordable apparel but lacked the time or fashion knowledge to shop on their own. She worked in a large metropolitan city and seemed popular among rising young female executives. Veronica was her newest client, also recently diagnosed with Avoidant Personality Disorder. Darnell found this diagnosis odd, since Veronica, an attorney by trade, advanced in quantum leaps up the executive ladder of a Fortune 500 company, requiring her to show fortitude, shark-like confrontational skills, and resilience against disputing enemies to the company. Still, in her personal life, Veronica was timid, self-doubtful, abhorred any partner relationship teetering on arguments, and she was clueless on outfitting herself to look attractive. Darnell spun her magic, in providing a wardrobe of chic and contemporary business suits with incredibly matching accessories. Veronica rejected the initial lot of designer clothes, complaining of looking too polished like a paid model. Within a week, her tone changed dramatically. Veronica told Darnell she had an unlimited expense account to assemble the most high-fashioned and slim-figured suits. Darnell abided by the request but did not really understand Veronica's odd change of heart.

A closer look into Veronica's peculiar shifts in decisions revealed understandable behavioral contingencies. When she first saw the portfolio of fashionable clothing, she felt embarrassed, humiliated, and too selfish to enjoy. She resisted becoming a store-manikin for other people to gawk at, tease, or repudiate as seemingly egocentric or greedy. However, her work drew the attention of several senior attorney females, who increasingly asked Veronica out for lunch and involved her in after-work activities. These experienced women attorneys dressed "to the 9's," in sparing no expense for luxury fashion and designer suits. *In seeking their approval,* Veronica sacrificed her own values of apparel to dress-like and morph into what these women attorneys looked like. Veronica's choice for expensive or classy attire did not reflect her own reform in clothing values; instead she capitulated to the fashions sported by women who she wanted to like her. Veronica became more than a good employee. Her motivation for high work productivity and now "looking more the part" almost exclusively depended on, not securing the approval of the women attorneys, b*ut of avoiding the rejection from the women attorneys.*

4. HISTORY OF TRANSIENT JOBS (LOW). Employment history for Cluster C personality types nearly always involves long durations at one particular job, often since high school years. Likewise, affiliation with any service or rehabilitation agency equally is extensive and typically exceeds reasonable periods; the length exceeds, for example, when most people might end, quit, or move beyond the service. Job security, in this respect, is a function of (a) feeling dedicated to the employer/provider, (b) avoiding fears of new jobs or services, and (c) accepting self-limitations that restrict or prohibit daring advancements. Self-refusal to advance in a job or service persists despite obvious oppression or other adversity (punishment) afflicting the consumer at the job or service agency.

Feeling dedicated. As indicated moments ago, benevolently-driven goals that support the employer or provider supersede any personal goals. Cluster C personality types self-impose obligations to emotionally *attach* and *preserve the attachment* to another person; they prove unequivocally how invaluable they are to the employer/provider. Responses that demonstrate such optimal dedication include (a) working overtime without pay; (b) overhelping coworkers and enabling their production quality or achievement of standards even at the expense of the consumer slacking on similar outcome measures; (c) buying gifts or preparing food for coworkers and supervisors; (d) listening to coworker issues and unconditionally consoling the coworkers; (e) serving as mediator in dispute resolutions among coworkers or among supervisor and worker; and (f) willingness to be used as bait or a pawn in luring unsuspected coworkers into traps of poor work ethics, or delinquent job performances. The intensity of dedication reflects a tunnel vision of adoration, undaunted by anything wrong the provider or employer does. This obsessive admiration is functionally similar to the psychopathology of erotomania, a condition of idealizing a secret love relationship inferred between a consumer and provider or employer. Preoccupation about the employer or provider is continuous, intense, and compels excessive appeasement behaviors.

Avoidance of new jobs or services. Job retention also frequently occurs to prevent the ambiguity of new jobs inside or outside of the current employment or services. Camille, for example, worked 30 years for the Department of Treasury in clerical support under four different bureau directors. Her years of service alone earned her the privilege to laterally transfer to another department within the state, or even advance to a different administrative track offering unlimited promotions. She declined these privileges and reconciled that her station in life was to facilitate the job success of her mentors and supervisors – the bureau directors. In truth, her real reason for staying put was to avoid the unpredictability and risk of failure associated with starting a new job outside, not of her own cubicle, but outside of her comfort zone. The anticipated steps of preparing a resume, passing an interview, making new friends, passing the probationary period, and relearning the nuances of the office, all felt meteoric and mortally frightened Camille. She felt safe, secure, and definite about intricacies of her current job. She resisted any job-altering decisions that might upset her stable apple cart.

Acceptance of self-limitations. A variation on this rigid thinking is when there are punitive consequences either for staying or leaving a job or provider. A Cluster C personality type in four years of therapy using a Rational-Emotive-Therapy modality may get chided each session for having ridiculous irrational beliefs; the disputation step a insult, badger, or even intimidate the consumer and bring him or her to the brink of tears (Lyons & Woods, 1991). Painfully hurt by this mistreatment, the consumer may *still remain a glutton for punishment by attending every session dutifully.* Why is this? Overobedient Cluster C types feel the punishment is instructive, valuable, and they will suppress insulted feelings while eagerly soliciting more punishment. To leave the provider, so it is believed, is to act selfishly and cause grief to the provider for the sudden termination of services. Then, too, fears abound infinitely when the consumer contemplates the choice of finding another provider. The consumer's fear is ostensibly this: "How will I find another provider *who would put up with my nonsense and chronic psychopathology as much as this provider has?"* Perceived value of therapy is crucial, largely support-ed by earlier research showing that 13 to 18 sessions are advisable to cure 50 percent to 60 percent of mental health issues (Connolly-Gibbons, Rothbard, Farris, Stirman, Thompson, Scott, Heintz, Gallop, & Crits-Christoph, 2011). However, psychotherapy utilization rates may also *increase* or *decrease* based on perceived value of therapy and perceived needs for that value.

Shanas loved music his entire life. He completed his masters and doctorate degrees in clarinet performance and orchestra conducting, but doubled at other woodwind instruments whenever he played in orchestra pits for community theatre musicals or in the city symphony. His doctorate, ideally, gave him the leverage for teaching at local col-leges and universities. It gave him the edge to compete against less qualified candidates for orchestra conductor positions. For years, Shanas received therapy for Obsessive-Compulsive personality disorder and Avoidant personality disorder, both regarded as limiting his persever-ance in the job market. He met with a life coach twice weekly, whose words of inspiration motivated Shanas to overcome his plateau of unsuitable, low-earning, and demeaning positions. He grew compla-cent teaching trombone at a local music store and also giving few pri-vate lessons. He also held a symphony position, but never competed for first chair in his section. Inspiration alone was not enough. Shanas *believed his musical skills were defective, inadequate, and that everybody else well exceeded his limited talents. He also hated to boast, self-promote, and pre-sent a fake image of himself in interviews, fearing an imposter image. He felt certain discerning interviewers would see through his transparent façade and nail him on the spot about his fakery.*

Fears aside, Shanas refused to leave the life coach, his therapist, or alter any current job circumstances. With the Obsessive-Compulsive personality, the need for order or perfection was paramount. Shanas feared exposure of his imprecision and consequently projected a cata-strophic scenario ahead in life, riddled with confusion and self-demor-alization. One possible intervention for Shanas was to structure his pro-jected risky world with a series of stepwise units of success, beginning at the simplest and least ostentatious (exhibitionistic) display of his musical talents. He could play a solo trombone number or accompany a voice or trombone student during a recital. He could play amid an instrumental trio or quartet, blending unnoticeably into the montage of sound. In addition, he was given relaxation techniques to make public announcements at recitals about his own or students' performance. For example, before the quartet begins, Shanas spoke a few words to introduce the history of the composer or relevance of the piece, or even emphasized the purpose of his particular trombone descant. Using a hierarchy of low-rated anxiety to high-rated anxiety musical risk behaviors, the next layer for Shanas' desensitization may entail increasing the number or diversity of the audience he performs for. At each step in the incremental anxiety-reducer process, barring unforeseen backsliding, Shanas' risk behaviors compete with the imposter syndrome of self-doubt, preconclusions of failure, and torturous humiliation.

5. COWORKER RELATIONS (HIGH). Coworker relations among Cluster C personalities nearly always are positive and durable. The employee, no matter his or her rank in the company, seeks fellowship for two reasons. First, fellowship offers a high dose of reinforcing exchange, in that kindness and generosity demonstrated to other coworkers (or supervisors) pays proportional dividends in acceptance, approval, and attenuation of any conflict. Cluster C employees maximize this dividend-payoff (reinforcing) effect. They idealize that their saccharine, unselfish demeanor will be insurance against *things going bad*. Second, fellowship permits normalcy, predictability, and a context for work stabilization. Cluster C individuals struggle in highly stressful or chaotic work environments, consisting of infrastructures of gossip, fierce competition, and infiltrations of sabotage, all randomly staggered over a week of work.

But there are flaws inherent in each of these two reasons for fellowship. One flaw is that the utopic picture of a happy and synergist staff who will like the kind-hearted Cluster C person premises on a simple contingency: that all coworkers enjoy being catered to. However, in lower and upper echelons of any business, from machinists in factories to executives in administration, there are very competent coworkers and superiors who may view the Pollyanna-pleasing worker as an annoyance or even a detriment to effective office systems. Why is this? One reason is that caretakers are on their own mission to preserve intraoffice peace. However, an office place may promote a "divide and conquer philosophy" such as in a law office, to motivate young ambitious associates to seek high-revenue cases and earn peer recognition. In such settings, the caretaker, who spreads goodwill and fig-leafs to maintain a détente, is actually undermining the *deliberate establishing operations responsible for building a competitively successful law practice.*

A second flaw with seeking fellowship may be called *the Unsinkable Molly Brown Syndrome*. The Unsinkable Molly Brown refers the Titanic ship survivor, Margaret Tobin, aka Brown, who indefatigably helped load women and children into lifeboats and beneficently cared for survivors once they boarded the *Carpathia*. She went over and above, exhaustively, to advocate for other people. Like Molly Brown, Cluster C caretakers are absorbers of excessive responsibility; they frequently "bite off more than they can chew." The downside of this caretaking is that it fosters a complacent work staff. In the psychosocial phenomenon of *social loafing*, people exert less effort to accomplish a goal when they work in a group versus when they work alone (cf. Karau and Williams. 1993). Groups defuse responsibility and tasks to few or *one* person eagerly agreeing to be the patsy and haul the logs of tasks for the entire group. The caretaker, or Cluster C personality type often is this prototypical patsy. Although this caretaker, in theory, appears a sucker who is pulling the weight of the entire group, the truth is just the opposite. Caretakers bask in the sheer delight of being *the sucker*. They refuse to see their overloaded tasks as exploitation. Instead, they interpret inundation of multiple tasks as the benevolent gesture to relieve other people of burdens. They draw more reinforcement (acceptance, approval) from how much people *need them to do more while others do less*.

A third flaw with seeking fellowship, in nonemployment settings such as in therapy or rehabilitation, is that it artificially protects against starting over again. Cluster C personality types quickly befriend office staff or volunteer time to prove they are indispensable; they seek insurance against being discharged or rejected. Zacharia, for example, was frequently homeless due to misspending his monthly SSDI checks. He also mismanaged his antianxiety medications, often overdrugging himself into sleep. Almost predictably when he faced the last days of an eviction, he sedated himself too much, causing vertigo and fainting on his hardwood floor. His injured forehead and other bruising from the fall typically required emergency admission into a unit in the hospital. There, he knew all of the nurses and felt "at home." His sweetness and ingratiation among the staff reinforced their care for him, allowing Zacharia to stay longer in the hospital than was medically necessary.

One intuitive strategy to break this rotative-door hospital habit and prevent the Cluster C caretakers' spell on coworkers to make them loaf is to (1) build team collaboration among staff and (2) increase identifiability of tasks. First, the goal would be to remove control of all of the tasks from the caretaker and return the control, equally, among co-workers, or staff. Under this practice, in accord with social facilitation research (Uziel, 2007), group productivity will increase when group members *identify* what projects belong to them. This is opposite to group members feeling they are anonymous and unidentifiable in the group. On the downside, there is a problem with social facilitation outcomes. It is not with its effects on restoring group cohesion and productivity. The problem lies instead with its exacerbation of the Cluster C personality pathology.

When equilibrium is restored to an office or agency system and the primary role of the caretaker (i.e., the Cluster C personality type) is removed, this displacement causes serious emotional and behavior side-effects for the caretaker. First, removal is viewed as a demotion, rejection, and abandonment. Cluster C personality types suffer acute anxiety and rally back with a surge of energy to appease the group that demoted them. They may engage in high production of tasks or offer to relieve a bewildered or busy coworker of their stress, all of which hint at reinstating duties they enjoyed beforehand. Or, when self-reinstatement fails, the caretaker may resort to clandestine strategies. They may passive-aggressively sabotage group projects or stir controversy and chaos for a short time, only to surface as the hero or heroine who defused the controversy and resolved the chaos. Second, removal of job tasks is viewed as self-demoralization. They feel profoundly depressed, useless, devalued, and are withdrawn, isolative, sullen, doleful, and suicidal. They take sick (medical) leave, consider job transfers or early retirement (if age applicable), or become lethargic and apathetic at their jobs. Diminished work performance lasts only as long as (a) the collective work group resists reinstatement of the caretaker as savior, and (b) the caretaker hunts for and finds a new, vulnerable group in which he or she can feel invaluable again.

Keegan, head veterinarian at a local cat clinic, employed Gary, a recently graduated veterinarian technician from the university. Gary's affinity for animals was impressively genuine and he instantly won the respect of customers and other staff members. Gary was also a very hard worker, staying after hours, including weekend overnights to care for the boarded felines, and also would *go out of his way* to research internet information for customers wanting medical explanations of their cat's diagnosis and treatment. Gary was a valuable asset and often relieved much of the ancillary work (like retrieval of internet materials) that fell on the shoulders of the five veterinarians in the clinic. Midway through Gary's second year, at a board meeting, the principal owners of the clinic decided they loaded Gary with too much responsibility. They decided that some of the duties he performed really belonged to the professionals, the veterinarians, like talking about the latest medical research of certain treatments with patients. Keegan, designated as the board spokesperson, informed Gary that while his services were exceptional, they wanted him only to perform duties consistent with a veterinarian technician. Gary, hiding his diagnosis of Avoidant personality disorder, politely acquiesced to Keegan's requests since, in fact, he was not being fired, but just demoted.

The next day, internet service in the clinic abruptly stopped. Gary announced the disaster and even reminded Keegan and others how devastating this internet loss meant for electronic recording of clinical cases, a system the clinic begrudgingly switched to only two months before. Panic rose among the staff, who imagined paying a fortune to some computer troubleshooter or hiring out clerical services to record the backlog of unrecorded treatments for that day, or for as many days as the internet was inoperable.

As the panic reached near-pandemonium, "a miracle occurred." Gary proudly announced he reactivated the hard-drive by using the backup file in DOS and bypassing the virus infecting the operation system. He brought the computers "back up" for immediate use by clerical and administrative staff, eliminating the impending office disaster and restoring normalcy to electronic recording of medical treatments. Gary was low-key about his powerful resurrection of the computer, and marginalized his computer programming talents to "just a couple of tricks he learned years ago taking computer classes." Despite his humbleness, the staff saw him as the messiah and were eternally indebted to Gary for his quick-acting skills.

Gary's role as miracle worker was nothing more than the clever genius of a prestidigitator. His trickery and illusions included the deliberate covert sabotage of the computer system, and then fixing it. His triumphs instantly earned him a hero status and, *in his mind,* re-elevated his value in the office that was lost from the demotion. Gary acted passive-aggressively, in secretly dismantling the Internet that caused momentary mayhem. His deception was in retaliation for lack of appreciation of his efforts. After artificially inducing an establishing operation among staff, he eliminated the urge (EO) just as quickly with his "miraculous" skills and became the savior. The collective group, whether superstitious or just from gratefulness, awarded Gary rein-statement of his caretaker role.

There are several methods touted to prevent intraoffice recidivism of sabotage by unsuspecting, overzealous caretakers (cf. Analoui & Kakabadse, 1992; Koch, 1999). The overriding approach applicable for Cluster C personality type employees is *kindly listening to their gripes*. Human resource policies, for example, may explicitly institute media-tors, mentor-listeners, and interceptors, whose job it is to create a (a) shared perceptions of reality, (b) result-oriented operating agreement, (c) clearer roles and accountabilities, (d) consensus decision-making, and (e) formalized conflict-resolution process. In effect, interventions promise a sensitive, more empathic, and complimentarity strategy of reaffirming the employee's integrity and dignity – their validation in the workplace. This validation is concurrent with crafting a new role for the employee in the company. Granting a creative role for the employ-ee is a milestone in the business world. It is very different from tradi-tional or vertical organizational systems that unilaterally pass down judgments and force subordinates into "take-it-or-leave-it" ultimatums. By contrast, the more egalitarian, horizontal organizational systems extend leverage to the subordinates to help in the decision process affecting their future. From a behavioral standpoint (i.e., *organizational behavioral management*), shifting the focus from coercion to autonomy *enables predictability and control over one's fate and gives a more reinforcing opportunity to make acceptable behavior changes.*

6. SUPERVISOR RELATIONS (HIGH). Worker relations with supervi-sors or perceived authorities is nearly always exceptionally high. Cluster C personality individuals are pacifists, orderly, people-pleasers, and regard their compliance to any structure as a harbinger of sustain-able employment. They equally remain unshakably loyal to a service or rehabilitation agency. *Authorities* play a critical role in the pattern of conformity behaviors. First, authorities represent symbolically (i.e., by metaphorical extension) a person similar to a parent, about whom the individual historically either adored or feared, but was unconditionally responsive to. In ACOA households, for example, exposed to aggres-sively violent alcoholic parents, children feared the parent's behaviors and learned to be unquestionably servitude. In conflict-free house-holds, equally as unrealistic and bubble-like in insulating children from normal family chaos, a child may adore his or her parents. The children

exhibit this adoration by unflinching altruism and conformity. In both households, perception and treatment of the parent is sacrosanct. The child is dedicated to the institution of catering to the authority and expecting, that with the right chemistry of kindness and self-sacrifice, the authority parent in return will reward the child with approval.

Into adulthood, like in childhood, Cluster C personalities work arduously, tirelessly, and volunteer beyond their job duties to convince authorities they are loyal and should be retained forever. In service or rehabilitation agencies, a similar response function appears. Loyalty comes from (a) spotless punctuality and attendance at sessions, (b) completion and precision of homework assignments, (c) evidence of progress using social media or other electronic communication (emails, video-attachments, texting, etc.), and (d) willingness to engage in a hierarchy of challenging improvement behaviors without any complaints.

Sex therapist Miranda met with a 54-year-old woman, Rashta, on a physician referral for Rashta's diagnosed secondary vaginismus. Miranda also learned Rashta premorbidly was diagnosed with Avoidant personality and Obsessive-Compulsive personality disorders. Miranda's goals were simple; she wanted to teach Rashta how to overcome any emotional barriers resisting intercourse while also instructing her on a pain-free use of dilators to slowly widen the vaginal opening (i.e., expand the pelvic floor). Vaginal tightness, Rashta confided, accounted for her unconsummated marriage and her husband's idle threats of seeking sexual relief from a third party unless Rashta sought medical treatment. Eager to show Miranda her enthusiasm for treatment, Rashta bought several self-help books on overcoming vagnismus and immediately purchased the dilator kit. She further informed Miranda of Rashta's husband's renewal of monogamy as he witnessed his wife's zealous commitment to fix their sexual problems. Two weeks into sex therapy, Rashta reported progress with the dilator assignments. Miranda viewed her client as a highly motivated pupil ready to advance to more complex levels of dilator usage and possibly even to attempt realistic intercourse with her husband.

And then the ruse ended. Miranda requested a session with Rashta and her husband, figuring she could coach the couple through the physical fragility and needed patience with postvagnismus coitus. The couple showed up punctually, consistent with Rashta's outsanding attendance record. When complimented for their mutual love and progress, Rashta's husband presented a strangely diametrical story about Rashta's lack of progress and her odd "hang-ups" about using the dilators. He explained, later corroborated by Rashta, that every time she sat on the couch and inserted the dilator, *she felt like a prostitute, it felt very unnatural, and she couldn't do it. It just felt wrong.* Likewise, when her husband offered to manipulate the dilator for her, resembling what he thought was similar to his foreplay ritual of digital-vaginal stimulation, Rashta dropped a bombshell saying she never found that foreplay ritual stimulating nor had she ever experienced an orgasm. Rashta further surprised her husband and therapist, Miranda, when she revealed a lack of *any libido and that she had no idea what people were talking about when they say they get "horny."* Miranda's clinical intake ruled out any prior sexual abuse, sexual trauma, or major surgeries (childbirth, etc.) accounting for emotional or behavioral painful sensations during intercourse. Rashta's disclosure shocked her husband and Miranda, both of whom operated under the presupposition that Rashta knew what sex was, enjoyed it at one time, and passionately wanted to restore healthy intimacy through treatment of vaginisumus. But both the husband and Miranda were wrong – dead wrong.

Why is this? A functional analysis of Rashta's behavior helps to explain her shocking disclosure. First, Cluster C personality types seek goals that are unselfish or appease other people. Despite the inherent health benefits from curing vaginismus, Rashta's *real* motivator for treatment was to *please her husband.* Second, Rashta faked knowledge and experience of sexual intimacy to pacify her husband's sexual requests, a concession she made to guarantee approval and acceptance (i.e., to avoid rejection and abandonment). Third, she similarly went to great lengths to fake progress for the sex therapist, from whom she sought admiration and affirmation of her "good client efforts." Fourth, from an etiological standpoint, Rashta's deficits in a sexual repertoire also meant she *never physiologically associated genital sensations* with oxytocin-sensations (i.e., the mammalian neurohypophysial hormone generated from an orgasm); hormonal and genital stimulation neither was learned nor did it pair respondently or operantly with other internal (proprioceptive) and external stimuli (cues). Such conditioning of evocative and elicitive cues, recurrently through adolescence and adulthood, would produce the establishing operations (EO) for sexual-seeking behavior. Without any of these cues conditioned, she felt asexual (i.e., hyposexual), indifferent toward, and even confused by people making sexual advances to her.

The solution for Rashta, from a clinical behavior therapy perspective, lies with many choices she makes about ending her deception about sex and desire to learn what sexual sensations feel like. However, the more serious issue here is her overobedience, both to the therapist and her husband. Discouragement of overobedience and encouragement of sharing problems faced along the path of treatment involves a threefold intervention. First, Miranda can design incentives of approval for risk-exposure disclosures. This entails weekly or intersession descriptions from the consumer of implementation difficulties, fears, or any other emotional, behavioral, or technical obstacles encountered with the homework assignment. Incidents of risk-exposure disclosure always accompany a fact-based or operational description of (a) what steps were attempted, (b) what went wrong, (c) what went right, and (d) how did the consumer or client manage the setbacks. Evidence of these disclosed setbacks and reparations are shared by email or in person. Second, as in many behavioral interventions, recruitment of a close or intimate partner (caregiver, spouse, etc.) is effective as a monitor of program implementation accuracy and consistency (cf. Zarit & Femla, 2008). Enlistment of a caregiver reduces or eliminates *reporting-fraud, or the probability of deceptive self-reporting of progress for attention seeking.* Her husband, in other words, can corroborate her updated reports on progress. Third, a method borrows from learner-centered teaching (Weimer, 2013). This variation is a system involving the consumer/client positioned to *teach or instruct other people on the methods used to cure the consumer's own problems.* These other people may appear, confidentially, in a group therapy or among extended family members, or in anonymous Internet chat rooms. In some cases, teaching of self-progress skills is not anonymous and involves proudly speaking to the general public.

7. Substance Abuse (Low). Misuse of alcohol and drugs may seem a high probable behavior for Cluster C personality disorders for obvious reasons. First, stimulants (e.g., cocaine, meta-amphetamines, psychostimulants, alcohol) can act as disinhibitors in artificially inducing social courage, happiness, hypomania, and surge of energy antithetical to a nondrug state of depression and self-suppression. Second, depressants (e.g., alcohol, barbiturates, opiate synthetics) often serve as self-medicators for symptomatic anxiety and panic. But a third reason why drug overuse frequently occurs is for depersonalization; the obliteration of any adverse physical or emotional sensations to a point of feeling

numb, disconnected, or in a self-hypnotic trance of "floating" (e.g., smoking cannabis). All three reasons for abusing alcohol or drugs predicate on the selfish premise that one's consumption of substances is more immediately favorable (reinforcing) than the immediate or remotely unfavorable social consequences of drug abuse. Carl, a nightly five-beer drinker at bars, who routinely becomes gregarious and a comedian in social groups, may enjoy the immediately rewarding effects of his liquid bravado over his timidity and social awkwardness when sober. He seemingly may ignore or discard his spouse's or children's negative opinion of him the following day when he suffers a hangover and is emotionally inaccessible to the family.

This assumption of enjoying the immediate pleasures over the distant negative effects of disapproval is very relevant in the behavioral conceptualization of Clusters A and B personality types. But not for Cluster C. Cluster C personality typologies entirely function on the *immediate and remote (anticipatory) effects of approval and disapproval, greatly reducing their risk-potential of drug abuse.* Such individuals are fearful that drug abuse may jeopardize their lifelines to stable interpersonal relationships, jobs, or other commitments, in which they are infinitely exerting efforts to maintain. At the slightest sign of social disapproval, damaging friendships or intimate partnerships from discovery of the consumer's excessive drinking, that consumer instantly will *try to* change. They will pledge a promise of abstinence and seek forgiveness from the offended parties who "busted them" for drinking. This contemplative stage of addiction recovery outwardly sounds viable but is fraught with alacrity (cf. Prochaska & DiClemente, 2005) Again, the lofty promises dangle so precariously on the tightrope of feeling reaccepted and avoidance of rejection. Should this proclamation of promises not pan out and instead incur more repudiations for the addiction, the consumer may withdraw further into depression, repeating the same cycle of abused drugs.

In the workforce, hypersensitivity to risk-potentials of drinking is doubled. Consumers make venerable commitments to their jobs and employers and are unlikely to disturb this covenant. Discovery of any on-the-job substance abuse sparks panic and a flurry of high-rate compensatory behaviors to quickly eradicate any trace of work-related impropriety threatening the covenant.

Larry worked for a local utility company for 20 years. He advanced slowly but progressively to a foreman position, overseeing the truck dispatch and equipment readiness for field workers handling electrical emergencies. On Saturday night, celebrating Independence Day, Larry spent five hours at a friend's house with several other guests and drank one beer. He was there for the barbeque and the host's delicious pastries. On Monday at work, he was selected for a random drug screening, as he had been several times during his successful employment. Results showed a positive level of THC, both surprising Larry and his supervisors. Larry was told the protocol involved being placed on job suspension while he underwent a substance abuse assessment in accord with the Federal Department of Transportation laws for safety-sensitive jobs. Larry obliged the protocol and nearly immediately figured out what had happened. Of the delicious pastries consumed, he probably ate one laced with marijuana. He called the host of the party to verify his suspicion and, adding salt to his wound, received verification of his suspension, that many of the pastries contained cannabis. Larry's embarrassment was only the tip of the iceberg. After he met therapy requirements and returned to his safety-sensitive job one month later, he (a) offered to work unlimited overtime, for no extra pay, for one month; (b) volunteered for projects at work that nobody else touched; and (c) unconditionally tolerated the haranguing by coworkers about his reckless oversight of eating THC-laced brownies.

Larry's voluntary subjection to harassment or mistreatment was his self-punishment, *not for using drugs*, but for violating the trust of approval he secured and enjoyed from his coworker and administrators. His self-sacrificing role as scapegoat for peer ridicule was equivalent to an adolescent's self-cutting to inflict punishment for egregious acts to peers (or their parents). Larry also engaged in extensive compensatory behaviors to rapidly remedy the situation and hopefully obliterate from the collective memories of his peers any recollection of his misdeed. Larry did not want his coworkers to think he was a drug abuser, nor did that image generate any benefits for Larry's world of appeasement.

Larry, like many C-type individuals, feel vulnerable. They are susceptible to acquiesce in tenuous situations in which they probably should discern as dangerous or at least decide to assertively set boundaries around themselves to prevent more susceptibility. Larry did neither of these behaviors, and lacked the reactional biography necessary to prevent his risk-potential for repeated, accidental drug contact. In the workplace, human resource personnel can spot Larry-like individuals – those who profusely apologize with martyrdom-like promises for restitution. In selecting appropriate interventions for Larry, focus is less on drug abuse prevention strategies, since most of his drug use was accidental or owing to improper judgment (i.e., he was not a drug *abuser*). Instead, return-to-work strategies should include a variation of response-exposure plus prevention, often used effectively in treating obsessive-compulsions and bulimiarexia (Rosen & Leitenberg, 1982; Whittal, Thordarson, & McLean, 2005). This is a two-step therapeutic process. First, the consumer faces or confronts some fear repeatedly until the fear subsides (habituation). Second, during this exposure to fear, the consumer refrains (or is prevented) from compulsions, avoidance, or escape behaviors to alleviate the anxiety associated with fear exposure. In clinical applications of bulimiarexia, for example, it requires a person after binge eating to sit at the table for 30 minutes to one hour while feeling the incredible waist-discomfort cues that typically compel purging. Bingers are prevented (or they self-refrain) from purging until the fear (and stomachache pain) subsides, reducing the probability of using avoidance and escape behavior to relieve the anxiety and stomach upset.

In the workplace, a similar application involves Larry, our accidental marijuana user, exposed to a crowded room of his coworkers. All the coworkers probably know the reason Larry was off work for one month and the protocol he passed to return to work. Larry is instructed *not to say anything to anybody about the reasons for his time off or to apologize. He further is instructed to refrain from any pledges for overproduction of work and from actually overworking to prevent compulsions to relieve anxiety.* In this respect, Larry habituates to the situation – his behavioral and autonomic sensory responses of anxiety anticipating disapproval disappear over time. He *learns to adjust and resolve his mistakes personally without enlisting other people as validators of his action.*

8. VIOLENCE (LOW). Aggressive violence in the workplace is indiscriminable among individuals no matter their diagnosis. Any person, under the right adverse conditions, can engage in amoralistic, illegal, unethical, or violent behaviors diametrical to their personalities. Nobody is perfectly immune to violence, regardless of their pacifism. Despite this ubiquity, the statistical percentage of violent workplace criminals who are passive and fit the Cluster C personality is very low (cf. Greenberg & Barling, 1999). Workplace crime, even for Cluster C

personality types, follows a Type III or worker-on-worker type of passive-aggressive offense. This is where the aggressor and victims are coworkers or within the same organization. Indirect, covert, or passive-aggressive crimes of this typology include thievery, task sabotage, or high absenteeism. However, approval-seeking individuals are reticent to disturb any pre-existing harmony among coworkers. They are rarely the instigators of any crime, but more likely the passive spectator of crimes, and may even align with whatever groups (criminal or non-criminal) represent the greater approval value. If the infiltrators and naysayers of crime give more approval than the conformers, preference for acceptance may lead to crime collaboration with infiltrators or at least being an accessory to workplace crimes.

Loretta prided herself on 30 years of civil service dedication to her current state job as tax auditor. She reviewed the tax returns of corporations against their previous records for any fraud or discrepancies in quarterly business payments. Loretta never received any verbal or written reprimands for job performance or related issues, and properly navigated through the political canals of coworker gossip and incantations of union or administration uproars. Her best coworker friend Amanda, also a veteran worker months away from retirement, confided in Loretta that two other tax auditors overlooked payment discrepancies of two businesses that were owned by family relatives of the coworkers. Loretta knew both of the conspiring coworkers and enjoyed their company both during work and after-work hours. Loretta believed, in her heart, that whatever oversight these coworkers made was their business and would not disrupt the viable good relationship Loretta enjoyed with them. Loretta always suffered low self-esteem and would do any favors for certain coworkers, whom she perceived as intimately close as her own sisters.

That said, Loretta was an accessory to workplace crime. Deliberately overlooking these tax returns for nepotistic reasons is a federal offense punishable by prison. These two friends engaged in tax audit fraud, about which Loretta fully had knowledge and intentionally opted to overlook. While Loretta may not lose her job per se over her passive-spectating of a work violence or crime, she did weigh the pros and cons or *valence* of social reinforcers. She concluded it more prudent to preserve the reinforcers deliverable by her crooked friends than from people who were not offenders of crime. Passive-spectators are frequently Cluster C personalities. Characteristic job features of this typology include that they (1) pursue other people's career agendas, (2) pursue the easy job of least resistance, (3) accept the salary they are offered, (4) don't show their worth and hope for occasional merit or longevity raises, (5) are completely dependent on others and outsource projects versus learning to do the projects themselves, (6) stay in the job way too long, (7) don't pursue side-income or self-employment, and (8) retire at a standard age because it is conventional.

Loretta's predicament of settling for the highest reinforcing valence is not unusual, and perhaps even the norm within highly complex bureaucratic systems. On the obverse, teaching her to be a whistle-blower is counterproductive and she would adamantly refuse this role. Alternatively, one behavioral solution to Cluster C passive spectators of violence and office crime is to generate new or a higher-valence of reinforcement. Supervisors suspecting a coworker fellowship that precludes honesty and even disguises job transgressions can alter the *worth and accessibility of competing social rewards.* For example, Loretta is a big baseball fan but lives too geographically far to attend a major league ball game. The supervisor may offer the incentive to Loretta for hanging around different coworkers (unlikely to commit crimes) in exchange for a certificate for free transportation to the baseball stadium. Here, the supervisor is enjoining (manding) Loretta to interact with low-crime coworkers incompatible to high-crime coworkers, under the establishing operation of free access to her favorite baseball team. Shifting the perception of reinforcer value partly is based on Vroom's expectancy theory of motivation (1964). He claimed that a (a) positive correlation existed between effort and performance, (b) favorable performance will result in desirable rewards, and (c) the reward will satisfy an important need. Reward valences made proportionally higher based on Loretta's increased or changed responses will be more attractive to Loretta. The reward most definitely satisfies an important need for social approval and, as an extra bonus, the opportunity to see her favorite ball club.

9. OFFICE CRIME (LOW). As suggested above, Cluster C personalities are mostly spectators and unintentional accessories to crime. They are rarely crime perpetrators. The valence of (social) reinforcers largely determines their susceptibility to crime participation or avoidance from crime. A second variable responsible for crime deterrence among Cluster C personality types is *threshold of criminal detection.* Crimes resulting in highly visible outcomes affecting several or even multitudes

of people are too risky and place the perpetrator into the possible spot-light. This spotlight, we mentioned earlier, generates damaging nega-tive attention to the consumer, who is already filled with excessive anx-iety and now fears the epitome of public prosecution, that of being tar and feathered in utter humiliation. However, crimes of a (a) lower threshold of visibility, (b) reduced or no traceability, and (c) low mag-nitude of impact effect seem more desirable to consider. For example, take the preponderance of adult and college students texting at vari-ously illegal times (e.g., Crosswhite, Rice, & Asay, 2014). Overtexting or *addictive texting* persists despite the clearly understood rule-governed beliefs about the inappropriateness of certain times or places to text. Texting may occur in the workplace, in school, while driving, or even when two people engage in sex; but the receiver of the text *does not know the parameters of the texter's behavior that make it appropriate or inap-propriate.* Sultan (2014) further insisted that receivers who respond back rapidly push text senders over the edge; the texters ignore social con-ventions and feed a hunger for instant gratification.

Telepsychologist Jethro ran a webpage offering paid online individ-ual therapy within his state of licensure, using a webcam for "personal contact." He ran a fairly successful web-psychology practice. His newest client, Paul, a 34-year-old, single male, employed as a factory worker at a local automotive plant, disclosed that he had a texting addiction. He frequently took pictures at work of attractive women and texted them to his friends. He considered using Twitter, Instagram, and snapchat but found it was easier to use electronic media already avail-able in his friends' cell phones and I-pods. He denied sexting but admitted that his cameo pictures of women sometimes focused on their more attractive features. Paul further admitted his live cell phone was a contraband at work. Employees were prohibited from using cell phones during work periods and even discouraged from texting or calling dur-ing their breaks. Paul figured his rapid finger texting while he kept the phone inside his pants pocket was inconspicuous and less likely to arouse suspicion.

Jethro's ethical obligation, of course, is to reduce or eliminate illegal behavior to prevent Paul from facing job jeopardy. He might offer, for example, different times of the day outside of work that are appropri-ate for texting and that may even draw similar reinforcing attention from his peers – the same peers who send Paul texts during the work-day. While this advice is prudent, it does not alter the relevant behavioral contingencies under which Paul responds. The more relevant contingencies include (a) the autonomic arousal stimulated from texting (illegally) during work, (b) the autonomic arousal stimulated from the clandestine or covert texting process, and (c) the reinforcing diversion the texting offers to escape the mundane assembly line work. As we saw earlier when introducing the technique on *evoked response arousal plus sensitization*, the method to replace or compete with a psychophysiological stimulant (e.g., viscerality of texting) is to match or exceed that stimulant in a different context, thereby maximizing this new reinforcement choice. According to the Matching Theory (Hernstein, 1961; Poling, Edwards, Weeden, & Foster, 2011), nonhuman organisms exposed to concurrent variable interval schedules (VIs) are likely to exert more responses proportional to the amount or duration of reinforcement delivered. Applying this principle to our example, it means Paul *is only likely to text at some later or variable time if the amount of reinforcement earned for texting later is equal to or better than the amount of reinforcement earned for texting during work.*

There are several ways to generate this different reinforcement schedule for Paul. First, Jethro, the telepsychologist, might suggest taking (decent) pictures of women *before work and after work*, storing the pictures, and then texting the pictures later. The snapping of pictures before and after work may still feel "covert" and arouse excitement. Second, Jethro can suggest Paul go to another venue entirely to take pictures and send them. While any picture taken of women, without their approval, may seem like stalking or voyeurism, one variation is to take snapshots of animals. But, Paul can take the animal pictures *without people seeing him take the pictures.* This secrecy preserves the excitement of a "covert operation" and provides an alternative for Paul's addictive texting pleasure.

10. PROGRAM COMPLIANCES (HIGH). All things said, the best trait of Cluster C personalities is program compliance. Workers are agreeable, passive conformers, people-pleasers, and blend into the workplace (or agency) invisibly without any semblance of rebelliousness. Outwardly, they are grateful, respectful, trustworthy, idolizers, low-maintenance, and tirelessly benevolent. From a boss's perspective, employment of Cluster C personalities offers the perfect blend of steady work production and rule-following enthusiasm. However, there is a serious problem inherent in the outward façade of compliance. The facade masks an underlying chronicity of fear and trembling, a state of mind

Kierkergaard (1985) characterized as anxiety from within. His existentialism aside, Kierkergaard was a behavioral visionary of sorts when he described subjectivity as going beyond objective facts to include how one relates to oneself to those matters of facts. That is, apart from logic or scientific analysis, people must experience inward reflection. Kierkergaard thought inward reflection evaded objective scrutiny, whereas it did just the opposite. One cannot appreciate inward reflection without first knowing the facts or events about which they reflect. Consequently, with Cluster C personalities, internal reflection is poor since the facts are elusive or ambiguous. This ambiguity (i.e., lack of facts) constantly stirs the irrational belief that coworkers, employers, and *everybody is upset with me and I must continuously work toward exoneration.*

Program compliance also appears as *eternal allegiance* to service providers or rehabilitation agencies. Pet therapist Cornelius provided psychiatric service dogs to anxiety-symptomatic individuals who found the canines soothing and capable of defusing panic attacks in public. He arranged for a service dog for Britt, a 42-year-old, divorced female who was diagnosed with obsessive-compulsive and avoidant personality disorders. Britt was not meticulous about her apartment, a place littered with paper debris and bordering on hoarding. However, she held strongly certain moral principles about people, and poorly tolerated any mistakes she made or that other people made. When her fears of mistakes soared, she panicked and ran out of stores. Cornelius assigned Britt a Labrador Retriever, who accompanied her in most public settings. Together with her Labrador Retriever, Britt ventured to unvisited places in the community not only to overcome anxiety but to generalize her self-control progress in similar settings.

Three months later, Cornelius praised Britt for her outstanding work and symptom-free control. He reminded her of the terms of the service-pet contract of releasing the Labrador Retriever after a period of measurable behavior stability. Both Cornelius and Britt amicably agreed this stability period was evident and that she could maintain her anxiety management on her own. That night, by herself with the Labrador Retriever, who she called Zoe, named after her younger sister Zoe who died of cancer two years earlier, Britt went into a full cycle of panic attacks, thinking she was losing Zoe, the sister – *all over again.*

She contacted Cornelius shortly after her panic subsided and reported her horrible relapse. She rationalized her relapse indicated the measurable period of stability was too short and she requested another two months for enhanced stabilization. Cornelius approved her request. Britt, in the safe company of Zoe, relieved her fear and trembling at the prospect of feeling abandonment.

The problem here is obvious: Attachment. Not attachment to the pet Zoe per se, although she possibly developed an attachment to Zoe from associating the pet metonymically with her deceased sister Zoe. But the major contingency of attachment was her *lifeline to therapy services and the fear that, without this lifeline, she will instantly relapse.* Britt even self-induced panic in anticipation of service termination. A solution for endless retention of therapy, as well as unconditional program compliance, is to predesignate the criteria for stepwise advancement through a series of levels. At each level, new duties, tasks, or challenges occur that may not buck the system but require some tenacity. This tenacity instills anxiety for a short duration until it subsides concurrent with reinforcement for meeting the task challenges. For example, with Britt, identify during baseline (pretherapy) a hierarchy of localities or high-risk panic settings (like in systematic desensitization). Identify that each steps will take approximately one week. When she desensitizes at each level of anxiety settings using Zoe, she uses Zoe less often during the week. For example, after meeting criteria for desensitization at level one, she works with Zoe for four days instead of seven days. After Britt completes the top level, and is anxiety-free in most social settings, she uses Zoe for only two days during the week. For steps in maintenance, Britt tries to visit the same places without using Zoe for one week. This systematic fading procedure enables more self-control and less reliance on her service pet. As a bonus, when she goes one week without Zoe, Britt can also give a public talk to other candidates for service pets on how she completed the program.

Similarly, in a job setting, an employee receives an incremental series of job tasks, each demanding slightly more effort and risk. At one level, for example, the task may involve premanagement duties of allocating jobs to other employees or making spot-decisions about product quality. At each new level, risks become tougher and may involve some decisions that are inconsistent with the organization's policies or long-standing conventions. However, as the consumer completes the difficult steps and wins praise for his or her mildly deviant decision making, a comfort level increases with not complying with all the programs.

The consumer quickly discovers that noncompliance is not only pre-scriptive, but it also is *safe, acceptable, and guarantees approval.*

PREDICTORS OF PERSONALITY FOR SPECIFIC VOCATIONAL OUTCOMES
CLUSTER C (AVOIDANT, DEPENDENT, OBSESSIVE-COMPULSIVE)

Program Attrition:	LOW
Absenteeism:	MILD TO LOW
Motivation:	HIGH TO MODERATE
Hx of Transient Jobs:	LOW
Coworker Relations:	HIGH
Supervisor Relations:	HIGH
Substance Abuse:	LOW
Violence:	LOW
Office Crime:	LOW
Program Compliance:	HIGH

Figure 5.3.

C'mon, remind me:
82. For Cluster C, absenteeism is very _____.
83. Supervisor relations, for Cluster BC, is usually very _____.
84. Program compliance is _____ for Cluster C.

REFERENCES

Ackerman, R. J. (1983). *Children of Alcoholics: A Guidebook for Educators, Therapists, and Parents.* Holmes Beach, FL: Learning Publications Inc.

Alsop, R. (2008). *The Trophy Kids Grow Up: How the Millennial Generation Is Shaping Up the Workplace.* New York: John Wiley & Sons.

American Psychiatric Association. (2013). *Diagnostic and Statistical Manual of Mental Disorders* (5th ed.). Arlington, VA: American Psychiatric Publishing (p. 302).

American Psychological Association (APA). (2010). *Ethical Principles of Psychologists and Code of Conduct.* Washington, DC: APA.

Analoui, F., & Kakabadse, A. (1992). Sabotage: *How to Recognize and Manage Employee Defiance.* New York: Mercury Books.

Ayllon, T., & Azrin, N. H. (1964). Reinforcement and instructions with mental patients. *Journal of the Experimental Analysis of Behavior, 7,* 327–331.

Ayllon, T., & Michael, J. (1959). The psychiatric nurse as a behavioral engineer. *Journal of the Experimental Analysis of Behavior, 2,* 323–344

Azrin, N. H., & Holz, W. C. (1966). Punishment. In W. K. Honig (Ed.), *Operant Behavior; Areas of Research and Application.* New York: Appleton Century Crofts (pp. 380–447).

BACB. (2004). *Professional and Ethical Compliance Code for Behavior Analysts.* Littleton. CO: Behavior Analyst Certification Board.

Bachrach, A. (1962). An experimental approach to superstitious behavior. *American Folklore Society, 75,* 1–9.

Baenninger, R., & Grossman, J. C. (1969). Some effects of punishment on pain-elicited aggression. *Journal of the Experimental Analysis of Behavior, 12,* 1017–1022.

Bagby, J. H., Wells, K., Edmondson, K., & Thompson, L. (2014). Montessori Education and Practice: A Review of the Literature, 2010–2013. *Montessori Life, 26*(1), 32–41.

Bailey, J., & Burch, M. (2011). *Ethics for Behavior Analysts* (2nd ed.). New York: Routledge Press.

Bankoff, S. M., Karpell, M. G., Forbes, H. E., & Pantalone, D. W. (2012). A systematic review of dialectical behavior therapy for the treatment of eating disorders. *Eating Disorders, 20,* 196–215.

Banks, R. K. (1965). Effect of pairing a stimulus with presentations of the UCS on extinction of an avoidance response in humans. *Journal of the Experimental Analysis of Behavior, 70,* 294–299.

Barneveld, P. S., Pieterse, J., de Sonneville, L., van Rijn, S., Lahuis, B., van Engeland, H., & Swaab, H. (2011). Overlap of autistic and schizotypal traits in adolescents with Autism Spectrum Disorders. *Schizophrenia Research, 126*, 231–236.

Barnhart, W. J., Makela, E. H., & Latocha, J. (2004). Selective serotonin reuptake inhibitor induced apathy syndrome: A clinical review. *Journal of Psychiatric Practice, 10*(3), 196–198.

Barratt, E. S., Stanford, M. S., Kent, T. A., & Felthous, A. (1997). Neuropsychological and cognitive psychophysiological substrates of impulsive aggression. *Biological Psychiatry, 15*, 1045–1046.

Barrer, A. E., & Ruben, D. H. (1984). *Readings in Head Injury.* Guilford, CT: Special Learning Corporation.

Berkowitz, L. (1993). Pain-induced aggression: An ethological perspective. *Motivation and Emotion, 17*, 277–293.

Billingsley, E. F., & Romer, L. T. (1983). Response prompting and the transfer of stimulus control: Methods, research, and a conceptual framework. *Journal of the Association for the Severely Handicapped, 8*, 3–12.

Black, C. (1982). *It Will Never Happen to Me.* Denver, CO: Medical Administration Company.

Bloom, C. M., Venard, J., Harden, M., & Seetharaman, S. (2007). Noncontingent positive and negative reinforcement schedules of superstitious behaviours. *Behavioural Processes, 75*, 8–13.

Bootzin, R., & Acocella, R. (1984). *Abnormal Psychology: Current Perspectives.* New York: Random House.

Brown, F., Holvoet, J., Guess, D., & Mulligan, M. (1980). The Individualized Curriculum Sequencing Model (III): Small group instruction. *Journal of the Association for the Severely Handicapped, 5*, 352–367.

Brown, P., & Jenkins, H. M. (1968). Auto-shaping of the pigeon's key peck. *Journal of the Experimental Analysis of Behavior, 11*, 1–8.

Brown, S. (1988). *Treating Adult Children of Alcoholics.* New York: Wiley Press.

Burke, L., Wang, J., & Sevick, M. A. (2011). Self-monitoring in weight loss: A systematic review of the literature. *Journal of the American Dietetic Association, 111*, 92–102.

Burns, J. (2009). *Goddess of the Market: Ayn Rand and the American Right.* New York: Oxford University Press.

Bush, D. M., & Autry, J. H. (2002). Substance abuse in the workplace: Epidemiology, effects, and industry response. *Occupational Medicine, 17*, 13–25.

Capaldi, D. M., Kim, H. K., & Shortt, J. W. (2007). Observed initiation and reciprocity of physical aggression in young, at-risk couples. *Journal of Family Violence, 22*, 101–111.

Catania, A. C. (1992). *Learning.* Englewood Cliffs, NJ: Prentice-Hall

Chambless, D. L., & Ollendick, T. H. (2001). Empirically supported psychological interventions: Controversies and evidence. *Annual Review of Psychology, 52*, 685–716.

Cherek, R. D., Sapiga, R., Steinberg, L. J., & Kelly, H. T. (1990). Human aggression responses maintained by avoidance or escape from point loss. *Journal of the Experimental Analysis of Behavior, 53*, 293–303.

Cipani, E., & Madigan, K. (1986). Errorless learning: Research and application for "difficult-to-teach" children. *Canadian Journal for Exceptional Children, 3*, 39–43.

Collinge, W., Yarnold, P., & Soltysik, R. (2013). Fibromyalgia symptom reduction by online behavioral self-monitoring, longitudinal single subject analysis and automated delivery of individualized guidance. *North American Journal of Medical Science, 9*, 546–553.

Connolly-Gibbons, M. B., Rothbard, A., Farris, K. D., Stirman, S. W., Thompson, S. M., Scott, K., Heintz, L. E., Gallop, R., & Critis-Christoph, P. (2011). Changs in psychotherapy utilization among consumers of services for major depressive disorder in the community mental health system. *Administrative Policy in Mental Health, 38*, 405–503.

Connor, D. (2002). *Aggression and Antisocial Behavior in Children and Adolescents: Research and Treatment.* New York: Guilford Press.

Crosswhite, J. M., Rice, D., & Asay, S. M. (2014). Texting among United States young adults: An exploratory study on texting and its use within families. *The Social Science Journal, 51*, 70–78.

Delapp., R. C. T., & Williams, M. T. (2015). Professional challenges facing African-American psychologists: The presence and impact of racial microaggressions. *The Behavior Therapist, 38*, 101–105.

Dannacker, E., & George, S. (2009). A comparison of laboratory measures of escape and avoidance behavior. *Journal of Pain, 10*, 53–59.

Davis, H., & McIntire, R. W. (1969). Conditioned suppression under positive, negative, and no contingency between condition and unconditioned stimuli. *Journal of the Experimental Analysis of Behavior, 12*, 633–640.

Deitz, D. E. D., & Repp, A. C. (1983). Reducing behavior through reinforcement. *Exceptional Education Quarterly, 3*, 34–46.

DeLeon, I. G., & Iwata, B. A. (1996). Evaluation of a multiple-stimulus presentation format for assessing reinforcer preferences. *Journal of Applied Behavior Analysis. 29*, 519–532.

Delprato, D. J. (1980). The reactional biography concept: Early contribution to a perspective for the psychology of aging. *Human Development, 23*, 314–322.

Delprato, D. J. (1986). Response patterns. In H. W. Reese & L. J. Parrott (Eds.), *Behavior Science: Philosophical, Methodological, and Empirical Advances* (pp. 61–113). Hillsdale, NJ: Lawrence Erlbaum Associates.

Delprato, D. J., & McGlynn, F. D. (1988). Interactions of response patterns and their implications for behavior therapy. *Journal of Behavior Therapy and Experimental Psychiatry, 19*, 199–205.

Delprato, D. J., & Smith, N. W. (2009). Sketch of J. R. Kantor's Psychological interbehavioral field theory. *Psychological Record, 59*, 671–678.

Dengerick, H. A., & Covey, M. K. (1983). Implications of an escape-avoidance theory of aggressive responses to attack. *Aggression: Theoretical and Empirical Reviews, 1*, 163–188.

Den Uyl, D., & Rasmussen, D. B. (1984). (Eds.). *The Philosophic Thought of Ayn Rand.* Chicago: University of Illinois Press.

Divac-Jovanovic, M., Svrakic, D., & Lecic-Tosevski, D. (1993). Personality disorders: Model for conceptual approach and classification. Part I: General model. *American Journal of Psychotherapy, 47*, 558–571.

Dixon, M. R., & Hayes, L. J. (1999). A behavioral analysis of dreaming. *The Psychological Record, 49*, 613–628.

Dolan, M., & Park, I. (2002). The neuropsychology of antisocial personality disorder. *Psychological Medicine, 32*, 417–427.

Dollard, J., & Miller, N. W. (1950). *Personality and Psychotherapy.* New York: McGraw-Hill.

Dugan, H. (2013). Crimes of the cubicle: 15 Desk Don'ts. *Houston Chronicle, February 12.*

Dworkin, S. I., & Smith, J. E. (1989). Assessment of neurochemical correlates of operant behavior. *Psychopharmacology, 13*, 741–785.

Dymond, S., & Roche, B. (2009). A contemporary behavior analysis of anxiety and avoidance. *Behavior Analysis, 32*, 7–27.

Ellis, A. (1962). *Reason and Emotion in Psychotherapy.* New York: Lye Stuart.

Eysenck, H. J. (1979). The conditioning model of neurosis. *The Behavioral and Brain Sciences, 2*, 155–166.

Ferentzy, P., & Turner, N. E. (2013). *A History of Problem Gambling: Temperance, Substance Abuse, Medicine, and Metaphors.* New York: Springer.

Ferster, C. B., Culberston, S., & Boren, M. C. P. (1975). *Behavior Principles.* Englewood Cliffs: NJ: Prentice-Hall.

Ferster, C. B., & Skinner, B. F. (1967). *Schedules of Reinforcement.* Englewood Cliffs, NJ: Prentice-Hall.

Foa, E., Yadin, E., & Lichner, T. (2012). *Exposure and Response (Ritual) Prevention for Obsessive-Compulsive Disorder: Therapist Guide.* New York: Oxford University Press.

Frances, A., & Widiger, T. (2012). Psychiatric diagnoses: Lessons from the DSM-IV past and cautions for the DSM-5 future. *Annual Review of Clinical Psychology, 8*, 109–130.

Franzen, M. D., & Getz, G. G. (2006). *Behavioral Neuropsychology.* New York: Academic Press.

Fryling, M. J., & Hayes, L. J. (2010). An interbehavioral analysis of memory. *European Journal of Behavior Analysis, 11*, 53–68.

Fuller, P. R. (1949). Operant conditioning of a vegetative human organism. *American Journal of Psychology, 62*, 587–590.

Garber, J., & Seligman, M. E. P. (Eds.). (1980). *Human Helplessness: Theory and Application.* New York: Academic Press.

Garcia, P., Mielke, M., Rosenberg, P., Bergey, A., & Rao, V. (2011). Personality changes in brain injury. *Journal of Neuropsychiatry and Clinical Neuroscience, 23*, E–14.

Gianoli, M. O., Jane, J. S., O'Brien, E., & Ralevski, E. (2012). Treatment for comorbid borderline personality disorder and alcohol use disorder: A review of the evidence and future recommendations. *Experimental Clinical Pharmacology, 20*, 333–344.

Gomes-Schwartz, B. (1979). The modification of schizophrenic behavior. *Behavior Modification, 3*, 439–468.

Greenberg, L., & Barling, J. (1999). Predicting employee aggression against coworkers, subordinates and supervisors: The roles of person behaviors and perceived workplace factors. *Journal of Organizational Behavior, 20*, 897–913.

Greenspoon, J. (1955). The reinforcing effect of two spoken sounds on the frequency of two responses. *American Journal of Psychology, 68*, 409–416.

Gross, A. (1981). Behavioral contrast and behavior therapy. *Behavior Therapy, 12*, 231–246.

Haase, J. M. (2009). Co-occuring antisocial personality disorder and substance abuse disorder: Treatment interventions. *Graduate Journal of Counseling Psychology, 1*, 57–64.

Hall, S. E., & Geher, G. (2003). Behavioral and personality characteristics of children with reactive attachment disorder. *Journal of Psychology, 137*, 145–162.

Harper, J., Iwata, B., & Camp, E. (2013). Assessment and treatment of social avoidance. *Journal of Applied Behavior Analysis, 46*, 147–160.

Harrison, M., & Pepitone, A. (1972). Contrast effects in the use of punishment. *Journal of Personality and Social Psychology, 11*, 398–404.

Hasin, D. S., Endicott, J., & Keller, M. B. (1989). RDC alcoholism in patients with major affective syndromes: Two–year course. *American Journal of Psychiatry, 146*, 218–323.

Hayes, S. C. (1987). *Rule-Governed Behavior: Cognition, Contingencies, and Instructional Control*. New York: Plenum Press.

Hayes, S. C., Brownstein, A. J., Zettle, R. D., Rosenfarb, I., & Korn, Z. (1986). Rule-governed behavior and sensitivity to changing consequences of responding. *Journal of Experimental Analysis of Behavior, 45*, 237–256

Herman, J. B., Brotman, A. W., & Rosenbaum, J. F. (1987). Rebound anxiety in panic disorder patients treated with shorter-acting benzodiazepines. *Journal of Clinical Psychiatry, 48*, 22–28.

Hernstein, R. J. (1961). Relative and absolute strength of responses as a function of frequency of reinforcement. *Journal of the Experimental Analysis of Behavior, 4*, 267–272.

Herrnstein, R. J. (1966). Superstition: A corollary of the principles of operant conditioning. In W. K. Honig (Ed.), *Operant behavior: Areas of Research and Application* (pp. 33–51). New York: Appleton-Century-Crofts.

Hoehn-Saric, R., Lipsey, J. R., & McLeod, D. R. (1990). Apathy and indifference in patients on fluvoxamine and fluoxetine. *Journal of Clinical Psychopharmacology, 10*, 343–350.

Hollis, J. H. (1973). "Superstition": The effects of independent and contingent events on free operant responses in retarded children. *American Journal of Mental Deficiency, 77*, 585–596.

Holvoet, J., Guess, D., Mulligan, M., & Brown, F. (1980). The Individualized Curriculum Sequencing Model (II): A teaching strategy for severely handicapped students. *Journal of the Association for the Severely Handicapped, 5*(4), 337–351.

Horton, A. M., & Wedding, D. (1984). *Clinical and Behavioral Neuropsychology.* New York: Springer.

Huibing, T., Lauzon, N. M., Bishop, S. F., Chi, N., Bechard, M., & Laviolette, S. R. (2011). Cannabinoid transmission in the basolateral amygdala modulates fear memory formation via functional inputs to the prelimbic cortex. *The Journal of Neuroscience, 31*, 5300–5312.

Ivancevich, J., & Konopaske, R. (2013). *Organizational Behavior and Management.* New York: McGraw-Hill.

Iwata, B. A., Wong, S. E., Riordan, M. M., Dorsey, M. F., & Lau, M. M. (1982). Assessment and training of clinical interviewing skills: Analogue analysis and field replication. *Journal of Applied Behavior Analysis, 15*, 191–203.

Jackson, K. C., & St. Onge, E. L. (2003). Antidepressant pharmacotherapy: Considerations for the pain clinician. *Pain Practitioner, 3*, 135–143.

Jann, M. W., & Slade, J. H. (2007). Antidepressant agents for the treatment of chronic pain and depression. *Pharmacotherapy, 27*, 1571–1587.

Jerome, J., Frantino, E. P., & Sturmey, P. (2007). The effects of errorless learning and backward chaining on the acquisition of internet skills in adults with developmental disabilities. *Journal of the Applied Behavior Analysis, 40*, 185–189.

Johnston, J. M., Foxx, R. M., Jacobson, J. W., Green, G., & Mulick, J. (2006). Positive behavior support and applied behavior analysis. *Journal of the Applied Behavior Analysis, 29*, 51–74.

Jones, R. B. (2007). The tonic immobility reaction of domestic fowl: A review. *World Poultry Science Journal, 42*, 82–96.

Kamin, L. J. (1969). Predictability, surprise, attention, and conditioning. In B. A. Campbell & R. M. Church (Eds.), *Punishment and Aversive Behavior* (pp. 279–296). New York: Appleton-Century-Crofts.

Kantor, J. R. (1921). A tentative analysis of the primary data of psychology. *Journal of Philosophy, 18*, 253–269.

Kantor, J. R. (1926). *Principles of Psychology* (Vol. 2). New York: Knopf.

Kantor, J. R. (1929a). *An Outline of Social Psychology.* Chicago: Follett.

Kantor, J. R. (1929b). Language as behavior and as symbolism. *Journal of Philosophy, 26*, 150–158.

Kantor, J. R. (1947). *Problems of Physiological Psychology.* Granville, OH: Principia Press.

Kantor, J. R. (1959). *Interbehavioral Psychology.* Granville, OH: The Principia Press.

Kantor, J. R. (1987). What qualifies interbehavioral psychology as an approach to treatment? In D. H. Ruben & D. J. Delprato (Eds.), *New Ideas in Therapy: Introduction to an Interdisciplinary Approach* (pp. 3–8). New York: Greenwood Press.

Karau, S. J., & Williams, K. D. (1993). Social loafing: A meta-analytic review and theoretical integration. *Journal of Personality and Social Psychology, 65*, 681–706.

Kawashima, K. (2003). Sequential dependencies in interresponse times and reinforcement/response cost. *The Psychological Record, 53*, 67–84.

Keller, F. (1968). "Goodbye teacher..." *Journal of Applied Behavior Analysis, 1*, 79–89.

Keller, M. B., Lavori, P. W., & Coryell, W. (1986). Differential outcome of pure manic, mixed/cycling, and pure depressive episodes in patients with bipolar illness. *Journal of the American Medical Association, 255*, 3138–3142.

Kierkegaard, S. (1985, first published translation). *Fear and Trembling.* New York: Penguin Books.

Kimble, M., Boxwala, M., Bean, W., Maletsky, K., Halper, J., Spollen, K., & Fleming, K. (2014). The impact of hypervigilance: Evidence for a forward feedback loop. *Journal of Anxiety Disorder, 28*, 241–245.

Kirwan, B., & Ainsworth, L. (Eds.). (1992). *A Guide to Task Analysis.* New York: Taylor and Francis.

Koch, J. (1999). Employee sabotage: Don't be a target. *Workforce, 78*, 32–47.

Koziol, L. F., & Ruben, D. H. (1993). In M. Squire, C. E. Stout, & D. H. Ruben (Eds.), *Current Advances in Inpatient Psychiatric Care* (pp. 249–262). Westport, CT: Greenwood Press.

Lancaster, L. C., & Stillman, D. (2003). *When Generations Collide: Who They Are, Why They Clash. How to Solve the Generational Puzzle at Work.* New York: HarperBusiness.

Leeies M., Pagura, J., Sareen, J., & Bolton, J. M. (2010). The use of alcohol and drugs to self-medicate symptoms of post-traumatic stress disorder. *Depression and Anxiety, 27*, 731–736.

Lamarre, J., & Holland, J. G. (1985). The functional independence of mands and tacts. *Journal of the Experimental Analysis of Behavior, 43*, 5–19.

Linehan, M. M. (1993). *Cognitive-behavioral Treatment of Borderline Personality Disorder.* New York: Guilford Press.

Linehan, M. M., Schmidt, H., Dimeff, L. A., Craft, J. C., Kanter, J., & Comtois, K. A. (1999). Dialectical behavior therapy for patients with borderline personality disorder and drug-dependence. *American Journal on Addiction, 8*, 279–292.

Lovaas, O. I., Newsom, C., & Hickman, C. (1987). Self-stimulatory behavior and perceptual reinforcement. *Journal of Applied Behavior Analysis, 20*, 45–68.

Lundin, R. W. (1961). *Personality: An Experimental Approach.* New York: Macmillan.

Lundin, R. W. (1969). *Personality: A Behavioral Analysis.* New York: Collier Macmillan.

Lundin, R. W. (1987). The interbehavioral approach to psychopathology. In D. H. Ruben & D. J. Delprato (Eds.), *New ideas in therapy: Introduction to an Interdisciplinary Approach* (pp. 37–51). Westport, CT: Greenwood Press.

Lyon, L. C., & Woods, P. J. (1991). The efficacy of rational-emotive therapy: A quantitative review of the outcome research. *Clinical Psychology Review, 11*, 357–369.

McClannahan, L. E., MacDuff, G. S., & Krantz, P. J. (2002). Behavior analysis and intervention for adults with autism. *Behavior Modification, 26*, 9–26.

Maham, H. C. (1968). *The Interactional Psychology of J. R. Kantor: An introduction.* San Marcos, CA: Project Socrates Press.

Malloy, P., & Levis, D. J. (1988). A laboratory demonstration of persistent human avoidance. *Behavior Therapy, 19*, 229–241.

Maxwell, W. A., Miller, F. D., & Meyer, P. A. (1971). The relationship between punishment and unavoidability in eliminating avoidance behavior in humans. *Psychonomic Science, 23*, 435–436.

Mellon, R. C. (2009). Superstitious perception: Response-independent reinforcement and punishment as determinants of recurring eccentric interpretations. *Behaviour Research and Therapy, 47*, 868–875.

Michael, J. (1982). Distinguishing between discriminative and motivational functions of stimuli. *Journal of the Experimental Analysis of Behavior, 37*, 149–155.

Michael, J. (1983). Evocative and repertoire-altering effects of an environmental event. *Verbal Behavior News, 2,* 19–21.

Michael, J. (1988). Establishing operations and the mand. *The Analysis of Verbal Behavior, 6,* 3–9.

Michael, J. (2000). Implications and refinements of the establishing operation concept. *Journal of Applied Behavior Analysis, 33,* 401–410.

Milgram, S. (1963). Behavioral study of obedience. *Journal of Abnormal and Social Psychology, 67,* 371–378.

Milgram, S. (1974). *Obedience to Authority: An Experimental View.* New York: HarperCollins.

Miller, W. R. (1983). Motivational interviewing with problem drinkers. *Behavioural Psychotherapy, 11,* 141–172.

Miller, W. R., & Rollnick, S. (2012). *Motivational Interviewing: Helping People Change.* New York: Guilford Press.

Miltenberger, R. (2012). *Behavior Modification, Principles and Procedures* (5th ed.). New York: Wadsworth.

Miltenberger, R. G., Fuqua, R. W., & Woods, D. W. (1998). Applying behavior analysis to clinical problems: Review and analysis of habit reversal. *Journal of Applied Behavior Analysis, 3,* 447–469.

Morris, E. K., & Midgley, B. D. (1990). Some historical and conceptual foundations of ecobehavioral analysis. In S. R. Schroeder (Ed.), *Ecobehavioral Analysis and Developmental Disabilities* (pp. 1–32). New York: Springer-Verlag.

Mowrer, O. H. (1950). *Learning Theory and Personality Dynamics.* New York: Roland Press.

Mulligan, M., Guess, D., Holvoet, J., & Brown, F. (1980). The Individualized Curriculum Sequencing Model (I): Implications from research on massed, distributed, or spaced trial training. *Journal of the Association for the Severely Handicapped, 5,* 325–336.

Nelson-Gray, R., & Farmer, R. F. (1999). Behavioral assessment of personality disorders. *Behaviour Research and Therapy, 37,* 347–368.

Nelson-Gray, R. C., Lootens, J. T., Mitchell, C. D., Robertson, N. E., Hundt, N. A., & Kimbrel, T. (2012). Assessment and treatment of personality disorders: A behavioral perspective. *The Behavior Analyst Today, 10,* 7–45.

Neylan, T. C., Marmar, C. R., Metzler, T. J., Weiss, D. S., Zatzick, D. F., Delucchi, K. L., & Schoenfeld, F. B. (1998). Sleep disturbances in the Vietnam generation: Findings from a nationally representative sample of male Vietnam veterans. *American Journal of Psychiatry, 155,* 929–933.

Noe, D. (2015). New York bans mistreatment of foreign manicurists. *Crime Magazine, May 12,* 3.

Olenick, D. L., & Pear, J. (1980). Differential reinforcement of correct responses to probe and prompts in picture-name training with severely retarded children. *Journal of Applied Behavior Analysis, 13,* 77–89.

Ono, K. (2013). Superstitious behavior in humans. *Journal of the Experimental Analysis of Behavior, 47,* 261–271.

Patterson, G. R., Reid J. B., & Dishion, T. J. (1992). *A Social Learning Approach: Antisocial Boys* (Vol. 4). Eugene, OR: Castalia.

Penzien, D. B., Rains, J. C., Lipchik, G. L., & Creer, T. L. (2004). Behavioral interventions for tension-type headache: Overview of current therapies and recommendation for a self-management model for chronic headache. *Current Pain Headache Reports, 8*, 489–499.

Peterson, A. L., Goodie, J. L., Satterfield, W. A., & Brimm, W. L. (2008). Sleep disturbance during military deployment. *Military Medicine, 173*, 230–235.

Pincus, S. M., Schmidt, P. J., Palladino-Negro, P., & Rubinow, D. R. (2008). Differentiation of women with premenstrual dysphoric disorder, recurrent brief depression, and healthy controls by daily mood rating dynamics. *Journal of Psychiatric Research, 42*, 337–347.

Piazza, C. C., Moes, D. R., & Fisher, W. W. (1996). Differential reinforcement of alternative behavior and demand fading in the treatment of escape-maintained and destructive behavior. *Journal of Applied Behavior Analysis, 29*, 569–572.

Poling, A., Edwards, T. L., Weeden, M., & Foster, T. (2011). The matching law. *The Psychological Record, 61*, 313–322.

Prasko, J., Diveky, T., Grambal, A., Kamaradova, D., Mozny, P., Sigmundova, Z., Slepecky, M., & Vyskocilova, J. (2010). Transference and countertransference in cognitive behavior therapy. *Biomedical Papers of Medical Facility of University Palacky Olomouc Czech Republic, 154*, 189–198.

Prochaska, J. O., & DiClemente, C. C. (2005). The transtheoretical approach. In J. C. Norcross & M. R. Goldfried (Eds.), *Handbook of Psychotherapy Integration* (2nd ed.) (pp. 147–171). New York: Oxford University Press.

Pronko, N. H. (1980). *Psychology from the Standpoint of an Interbehaviorist.* Monterey, CA: Brooks/Cole.

Puente, A. E., & Horton, A. M. (1986). Behavior therapy and clinical neuropsychology: Behavioral neuropsychology. *The Behavior Therapist, 2*, 30–31.

Ratner, S. C. (1977). Immobility of invertebrates: What can we learn? *Psychological Record, 27*, 1–13.

Rescorla, R. A., & Wagner, A. R. (1972). A theory of Pavlovian conditioning: Variations in the effectiveness of reinforcement and nonreinforcement. In A. H. Black & W. F. Prokasy (Eds.), *Classical Conditioning II* (pp. 64–99). New York: Appleton-Century-Crofts.

Richards, M., Rubinow, D. R., Daly, R. C., & Schmidt, P. J. (2006). Premenstrual symptoms and perimenopausal depression. *American Journal of Psychiatry, 163*, 133–137.

Rincover, A., Cook, R., Peoples, A., & Packard, D. (1979). Sensory extinction and sensory reinforcement principles for programming multiple adaptive behavior change. *Journal of Applied Behavior Analysis, 12*, 221–233.

Rogers, C. R. (1961). *On Becoming a Person.* Boston: Houghton-Mifflin.

Rosen, J. C., & Leitenberg, H. (1982). Bulimia nervosa: Treatment with exposure and response prevention. *Behavior Therapy, 13*, 117–124.

Ruben, D. H. (1983a). Interbehavioral implications for behavior therapy: Clinical perspectives. In N. W. Smith, P. T. Mountjoy, & D. H. Ruben (Eds.), *Reassessment in Psychology: The Interbehavioral Alternative* (pp. 445–469). Washington, DC: University Press of America.

Ruben, D. H. (1983b). The effects of praise and ignoring on relevant and irrelevant verbalizations by preschool children within a classroom setting. In P. T. Mountjoy & D. H. Ruben (Eds.), *Behavior Genesis: Readings in the Science of Child Psychology* (pp. 169–181). MA: Ginn.

Ruben, D. H. (1983c). Analogue assessments in the behavioral treatment of drug addictions. *The Catalyst, 2,* 69–77.

Ruben, D. H. (1984). Comparison of two analogue measures for assessing and teaching assertiveness to physically disabled elderly: An exploratory study. *Gerontology and Geriatrics Education, 5,* 63–71.

Ruben, D. H. (1984b). *Drug Abuse and the Elderly: An Annotated Bibliography.* New Jersey: Scarecrow Press.

Ruben, D. H. (1986a). Sudden impact: loss of language in aphasia. In D. Ruben & N. Macciomei (Eds.), *Readings in Aphasia* (pp. 17–22). New York: Longman Press.

Ruben, D. H. (1986b). Alcoholism/drug abuse counselors in industry: Do they need interpersonal skills? *Employee Assistance Quarterly, 1,* 57–62.

Ruben, D. H. (1986c). The management of role ambiguity in organizations. *Journal of Employment Counseling, 23,* 120–130.

Ruben, D. H. (1987a). On the origins of selfishness. *Behavioural Approaches with Children, 11,* 116–127.

Ruben, D. H. (1987b). Improving communication between the elderly and pharmacies: A self-initiative training program. *Journal of Alcohol and Drug Education, 32,* 7–12.

Ruben, D. H. (1988). Private events revisted: Does unobservable mean private? *Journal of Contemporary Psychotherapy, 18,* 16–27.

Ruben, D. H. (1989). Managing without managers: The participative way. *Supervision,* November, 17–19.

Ruben, D. H. (1990). *The Aging and Drug Effects: A Planning Manual for Medication and Alcohol Abuse Treatment of the Elderly.* Jefferson, NC: McFarland.

Ruben, D. H. (1992a). Interbehavioral analysis of adult children of alcoholics: Etiological predictors. *Alcoholism Treatment Quarterly, 9,* 1–21.

Ruben, D. H. (1992b). Behavioral Systems Approach. In C. Stout, J. Levitt & D. H. Ruben (Eds.), *Handbook for Assessing and Treating Addictive Disorders* (pp. 3–24). Westport, CT: Greenwood Press.

Ruben, D. H. (1993a). A behavior analysis of impulsive child behavior. In L. K. Koziol, C. E. Stout, & D. H. Ruben (Eds.), *Handbook of Childhood Impulse Disorders and ADHD* (pp. 78–107). Springfield, IL: Charles C Thomas.

Ruben, D. H. (1993b). *Avoidance Syndrome: Doing Things Out of Fear.* St Louis, MO: Warren Green.

Ruben, D. H. (1993c). Traumatic brain injured: Transitional stages of inpatient recovery. In M. Squire, C. E. Stout, & D. H. Ruben (Eds.), *Current Advances in Inpatient Psychiatric Care* (pp. 215–223). Westport, CT: Greenwood Press.

Ruben, D. H. (1993d). Transitional living centers for the multiply disabled. In D. H. Ruben & C. E. Stout (Eds.), *Transitions: Handbook of Managed Care for Inpatient to Outpatient Treatment* (pp. 101–113). New York: Praeger Press.

Ruben, D. H. (1998). Social exchange theory: Dynamics of a system governing the dysfunctional family and guide to assessment. *Journal of Contemporary Psychotherapy, 28*, 307–325.

Ruben, D. H. (1999). Behavioral systems approach: Case response. In E. T. Dowd & T. Rugle (Eds.), *Comparative Treatments of Substance Abuse* (pp. 79–95). New York: Springer.

Ruben, D. H. (2000). Sensitizing drug dealers to victim impact using mandatory psychoeducation. *Offender Program Reports, 3*, 68.

Ruben, D. H. (2001). *Treating Adult Children of Alcoholics: A Behavioral Approach.* New York: Academic Press.

Ruben, D. H. (2002). *Therapist Desk Reference of Behavioral Interventions.* Okemos, MI: Best Impressions International.

Ruben, D. H. (2004). Drug Dependence. In C. Spielberger (Ed.), *Encyclopedia of Applied Psychology* (pp. 645–653). San Diego, CA: Academic Press.

Ruben, D. H. (2009) Evoked response arousal plus sensitization. In I. Marks & M. Fullana (Eds.), *Common Language for Psychotherapy (CLP) Procedures.* Retrieved 8, 20, 2009 from CLP: www.commonlanguagepsychotherapy.org.

Ruben, D. H. (2013). *Effects of Bad Parenting and What to Do About It.* Okemos, MI: Best Impressions International.

Ruben, D. H. (2014). *Tantrum Survival Kit: The Definitive Guide to Tantrum Management.* Denver, CO: Outskirts Press.

Ruben, D. H., & Ruben, M. J. (1985a). Behavioral implications of the postpartum blues (depression). *Birth Psychology Bulletin, 6*, 1–9.

Ruben, D. H., & Ruben, M. J. (1985b). Behavioral principles on the job: Control or manipulation? *Personnel Magazine, 62*, 61–65.

Ruben, D. H., & Ruben, M. J. (1987). Assumptions about teaching assertiveness: Training the person or behavior? In D. H. Ruben & D. J. Delprato (Eds.), *New Ideas in Therapy: Introduction to an Interdisciplinary Approach* (pp. 107–118). Westport, CT: Greenwood Press.

Ruben, D. H., & Such, M. J. (1993) Participative management of multiple priorities in hospital administration. In M. Squire, C. E. Stout, & D. H. Ruben (Eds.), *Current advances in inpatient psychiatric care* (pp. 29–40). Westport, CT: Greenwood Press.

Ryan, V., Popour, J., Arneson, A., & Ruben, D. H. (Eds.). (1983). *Fundamentals of Substance Abuse Counseling.* Lansing, MI: ARIS.

Sato, M. (2001). A behavioral analysis of personality. In M. Sato (Ed.), *Contemporary Neuropsychiatry* (pp. 417–419). Japan: Springer.

Scheel, K. R. (2000). The empirical basis of dialectical behavior therapy: Summary, critique, and implications. *Clinical Psychology Science and Practice, 7*, 68–86.

Schmajuk, N. (2010). *Computational Models of Conditioning.* UK: Cambridge University Press.

Schneider, J. P., Sealy, J., & Montgomery, J. (2005). Ritualization and reinforcement: Keys to understanding mixed addiction involving sex and drugs. *Sexual Addiction and Compulsivity, 12*, 121–148.

Schuckit, M., & Raimo, E. B. (1998). Alcohol dependence and mood disorders. *Addictive Behaviors, 23*, 933–946.

Seeling, A., Jacombson, I., Smith, B., Hooper, T., Boyko, E., Gackstetter, G., Gehrman, P., Macera, C., & Smith, T. (2010). *Sleep patterns before, during, and after deployment to Iraq and Afghanistan* (33rd ed., Vol.12) (pp. 1615–1622).

Seligman, M. E. P., & Campbell, B. A. (1965). Effect of intensity and duration of punishment on extinction of an avoidance response. *Journal of Comparative & Physiological Psychology, 59,* 295–297.

Seligman, M. E. P., & Johnston, J. C. (1973). A cognitive theory of avoidance learning. In F. J. McGuigan & D. B. Lumsden (Eds.), *Contemporary Approaches to Conditioning and Learning* (pp. 69–110). Washington, DC: Winston.

Seligman, M. E., Maier S. F., & Greer, J. J. (1968). Alleviation of learned helplessness in the dog. *Journal of Abnormal Psychology, 73,* 256–262.

Skinner, B. F. (1948). 'Superstition' in the pigeon. *Journal of Experimental Psychology, 38,* 168–172.

Skinner, B. F. (1953). *Science and Human Behavior.* New York: The Free Press.

Skinner, B. F. (1957). *Verbal Behavior.* New York: Appleton-Century-Crofts.

Skinner, B. F. (1966). An operant analysis of problem solving. In B. Kleinmuntz (Ed.), *Problem Solving: Research, Method and Theory* (pp. 133–171). New York: John Wiley & Sons.

Skinner, B. F. (1968). *The Technology of Teaching.* New York: Appleton-Century-Crofts.

Skinner. B. F. (1969). *Contingencies of Reinforcement: A Theoretical Analysis.* New York: Appleton-Century Crofts.

Skinner, B. F. (1974). *About Behaviorism.* New York: Vintage Books.

Solomon, R. W., & Wynne, L. C. (1954). Traumatic avoidance learning: The principle of anxiety conservation and partial irreversibility. *Psychological Review, 61,* 353–385.

Sue, D. W., Capodilupo, C. M., Torino ,G., Bucceri, J. M., Holder, A., Nadal K. L., & Esquilin, M. (2007). Racial microaggressions in everyday life: Implications for clinical practice. *American Psychologist, 62,* 271–286.

Sundberg, M. L. (2004). A behavioral analysis of thinking. *VB News, 4,* 4–5.

Sundberg, M. L., Ray, D. A., Braam, S. E., Stafford, M. W., Reuber, T. M., & Braam, C. A. (1979). A manual for the use of B. F. Skinner's analysis of verbal behavior for language assessment and programming. *Western Michigan University Behavioral Monograph #9,* Kalamazoo, MI.

Sundberg, M. L., & Partington, J. W. (2010). *Teaching Language to Children with Autism or Other Developmental Disabilities.* Concord, CA: AVB Press.

Stampfl, T. G. (1987). Theoretical implications of the neurotic paradox as a problem in behavior theory: An experimental resolution. *The Behavior Analyst, 10,* 161–173.

Stampfl, T. G., & Levis, D. J. (1967). The essentials of implosive therapy: A learning theory-based psychodynamic behavior therapy. *Journal of Abnormal Psychology, 72,* 496–503.

Strauss, W., & Howe, N. (2000). *Millennials Rising: The Next Generation.* New York: Vintage Press.

Sullivan, M. D., & Robinson, J. P. (2006). Antidepressant and anticonvulsant medication for chronic pain. *Physical Medicine Rehabilitation Clinic of North America, 17,* 381–400.

Sultan, A. J. (2014). Addiction to mobile text messaging applications is nothing to "lol" about. *The Social Science Journal, 51*, 57–69.

Terrace, H. S. (1963). Discrimination learning with and without "errors." *Journal of the Experimental Analysis of Behavior, 6*, 1–27.

Tharp, R. G., & Wetzel, R. J. (1969). *Behavior Modification in the Natural Environment.* New York: Academic Press.

Timberlake, W., & Lucas, G. A. (1985). The basis of superstitious behavior: Chance, contingency, stimulus substitution, or appetitive behavior? *Journal of the Experimental Analysis of Behavior, 44*, 279–299.

Torueke, N., Luciano, C., & Salas, S. V. (2008). Rule-governed behavior and psychological problems. *International Journal of Psychology and Psychological Therapy, 8*, 141–156.

Ullman, L., & Krasner, L. (1975). *Psychological Approach to Abnormal Behavior.* Englewood Cliffs, NJ: Prentice-Hall.

Ulrich, R. E. (1966). Pain as a cause of aggression. *American Zoologist, 6*, 643–662.

Ulrich, R. E., & Azrin, N. H. (1962). Reflexive fighting in response to aversive stimulation. *Journal of the Experimental Analysis of Behavior, 5*, 511–520.

US Department of Justice. (2011). Workplace Violence. *Special Report*, 1993–2011. March, 1–17.

US Department of Transportation. (2015). *49 CFR, Part 40.* Washington, DC.

Uziel, L. (2007). Individual differences in the social facilitation effect: A review and meta-analysis. *Journal of Research in Personality, 41*, 579–601.

Van Gelderen, B. F., & Bakker, A. B. (2011). Daily suppression of discrete emotions during the work of police service workers and criminal investigation officers. *Anxiety, Stress & Coping: An International Journal, 24*, 515–537.

Van Hamme, L. J., & Wasserman, E. A. (1994). Cue competition in causality judgements: The role of nonpresentation of compound stimulus elements. *Learning and Motivation, 25*, 127–151.

Van Minnen, A., Harned, M. S., Zoellner, L., & Mills, K. (2012). Examining potential contraindications for prolonged exposure therapy for PTSD. *European Journal of Psychotraumatology, 3*, 18805–18807.

Vroom, V. (1964). *Work and Motivation.* New York: Wiley.

Whittal, M. L., Thordarson, D. S., & McLean, P. D. (2005). Treatment of obsessive-compulsive disorder: Cognitive behavior therapy vs. exposure and response prevention. *Behaviour Research and Therapy, 43*, 1559–1576.

Wann, T. W. (1965). *Behaviorism and Phenomenology.* Chicago: University of Chicago Press.

Weimer, M. (2013). *Learner-centered Teaching: Five Key Changes to Practice* (2nd ed.). San Francisco: Jossey-Bass.

Wilson, N., & Lud Cadet, J. (2009). Comorbid mood, psychosis, and marijuana abuse disorders: A theoretical review. *Journal of Addictive Disorders, 28*, 309–319.

Wolff, C., & Cull, A. (1986). Schizoid personality and antisocial conduct: A retrospective case note study. *Psychological Medicine, 16*, 677–877.

Wolpe, J. (1958). *Psychotherapy by Reciprocal Inhibition.* Stanford, CA: Stanford University Press.

Wong, M., Gardiner, E., Lang, W., & Coulon, L. (2008). Generational differences in personality and motivation: Do they exist and what are the implications for the workplace. *Journal of Managerial Psychology, 23*, 878–890.

Zarit, S., & Femla, E. (2008). Behavioral and psychosocial interventions for family caregivers. *American Journal of Nursing, 108*, 47–53.

Zeiler, M. D. (1968) Fixed and variable schedules of response-independent rein-forcement. *Journal of the Experimental Analysis of Behavior, 11*, 405–414.

Zeiler, M. D. (1972). Superstitious behavior in children: An experimental analysis. In H. W. Reese (Ed.), *Advances in Child Development and Behavior* (pp. 1–29). New York: Academic Press.

Zettle, R., & Hayes, S. C. (1982). Rule-governed behavior: A potential theoretical framework for cognitive-behavioral therapy. *Advances in Cognitive-Behavioral Research and Therapy, 1*, 73–117.

NAME INDEX

H

Harrison, M., 197

K

Kantor, J. R., 4, 65, 91, 117, 121, 131
Kierkergaard, S., 229

L

Lancaster, L. C., 202
Linehan, M. M., 116–117
Lundin, R. W., 4, 91

M

Madoff, B., 157
Milgram, S., 197

P

Patterson, G. R., 168

P (cont.)

Pepitone, A., 197
Pronko, N. H., 65

R

Rescorla, R. A., 45

S

Skinner, B. F., 31, 50–52, 91
Stillman, D., 202
Sultan, A. J., 227

V

Van Hamme, L. J., 45
Vroom, V., 226

W

Wagner, A. R., 45
Wasserman, E. A., 45

SUBJECT INDEX

A

Abandonment, 139, 216
 See also Fear of abandonment
Absenteeism, 152–153, 160–161,
    174–176, 207–209
Accommodations and exceptions with
    Cluster C personalities, 146–147
Addiction, 38
 See also Substance abuse
Adult Children of Alcoholics (ACOAs),
    33–39, 209, 218–219
 See also Avoidant Personality Disorder
Adult Children of Family Abuse
    (ACOFA), 33–39
 See also Avoidant Personality Disorder
Age duration of personality disorders, 3
Aggression
 See also Anticipatory aggression;
        Violence in the workplace
    aggressive personalities, 34–35
    in avoidance and escape patterns,
        168–169
    in Cluster B Personality Disorders,
        182
    following TBI, 91, 92
    microaggressions, 205–206
    visceral gratification type, 77
Altruism, 177, 210
Ambivalence, 159
Ancillary contingencies, 153
Anger
    in aggressive ACOAs and
        ACOFA, 34

following TBI, 92–93
    impulsiveness of, 199
    parental, 39
    in personality management decision
        tree, 99
    as response to paranoia, 189–190
    schizoid and schizotypal personali-
        ties responses to, 112
    self-medicating with, 86
    self-stimulating, 25, 47, 87, 199
Anorexia, 50
Anosognosia, 94–95
Anticipatory aggression, 19, 31, 51, 77,
    190, 199
 See also Aggression
Anticipatory anxiety, 31, 200
Anticipatory fear, 128
Antisocial Personality Disorder (Cluster B)
    characteristics of, 8, 17–19, 85
    decision tree criteria for, 99
    Don'ts for Cluster B Personality
        Disorders, 123–130
    Dos for Cluster B Personality
        Disorders, 116–123
    Gambling Disorder comorbid
        with, 89
    Impulse Control Disorder comorbid
        in, 77
    Learning Theory on etiology of,
        18–19
    movie characters as examples of,
        19–20
    risky substance use in, 80
    substance use comorbid with, 82,

85–86
Antisocial Personality Disorder (Cluster B), vocational, therapy, and rehabilitation outcomes for
absenteeism, 174–176
coworker relations, 187–188
job transience, 178–187
motivation, 176–178
office crime, 199–201
program attrition, 172–173
program compliance, 201–204
substance abuse, 194–196
supervisor relations, 188–194
violence in the workplace, 196–199
Anxiety
See also Panic-mode; Social anxiety
anger resulting from, 168–169
in Avoidant Personality Disorder, 31, 71–72
in Cluster B Personality Disorders, 17, 183
in Cluster C Personality Disorders, 216
complexity of, 87–88
in conflict-deprived (adult) children, 34
hypervigilance and hyper-awareness during, 192–193
Kierkergaard on, 229
in Paranoid Personality Disorder, 11
in personality management decision tree, 85
rebound anxiety, 85
response-exposure plus prevention treatment, 224
separation anxiety, 139
underlying substance abuse, 84, 86, 194–195
Applied Behavior Analysis (ABA), 138
Asocial, 18
Attachment, 21
Autism Spectrum Disorder (ASD), 13, 66–67, 164, 191–194
Autoclitic mands and tacts, 56, 121, 190
Autonomic arousal, 25, 47, 87–88, 167,

190–194
Avoidance and escape patterns
See also Absenteeism
in Cluster B Personality Disorders, 126, 184
in Cluster C Personality Disorders, 131–132
detachment, 180
managing, 183
metonymical events, 163
mutual aggression in, 168–169
theoretical discussion of, 52
Avoidant Personality Disorder (Cluster C)
See also ACOAs and ACOFA
autism traits in, 67
characteristics of, 8, 29–33, 93, 126
comorbid depressive disorders in, 68–69, 71–72
decision tree criteria for, 99
Don'ts with Cluster C Personality Disorders, 142–150
Dos with Cluster C Personality Disorders, 132–142
etiology of, 30–32
example of, 65–66
hoarding comorbid with, 73
movie characters as examples of, 32
substance use comorbid with, 79, 86
TBI comorbid with, 93–94
Avoidant Personality Disorder (Cluster C), vocational, therapy and rehabilitation outcomes for
absenteeism, 207–209
coworker relations, 214–218
job transience, 211–214
motivation, 209–211
office crime, 226–228
program attrition, 205–207
program compliance, 228–231
substance abuse, 221–224
supervisor relations, 218–221
violence, 224–226

B

Backward conditioning, 45–46
Behavioral contrast effects, 197
Behavior constellations in ACOAs and ACOFA, 34–38
Behavior potentials, 151
Bidirectional relationships, 111
Bipolar and related disorders, 71–72
Blame, 27
Borderline Personality Disorder (Cluster B)
  bipolarity comorbid with, 71
  characteristics of, 8, 17, 20–22, 85
  comorbid depressive disorders in, 68–69
  decision tree criteria for, 99
  Don'ts for Cluster B Personality Disorders, 123–130
  Dos for Cluster B Personality Disorders, 116–123
  Gambling Disorder comorbid with, 89
  Impulse Control Disorder comorbid in, 77
  Learning Theory on etiology of, 21
  movie characters as examples of, 22
  substance use comorbid with, 80, 85–86
Borderline Personality Disorder (Cluster B), vocational, therapy, and rehabilitation outcomes for
  absenteeism, 174–176
  coworker relations, 187–188
  job transience, 178–187
  motivation, 176–178
  office crime, 199–201
  program attrition, 172–173
  program compliance, 201–204
  substance abuse, 194–196
  supervisor relations, 188–194
  violence in the workplace, 196–199
Boundaries, 118, 120
Brief Psychotic Disorder, 68
Bulimiarexia, 224

C

Cannabis use, 61, 62–63
Caretaking, 36
Case manager change, 142–143
Catatonia, 68
Cavalierty, 174–175
Circadian Rhythm Disorder, 75
Classical conditioning, 87
Classification of personality disorders, 3–7
Cluster A Personality Disorders. *See* Paranoid Personality Disorder; Schizoid Personality Disorder; Schizotypal Personality Disorder
Cluster B Personality Disorders. *See* Anti-social Personality Disorder; Borderline Personality Disorder; Histrionic Personality Disorder; Narcisstic Personality Disorder
Cluster C Personality Disorders. *See* Avoidant Personality Disorder; Dependent Personality Disorder; Obsessive-Compulsive Personality Disorder
Coaching, 107, 136–137, 144–145, 160
Comorbid disorders (DSM-5 changes to)
  Bipolar and Related Disorders, 71–72, 74
  Depressive Disorders, 68–70, 74
  Disruptive and Impulsive Control Disorders, 77, 96
  Gambling Disorder, 88–89
  Neurocognitive Disorders, 89–96
  Neurodevelopmental Disorders, 66–67, 74
  Obsessive-Compulsive and Related Disorders, 72–74
  Schizophrenia Spectrum and Other Psychoses, 67–68, 74
  Sleep-Wake Disorders, 74–76, 96
  Substance-Related and Addictive Disorders, 78–83, 96
Compliments, 135, 175, 188
Compulsivity, 38
Conditioning, 43–46
Conduct Disorder, 18

Conflict avoidance, 34–35, 37
Contingency management, 110, 171
Contingent effects of punishment,
       43–48, 132–133
Control reinstatement, 195–196, 218
Countertransference, 120–122
Coworker relations, 154, 164–165,
       187–188, 214–218
Crimes of the cubicle, 157
Criticism, 144
Cues, 31, 32, 43, 51, 53–54
Cultural diversity, 138–139
Cultural syndrome of personality, 4–5
Culture, 4
Cyclothymic Disorders, 71–72

D

Decision making, 56
Decision tree for personality manage-
       ment. *See under* Personality man-
       agement
Delayed conditioning, 44
Delirium, 90
Delusional Disorder, 68
Department of Transportation, 194
Dependent Personality Disorder (Cluster C)
   characteristics of, 8, 40–41, 94
   comorbid depressive disorders in,
       68–70
   decision tree criteria for, 99, 101
   Don'ts with Cluster C Personality
       Disorders, 142–150
   Dos with Cluster C Personality
       Disorders, 132–142
   substance use comorbid with, 79–80,
       86
   TBI comorbid with, 94
Dependent Personality Disorder (Cluster
       C), vocational, therapy and reha-
       bilitation outcomes for
   absenteeism, 207–209
   coworker relations, 214–218
   job transience, 211–214
   motivation, 209–211

office crime, 226–228
program attrition, 205–207
program compliance, 228–231
substance abuse, 221–224
supervisor relations, 218–221
violence, 224–226
Depersonalization, 73, 90, 97, 167,
       221–222
Depression
   in Border Personality Disorder, 21
   Disruptive Mood Dysregulation
       Disorder, 69
   Dysthymic Disorder, 69
   iatrogenic causes of, 61
   Premenstrual Dysphoric Disorder, 70
   tolerance as prodromal step to, 34
   underlying substance abuse, 84
Desensitization, 132
Design of motivators, 106–107
Detachment, 180
*Diagnostic and Statistical Manual of Mental
       Disorders (DSM)*, 3–7
Dialectical Behavior Therapy (DBT),
       116–117
Dialectics, 117
Differential Reinforcement of
       Alternative Behaviors (DRA),
       182–183
Disclosure, 122
Discriminative control, 163–164
Disruptive and Impulsive Control
       Disorders, 77, 96
Disruptive Mood Dysregulation
       Disorder, 69
Domestic abuse, 79, 168
Dos and Don'ts. *See under* Personality
       management application
Dreaming, 76
Drug classifications in DSM-5, 78
Drug replenishment, 81
Dysthymia, 69

E

Empathy, 108–110, 122, 129–130

Empathy skills, 188
Employment. *See Job* transience
Enabling, 36, 144–145
Erotomania, 212
Errors of fact and judgement, 144
Escape patterns. See Avoidance and
    escape patterns
Establishing Operations (EOs)
    See also Motivation
    cues in, 53–54
    defined, 53
    erroneous, 113–114
    rule-governed behavior and, 56
    in substance abuse, 78, 80
    of therapy practitioners, 106, 111
Ethical codes, 119
Evoked response arousal plus sensitiza-
    tion, 191–194, 228
Exceptions and accommodations with
    Cluster C personalities, 146–147
Excuses, 113
Expectancy theory of motivation, 226
Expectations, 148–149, 178
Expression of feelings, 35–36

F

Fading procedures, 145–146, 230
False promises, 126–127
Family resistance, 146–147
Fear, 99, 131–133, 135
Fear-based learning, 63
Fear of abandonment
    in ACOAs and ACOFA, 36, 37, 209
    in Avoidant Personality Disorder, 30
    in Borderline Personality Disorder,
        20–21, 75
    in Cluster C Personality Disorders,
        147–148, 216
    in Dependent Personality Disorder,
        40, 132, 147–148
    by service termination, 129
    substance abuse to alleviate, 79–80,
        85
Feedback

importance of, 108–109
intersession, 116–118
positive and negative, 138–139, 178,
    181–183
psychotic responses impacted by, 68
reactions to, 180
realistic, 175–176
staff changes and, 143
Flooding, 132
Functional outcomes of punishment,
    49–51

G

Gambling Disorder, 88–89
Generalization, 50–51, 143
Generational experts, 202–203
Generation Y, 202
Goal setting, 173

H

Helpfulness, 144–146
Helplessness
    in ACOAs and ACOFA, 33–34, 209
    avoiding, 77
    in Borderline Personality Disorder,
        21, 182
    in Cluster B Personality Disorders,
        182
    in Cluster C Personality Disorders,
        148
    in employee relationships, 155
    in Gambling Disorder, 88
    in Histrionic Personality Disorder,
        126
    victim-centered, 116
Histrionic Personality Disorder (Cluster B)
    characteristics of, 8, 17, 23–25, 85
    comorbid depressive disorders in,
        68–70
    decision tree criteria for, 99
    Don'ts for Cluster B Personality
        Disorders, 123–130
    Dos for Cluster B Personality

Disorders, 116–123
movie characters as examples of, 25
substance use comorbid with, 85
Histrionic Personality Disorder (Cluster
    B), vocational, therapy, and reha-
    bilitation outcomes for
absenteeism, 174–176
coworker relations, 187–188
job transience, 178–187
motivation, 176–178
office crime, 199–201
program attrition, 172–173
program compliance, 201–204
substance abuse, 194–196
supervisor relations, 188–194
violence in the workplace, 196–199
Hoarding Disorder, 72–73
Hope, 161
Hysteria, 99

I

Iatrogenic personality disorders symp-
    tom subclassfication, 60–64
Immobilization, 182
Imperturbability, 158
Implicit interactions, 91
Impulsiveness, 177–178, 199
*Individualized Curriculum Sequencing (ICS)
    Model,* 143
Instrumental (operant) conditioning, 46
Intermittent Explosive Disorder, 77, 96
Interpersonal deficits, 32
Intersession feedback, 116–118
Inter-trial-intervals (ITIs), 43, 82
Introversion, 32

J

Job transience, 153–154, 162–164,
    178–187, 211–214
See also Self-termination

L

Learner Centered teaching, 221
Learning Theory in etiology of
    Anti-Social Personality Disorder,
        18–19
    Borderline Personality Disorder, 21
    Dependent Personality Disorder, 40
    Narcissistic Personality Disorder,
        25–27
    Schizoid Personality Disorder, 13
    Schizotypal Personality Disorder, 15
Learning Theory in Lundin's behavioral
    perspective, 4
Loss of control, 37
Loyalty, 36

M

Magical mands, 185–186, 200
Managing personality. *See* Personality
    management
Marijuana use, 61, 62–63
Markers in *cultural syndrome of personality,*
    4–5
Massively multiplayer online role-play-
    ing games (MMORPGs), 32
Matching Theory, 228
Medication administration, 167
Memorial behavior, 121
Meta-rules, 57
Metonymical extension, 51, 189
Microaggressions, 205–206
Micromanagement, 127–128
Millennials, 202, 204
Millon Clinical Multiaxial Inventory
    (MCMI), 99–100
Misanthropy, 158
Montessori-curriculum training, 161
Mood swings, 126
Motivation
    See also Establishing Operations (EOs)
    with Cluster A Personality Disorders,
        161–162, 170
    with Cluster B Personality Disorders,
        176–178
    with Cluster C Personality Disorders,

209–211
designing motivators, 106–107
overview of, 153
Vroom's expectancy theory of, 226
Motivational Interviewing, 159–160
Multigenerational workplaces, 202–203
Musterbation, 37–38

N

Narcissistic Personality Disorder (Cluster B)
comorbid depressive disorders in, 71
decision tree criteria for, 99
Don'ts for Cluster B Personality Disorders, 123–130
Dos for Cluster B Personality Disorders, 116–123
etiology of, 25–28
Gambling Disorder comorbid with, 89
Learning Theory on etiology of, 25–27
managing behaviors, 118
movie characters as examples of, 28
substance use comorbid with, 80–82, 85
traits shared by Cluster B, 8, 17
Narcissistic Personality Disorder (Cluster B), vocational, therapy, and rehabilitation outcomes for
absenteeism, 174–176
coworker relations, 187–188
job transience, 178–187
motivation, 176–178
office crime, 199–201
program attrition, 172–173
program compliance, 201–204
substance abuse, 194–196
supervisor relations, 188–194
violence in the workplace, 196–199
Negative punishment, 46–47
Neurocognitive Disorders, 89–96
Neurodevelopmental Disorders, 66–67
Noncontingent effects of punishment, 48–49

O

Obsessive-compulsion treatment, 224
Obsessive-Compulsive Personality Disorder (Cluster C)
characteristics of, 8, 42–43, 59
decision tree criteria for, 99, 101
Don'ts with Cluster C Personality Disorders, 142–150
Dos with Cluster C Personality Disorders, 142–150
movie characters as examples of, 59–60
rule use in, 57–59
substance use comorbid with, 86
TBI comorbid with, 94–95
Obsessive-Compulsive Personality Disorders (Cluster C), vocational, therapy and rehabilitation outcomes for
absenteeism, 207–209
coworker relations, 214–218
job transience, 211–214
motivation, 209–211
office crime, 226–228
program attrition, 205–207
program compliance, 228–231
substance abuse, 221–224
supervisor relations, 218–221
violence, 224–226
Office crime, 157–158, 169–170, 199–201, 226–228
Operant conditioning, 43–44, 46, 87
Operation behavior segments, 65
Oppositional Defiant Disorder, 51
Overconfidence, 174–175, 201–202
Overprecision, 147–148

P

Pain, 62
Pain management, 81
Panic-mode, 125, 195–196

See also Anxiety
Paranoia, 189
Paranoid Personality Disorder (Cluster A)
  characteristics of, 7–12, 84, 90
  decision tree criteria for, 99
  Don'ts for Cluster A Personality
    Disorders, 110–115
  Dos for Cluster A Personality
    Disorders, 106–110
  hoarding comorbid with, 72
  mood swings comorbid with, 71
  movie characters as examples of, 12
  sleep disorders comorbid with, 76
  substance abuse comorbid with,
    84–85
Paranoid Personality Disorder (Cluster
  A), vocational, therapy and rehabilitation outcomes for
  absenteeism, 160–161
  coworker relations, 164–165
  job transience, 162–164
  motivation, 161–162
  office crime, 169–170
  program attrition, 158–160
  substance abuse, 166–167
  supervisor relations, 165–166
  violence, 167–169
Passive-aggressiveness, 27, 174, 187,
  207–208, 217–218
Passive personalities, 35
Pathology, 79
Patience, 106, 118–119
Personality Disorders
  See also specific disorders
  Cluster characteristics, 7–10, 17, 29
  DSM criteria for, 3
  Other Specific Personality Disorders
    of iatrogenic causes, 60–64
  Unspecified Personality Disorders, 60
Personality management, 97–98,
  100–104
Personality management application
  Cluster A personality disorders
    overview, 106
  Cluster B personality disorders

  overview, 115–116
  Cluster C personality disorders
    overview, 131–132
  Don'ts for Cluster A Personality
    Disorders, 110–115
  Don'ts for Cluster B Personality
    Disorders, 123–130
  Don'ts for Cluster C Personality
    Disorders, 142–150
  Dos for Cluster A Personality
    Disorders, 106–110
  Dos for Cluster B Personality
    Disorders, 116–123
  Dos for Cluster C Personality
    Disorders, 132–141
  overview of, 105–106
Positive punishment, 46–47
Positive reinforcement, 47
Post-Traumatic Stress Disorder (PTSD),
  194
Praise, 134–136, 161
Premenstrual Dysphoric Disorder, 70
Premenstrual Syndrome (PMS), 70
Process behavior segments, 65
Procrastination, 124–125
Profanity, 112
Program attrition, 152, 158–160,
  172–173, 205–207
Program compliance, 158, 170–171,
  201–204, 228–231
Program development, 107–108
Prompts, 145–146
Proprioceptive stimuli, 25, 47, 87–88
Psychotic Disorders due to another med-
  ical condition, 68
Punishment
  affecting supervisor relations, 155
  anticipatory aggression and, 199
  in Cluster C Personality Disorders,
    212
  contingent effects of, 43–48, 132–133
  in development of Anti-social
    Personality, 18–19
  in development of Avoidant
    Personality, 30–31

in development of Borderline
  Personality, 21
in development of Paranoid
  Personality, 11
in development of rule-governed
  behavior, 11
in development of Schizoid
  Personality, 18–19
functional outcomes of, 49–51
noncontingent effects of, 48–49,
  181–182
paranoia related to, 189
positive and negative, 46–47
risk potential and, 140–141
time schedule of punishment contingencies, 47–48, 132, 135

R

Racism, 205–206
Rapid Eye Movement (REM) Sleep
  Behavior Disorder, 75–76
Reactional biography, 57, 111, 151–152
Reaction Attachment Disorder (RAD),
  40
Reality orientation, 98–99
Rebound anxiety, 85
Reinforcers
  See also Self-monitoring
  behavioral contrast effects, 197
  for Cluster C Personalities, 214
  in development of Antisocial
    Personality Disorder, 18–19
  in development of Narcissistic
    Personality Disorder, 25–26
  in development of Schizoid
    Personality Disorder, 13
  differential reinforcement, 129–130
  effective for Cluster B Personality
    Disorders, 176–178, 181
  evoked response arousal plus sensiti-
    zation, 191–194, 228
  maintaining motivation with, 162
  specificity of, 122
  on verbal content, 111

Rejection avoidance, 211
Relationship difficulties, 37
Relaxation, 36
Repeating yourself, 128
Respondent conditioning, 43–44
Response-exposure plus prevention
  intervention, 224
Response patterns, 82–83
Responsibility, 36, 38, 215
Retribution, 199–200
Risk, 80–81
Risk potential, 140–141
Rituals, 45–48, 52, 53, 60, 72
Rule-governed behaviors, 11, 15
  adventitious rule-following, 55
  development of, 55–58
  etiology of in Obsessive-Compulsive
    Personality Disorder, 43
  musterbations, 37
  operationalization of, 54–55, 73
  self-evaluatory, 58–59
  self-generative, 56

S

Safety, 109
Samplers, 134–135
Schizoaffective Disorder, 68
Schizoid Personality Disorder (Cluster A),
  7–10
  characteristics of, 13–14, 84, 90
  comorbid conditions, 68
  decision tree criteria for, 99
  Don'ts for Cluster A Personality
    Disorders, 110–115
  Dos for Cluster A Personality
    Disorders, 106–110
  exclusions of, 14
  hoarding comorbid with, 72–73
  Learning Theory on etiology of, 13
  movie characters as examples of, 14
Schizoid Personality Disorder (Cluster
  A), vocational, therapy and rehabilitation outcomes for
  absenteeism, 160–161

coworker relations, 164–165
job transience, 162–164
motivation, 161–162
office crime, 169–170
program attrition, 158–160
program compliance, 170–171
substance abuse, 166–167
supervisor relations, 165–166
violence, 167–169
Schizophrenia, 68
Schizophrenia spectrum and other psychoses, 67–68
Schizophreniform Disorder, 68
Schizotypal Personality Disorder (Cluster A)
    autism traits in, 67
    characteristics of, 7–10, 15–17, 84, 90
    comorbid conditions, 67–68
    decision tree criteria for, 99
    Don'ts for Cluster A Personality Disorders, 110–115
    Dos for Cluster A Personality Disorders, 106–110
    exclusions of, 16–17
    hoarding comorbid with, 72–73
    Learning Theory on etiology of, 15
    movie characters as examples of, 16
    substance abuse comorbid with, 85
Schizotypal Personality Disorder (Cluster A), vocational, therapy and rehabilitation outcomes for
    absenteeism, 160–161
    coworker relations, 164–165
    job transience, 162–164
    motivation, 161–162
    office crime, 169–170
    program attrition, 158–160
    program compliance, 170–171
    substance abuse, 166–167
    supervisor relations, 165–166
    violence, 167–169
Secure Continuous Remote Alcohol Monitor (SCRAM), 195
Self-criticism, 37–38, 58
Self-medication, 84–88, 194

Self-monitoring, 162, 179–181
    See also Reinforcers
Self-termination
    disapproval, 180–181
    illusions behind, 184–187
    negative feedback, 181–183
    overview of, 178
    performance failure, 183–184
    short-term expectations, 179–180
Separation anxiety, 139
Serial Partner Attraction Syndrome (SPAS), 40
Shame, 27
Shaping, 107, 108, 139–140, 145
Simultaneous conditioning, 45
Sleep-Wake Disorders, 74–76, 96
Social anxiety, 15, 84, 101, 205
    See also Anxiety
Social exchange theory, 176
Social facilitation, 216
Social loafing, 215
Social skills
    coworker relations and, 154
    deficits in Avoidant personalities, 32
    deficits in Cluster A personalities, 10
    deficits in Cluster A personalties, 84, 106, 112
    deficits in Cluster C personalities, 205
    as precondition for evoked response arousal plus sensitization, 191
Solicitation, 133–134
Splitting, 20, 71
Spontaneous recovery, 87
Stimulant-Depressant Effects in substance abuse, 84
Stimulus generalization, 120
Structure and specificity of interventions, 132–133
Subcultures, 138–139
Substance abuse
    See also Addiction
    in Cluster A Personality Disorders, 166–167
    in Cluster B Personality Disorders, 194–196

in Cluster C Personality Disorders, 221–224
risky, 80
stimulant-depressant effects, 84
Substance-Related and Addictive Disorders, 78–83, 96
therapy and employment outcomes impacted by, 155–156
tolerance level, 81
Substance-induced disorders, 68, 79
Successive approximation, 107, 108, 139–140, 145
Superstition, 15
Superstitious behaviors, 52–53, 88, 182
Supervisor relations, 155, 165–166, 188–194, 218–221

T

Task analyses, 133
Task size, 148–149
Temporal parameters of conditioning, 44
Termination, 52, 128–129
Texting, 227
Threshold of criminal detection, 226–227
Time schedule of punishment contingencies, 47–48

Tolerance, 31, 34
Tolerance levels in substance abuse, 81
Trace conditioning, 44
Trace intervals, 44–45
Traumatic Brain Injury (TBI), 91–95
Trust, 161–162
Typology of personality disorder symptoms with iatrogenic causes, 60–64

U

Unsinkable Molly Brown Syndrome, 215

V

Victimization, 185
Violence in the workplace, 156–157, 167–169, 196–199, 224–226
See also Aggression
Vulnerability, 37

W

Withdrawal symptoms, 81
World Health Organization Disabilities Assessment Schedule (WHODAS), 6

CHARLES C THOMAS • PUBLISHER, LTD.

THE PROFESSIONAL HELPER
(2nd Ed.)
By Willie V. Bryan
2015, 354 pp. (7 x 10)
$53.95 (paper), $53.95 (ebook)

CRISIS INTERVENTION AND COUNSELING BY TELEPHONE AND THE INTERNET *(3rd Ed.)*
By David Lester & James R. Rogers
2012, 460 pp. (7 x 10), 12 tables.
$49.95 (paper), $49.95 (ebook)

SOLVING THE PUZZLE OF YOUR ADD/ADHD CHILD
By Laura J. Stevens
2015, 266 pp. (7 x 10), 7 il., 13 tables.
$35.95 (spiral), $35.95 (ebook)

WHEN PARENTS HAVE PROBLEMS *(2nd Ed.)*
By Susan B. Miller
2012, 120 pp. (7 x 10)
$19.95 (paper), $19.95 (ebook)

INTERNATIONAL PERSPECTIVES IN MUSIC THERAPY EDUCATION AND TRAINING
By Karen D. Goodman
2015, 364 pp. (7 x 10), 19 il., 3 tables.
$69.95 (hard), $69.95 (ebook)

THE DYNAMICS OF ART AS THERAPY WITH ADOLESCENTS *(2nd Ed.)*
By Bruce L. Moon
2012, 308 pp. (7 x 10), 29 il.
$39.95 (paper), $39.95 (ebook)

THE UNDECIDED COLLEGE STUDENT *(4th Ed.)*
By Virginia N. Gordon & George E. Steele
2015, 308 pp. (7 x 10), 4 il.
$44.95 (paper), $44.95 (ebook)

PERSONAL COUNSELING SKILLS *(Rev 1st Ed.)*
By Kathryn Geldard & David Geldard
2012, 340 pp. (7 x 10), 20 il., 3 tables.
$45.95 (paper), $45.95 (ebook)

THE USE OF CREATIVE THERAPIES IN TREATING DEPRESSION
By Stephanie L. Brooke & Charles Edwin Myers
2015, 368 pp. (7 x 10), 38 il.
$69.95 (hard), $69.95 (ebook)

FOUNDATIONS OF MENTAL HEALTH COUNSELING *(4th Ed.)*
By Artis J. Palmo, William J. Weikel & David P. Borsos
2011, 508 pp. (7 x 10), 6 il., 3 tables.
$87.95 (hard), $64.95 (paper), $64.95 (ebook)

CRISIS INTERVENTION *(6th Ed.)*
By Kenneth France
2014, 338 pp. (7 x 10), 3 il.
$54.95 (paper), $54.95 (ebook)

DECODING CHALLENGING CLASSROOM BEHAVIORS
By Ennio Cipani
2011, 240 pp. (7 x 10), 9 il., 72 tables.
$34.95 (paper), $34.95 (ebook)

TRAUMA-INFORMED DRAMA THERAPY
By Nisha Sajnani & David Read Johnson
2014, 414 pp. (7 x 10), 16 il., 16 tables.
$72.95 (hard), $52.95 (paper), $52.95 (ebook)

THE USE OF TECHNOLOGY IN MENTAL HEALTH
By Kate Anthony, DeeAnna Merz Nagel & Stephen Goss
2010, 354 pp. (7 x 10), 6 il., 5 tables.
$79.95 (hard), $54.95 (paper), $54.95 (ebook)

ACTIVITIES TO ENHANCE SOCIAL, EMOTIONAL, AND PROBLEM-SOLVING SKILLS *(3rd Ed.)*
By John M. Malouff & Nicola S. Schutte
2014, 290 pp. (8.5 x 11), 3 il.
$46.95 (spiral), $46.95 (ebook)

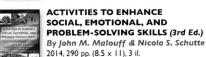

Find us on Facebook
FACEBOOK.COM/CCTPUBLISHER   **TO ORDER:** 1-800-258-8980 • books@ccthomas.com • www.ccthomas.com

SETON HALL UNIVERSITY
UNIVERSITY LIBRARIES
SOUTH ORANGE, NJ 07079